POLITICAL CHILDREN

POLITICAL CHILDREN

Violence,
Labor,
and Rights
in Peru

Mikaela Luttrell-Rowland

STANFORD UNIVERSITY PRESS
Stanford, California

Stanford University Press
Stanford, California

© 2023 by Mikaela Luttrell-Rowland. All rights reserved.

No part of this book may be reproduced or transmitted in any form or by any means, electronic or mechanical, including photocopying and recording, or in any information storage or retrieval system, without the prior written permission of Stanford University Press.

Printed in the United States of America on acid-free, archival-quality paper

Library of Congress Cataloging-in-Publication Data
Names: Luttrell-Rowland, Mikaela, author.
Title: Political children : violence, labor, and rights in Peru / Mikaela
    Luttrell-Rowland.
Description: Stanford, California : Stanford University Press, 2023. | Includes
    bibliographical references and index.
Identifiers: LCCN 2022014930 (print) | LCCN 2022014931 (ebook)
    | ISBN 9781503633360 (cloth) | ISBN 9781503634022 (paperback) |
    ISBN 9781503634039 (ebook)
Subjects: LCSH: Children—Political activity—Peru—Lima. | Children—
    Peru—Lima—Social conditions. | Teenagers—Political activity—
    Peru—Lima. | Teenagers—Peru—Lima—Social conditions. | Child
    labor—Peru—Lima. | Children's rights—Peru—Lima.
Classification: LCC HQ792.P4 L88 2023 (print) | LCC HQ792.P4 (ebook) |
    DDC 305.230985/255—dc23/eng/20220404
LC record available at https://lccn.loc.gov/2022014930
LC ebook record available at https://lccn.loc.gov/2022014931

Cover photo: Mural in Lima, Peru. Photo by author.
Cover design: Rob Ehle
Typeset by Elliott Beard in Adobe Caslon Pro 10/14.5

For Jacob

Contents

Acknowledgments	ix

INTRODUCTION
Learning How to Describe the State   1
The Everyday Lives of Young People in Lima

PART I

1 **Listening Between Generations**   23
Past and Present Violence in Lomas

2 **Deferred Promises**   51
How Young People Describe Injustice in Lomas

3 **Stories of a Visual Landscape**   77
Murals, Slogans, and Margins in Lomas

PART II

4 **Young People Together**   107
Children, Protagonism, and Organized Labor

5 **Child Workers and Child Citizens**   137
Rights, Recognition, and the Language of Equality

viii Contents

PART III

6 **Looking for the State**   165
   The Politics of Children's Participation in Peru

AFTERWORD   185

Notes   189

Works Cited   219

Index   237

Acknowledgments

I BEGAN RESEARCH FOR THIS book in 2007. Writing a book over such a long period of time necessitates a lot of help, starts and stops, and profound indebtedness. This project truly is a layered one, a collective conversation, an expansive testimony to so many people's generosity, sharing, and generative insights. It is not mine alone, but rather represents years of relational listening and critical engagements.

The young people featured in this book, both in Lomas de Carabayllo and with Movimiento de Adolescentes y Niños Trabajadores Hijos de Obreros Cristianos (MANTHOC), shared their time, their trust, their wisdom. I don't identify them by individual name here for safety and confidentiality, but this book is written to honor their critical interventions for these times. With the children of Lomas de Carabayllo, many were quite young when I first met them and their families. Staying in touch with them over such a long stretch of years and hearing how their observations have changed, as have mine, has been deeply moving. My first and most enormous thanks goes to each of these groups of young people.

In Lima, I owe a debt of thanks to a wide circle of colleagues and friends, only some of whom I can name, who opened up their homes, made

x Acknowledgments

and shared delicious meals, and helped me to better understand the political, cultural, and social landscape. Special thanks to María Balarin, who supported the development of this project since it was just in early planning stages, and whose research and ethical practices with young people has been foundational and influential. Alejandro Cussiánovich was so generous with his time, and our memorable discussions of theory, practice, and history were paramount. Patricia Ames, Bethsabe Huamán Andía, and Sonia Martinez helped in multiple ways through their rich engagements and insights. Early in this research, I had the good fortune to meet and share ideas with the late María Eugenia Mansilla. Our fiery conversations have stayed with me over all these years.

Multiple colleagues and contacts at various children's rights institutions in Peru aided in this research, even if and while some of them may disagree with my positions. They helped me track down historical documents, explain legal texts, and provided critical context for this work. In particular I give thanks for the time and the work of colleagues at Acción por los Niños, el Centro de Estudios Sociales y Publicaciones (CESIP), Instituto de Formación para Educadores de Jóvenes y Niños Trabajadores de America Latina y el Caribe (IFEJANT), Grupo de Iniciativa Nacional por lost Derechos del Niño (GIN), Dirección General de Niños Niñas y Adolescentes, Ministerio de la Mujer y Poblaciones Vulnerables (MIMP), MANTHOC, and UNICEF Peru, among others. My heartfelt thanks to the archives team at IFEJANT, where I continually lost track of time and learned so very much. And a special thanks to CESIP for engaging early in the research and for their tremendous collaboration and support.

This project simply could not be possible without the man I call Enrique in the book, my partner for all research exchanges and whose belief in this project has been fundamental to the content, methods, and insights. I respect his wish to not be named, while also seeing the centrality of the role he played. My sincere thanks also to observations and comments by Fredy and Imelda, who have been so helpful over such a long stretch of time and whose insights were instrumental.

Fellow Latin American scholars and friends inspired me along the way. Cristina Alcalde provided early encouragement, read early drafts, and offered important questions. Stephanie McNulty, Julia Paulson, and Tamara Walker, treasured writing partners and friends, each read and commented on parts of this book, over many years. Writing side by side with them, as we all forwarded our own projects about Peru, made this book better, and possible. A special thanks to Tamara Walker, whose scholarship has been influential and who ensured that I got over the finish line, even when I thought it may not be doable. My intellectual partnership and friendship with Mariana Prandini Assis, who offered critical interventions in many early and then later drafts, has continued to enrich my life and work.

I was lucky early in this research to learn from and with Sarah White, whose scholarship on childhood and well-being inspired and fundamentally shifted my thinking. Similarly, Jo Boyden and Jason Hart were crucial touchstones for my early questioning and de-centering of U.S.-centric thought. I see their influences in these pages.

Dialogue has been crucial to the life and completion of this book. Working across a range of disciplines, and over such a long period of time, meant presenting this work over many years at various conferences, workshops, and interdisciplinary spaces. Many friends, colleagues, and mentors read or discussed early drafts and parts of this manuscript, helped me to work through its ideas at different iterations, or offered professional advice at critical moments. Thank you especially to Adelle Blackett, Pascha Bueno-Hansen, Carolyn Chernoff, Elora Chowdhury, Alexandra Cox, Eve Darian-Smith, Julia Dehm, Michelle Forrest, Alison Kibler, César Rosado Marzan, Suzanne McCullagh, Zinaida Miller, Bill Mullen, Leigh Payne, Ian Reilly, Leanne Roncolato, Robert Ross, Valerie Sperling, Shobhana Xavier, and Nurfadzilah Yahaya. Friends near and far puzzled with me over translation questions, concepts, and ideas: Aldo Crossa, Chloe Waters, and Holly Anger. Thomas Hilbink urged me to think broadly about the implications of this work, and his comments have been of consequence ever since. I give a warmest thanks to Jothie Rajah, who has believed in, encouraged, and commented on this project in a multitude of intellectually generous ways. It is also Jothie who gifted me with workshopping the book's title. The influence of the late Lee Ann Fujii is present across the pages of this book; our important conversations about relational methods were invaluable but too short.

The teachings and scholarship of Patricia Ewick had a profound influence on my early thinking about this book. Likewise, Mariah Zeisberg read the entire manuscript at different early junctures and believed in the ideas.

xii   Acknowledgments

The unwavering support and gracious comments from both of them at multiple stages has meant more than they may know. Matthew Canfield was unstinting in his generosity of multiple readings and as a thought partner and activist-scholar. Cynthia Enloe—whose feminist voice and instincts shape much of how I think about and understand power—read multiple early portions of this manuscript and pushed me to rethink and rewrite. Joni Seager brought humor, rigor, and specificity. I am a better thinker and writer because of them both. Along this same vein, I am especially indebted to Nick Cheesman, who was unbelievably generous with his time and support, and whose discernments and questions continually pushed me towards greater clarity. Our rich exchanges and his advice proved vital to the completion of this project. Cameron Rowland's consistent engagement was invaluable both in terms of content and unwavering support, but also as one of my closest friends and favorite thinkers. With each of these colleagues and friends, I can only hope I have done justice to such generous and brilliant comments.

I have been fortunate to join a number of sustaining intellectual communities across space and time. The Sara Ahmed Reading Group—with colleagues across disciplines and geographic places—provided comfort and new understandings across seas. Gina Heathcote and I joined forces for virtual accountability and intellectual motivation, and her advice, comradeship, and encouragement made all the difference. Joseph Clark, my productive and inspiring writing partner for many stretches, was steadfast and animating.

In 2016, I had the good fortunate to begin to work with and alongside a powerful network of grassroots activists-scholars who made me rethink many parts of this book. My great and wide thanks to Nuria Abdi, the late Kathy Boudin, Martha Mutisi, Ruth Ochieng, Margo Okazawa-Rey, Puleng Segalo, María Elena Torre, and Cheryl Wilkins for the ways they both facilitate spaces, and listen, and for what such affective teachings mean and create in the world. As part of this work, I also have had the privilege and joy to work alongside Nobel Peace Laureate Leymah Gbowee, who reminds me of the politics of writing in clear and accessible ways and to ground all work, both academic and social, in an ethos of care. Michelle Fine, from whom I have learned so much, also taught me this lesson and continually inspires me to think in new and ever-expanding ways about collective voice.

This book has been written in many physical places. For opening their home, I am tremendously grateful to dear friends Catherine Baker Pitts and Will Pitts, and later, Catherine's office, for giving me a writing refuge. Their friendship and belief in this project have been buoying and critical. Special thanks to Esther Rowland, and to the late Lewis "Bud" Rowland, beloved grandparents, for their support of this project in multiple ways, including spaces to write. Finally, this manuscript would not have been completed without the loving support of Debórah Dwork and Ken Marek, my godparents, who provided me a home in multiple senses.

Funding and scholarship at various stages made this research possible. I am grateful for funding from the British Research Council; the Society of Latin American Studies; the Committee on Grants Funding at Franklin and Marshall College; the Buckley Summer Institute, a joint initiative of Harvard Kennedy School and the University of Manchester; the Early Career workshop of the Law and Society Association; and a travel grant with the Institute for Global Law and Policy, Harvard Law School.

For editorial support and assistance over various stages, I thank Inés Rénique, Cecelia Cancellaro, and a special thanks to Christopher Lura who really pushed this project and helped transform its prose. At Stanford University Press, I am enormously grateful to Dylan Kyung-lim White, Sunna Juhn, Emily Smith, Gigi Mark, and Kate Wahl. A terrific thanks to Jennifer Gordon for her careful eye and thoughtful edits. I also thank Mark Goodale and two immeasurably helpful and smart anonymous reviewers.

I don't have adequate words to thank my wide circle of dear family, friends, and colleagues who nourished me, and this work, over many years. While I have named some, there are many more who have held this project, and me, as I have puzzled it through. The patience has been immense, as has the encouragement. My deepest thanks. And to my son Jacob, to whom this book is dedicated, with love.

POLITICAL CHILDREN

INTRODUCTION

Learning How to Describe the State

The Everyday Lives of Young People in Lima

ELENA'S MEMORIES OF HER CHILDHOOD growing up as a little girl in the northern highlands of Peru came to her in waves. She remembered the animals, the bird sounds, the clean air (*aire puro*). She remembered the lush green landscape, how you could pick fruit off of trees. Prompted by the death of her grandfather on her mother's side, when Elena was 9 years old, her family migrated from the highlands of Peru to Lomas de Carabayllo in search of work in an area where Elena and her siblings could also go to school. Elena, three of her siblings, and her father moved first. Her mother came later with their youngest child. At the time, Elena was the eldest of their five children, which would later become seven.

When Elena and her family moved to Lomas de Carabayllo in 2010, the area was home to the largest landfill in Lima. Located in the northern margins of the capital city Lima, Lomas is largely an urban shantytown. Previously considered an industrial garbage zone, much of the infrastructure necessary for habitation was not provided, despite the large numbers of people who had lived there for some time. In the early 1990s, families like

1

2   Introduction

Elena's migrated from the highlands and began to occupy the neighborhood while they worked at the landfill or in recycling jobs. It wasn't until the early 2000s that the area became recognized by the state as a residential zone, more than a decade after Elena's family, and others like hers, had been living there.[1] Lomas was marked by a large garbage dump and landfill on one side, and a large rubber factory on the other.

In Lomas, Elena's father secured work at the landfill driving a garbage truck. Her grandfather, on her father's side, found work at the landfill sorting trash and looking for items that could be sold as recycling. Elena also worked, both inside the home and outside, doing a range of jobs from sewing clothes, to selling breads, to working at a small restaurant adjacent to the landfill. The transition to life in Lomas wasn't easy for Elena—the shift in landscape from the highlands where they had been living to the dusty shantytown was jarring, and she didn't like the smells of burning plastic and trash in the air. She described the move from the highlands to Lomas as one of the most difficult and transformative moments of her life.

"I couldn't get used to it here," Elena told me when I met her several years after she migrated to Lomas. "When I was a girl, I used to say, no, here I don't see the hills. These are not hills. These hills are naked. There [in the highlands], it was all green. Here, you wanted to play, but you couldn't. It is pure rocks."[2]

When I first met Elena, it was just before her 18th birthday, and by then she had lived in Lomas for eight years. As the oldest child in her family, she had many daily responsibilities, and she was a major caretaker for her six younger brothers and sisters. With no running water or sewer system in Lomas, her daily tasks such as cooking and cleaning took up a great deal of her day. These tasks required significant physical labor, such as fetching water for the family from the large plastic bins that sit throughout the neighborhood. At the time, the blue water bins were the only source of water for many of the people who lived in the area—a fixture of the neighborhood, their bright blue color a notable contrast to the gray, sandy hills.

Elena wasn't alone in her longing for clean air, water, and plants. The families of Lomas had begun to organize, calling on the local municipal government to provide running water and a sewer system in the area. In April 2014, after more than two decades of habitation, then-President Ollanta Humala made a rare appearance in Lomas de Caraballo. He announced that his administration would bring infrastructure for running water and a sewer system to the district. He told the crowd:

> We are performing this work with money that comes from every Peruvian who pays taxes, but it is worth the effort so that our children won't have the same lives as us. They won't have to be searching for water in water tanks. Now they will have pipes [in their houses] and this is improved quality of life.[3]

Despite wishing for the kind of improvements Humala was proposing, Elena told me she had long been skeptical of such politicians and their promises. While political slogans fill the walls and neighborhood murals surrounding Lomas, Elena felt it was just talk—"propaganda" she called it—and that it was politicians in search of votes. When multiple Peruvian news outlets covered President Humala's speech and his visit to Lomas, they did not mention the many young people like Elena present in the audience. Nor did the journalists report on the years of ongoing organizing and lobbying by Lomas residents that had preceded the president's announcement. Instead, Peruvian news outlets focused on the words that Humala spoke, including "our" children "searching for water."

In development discourse, state actors and politicians, like Humala, often call forth images of vulnerable children and their futures when promising to deliver basic services to marginalized areas or when evoking images of nation building. Categories of childhood, and children, are often used to elicit calls for economic and political investment, and to legitimize state development projects.[4] Dominant policy discourse and metaphors of children as representatives of hope for the future—and stereotypical tales of innocent girls and boys in need of protection by the state—are all familiar. It is less common, however, to hear politicians talking about the actual lives of young people, the physical conditions in which they live, the concrete economic and political interests of the state that shape such conditions, and the specific historical processes and environmental factors that influence such quotidian experiences.[5] Even less common: to hear of politicians listening to how children themselves describe and talk about these everyday state processes, especially in ways that move beyond only symbolic participation.

4   Introduction

Based on research conducted during different periods over a ten-year span in Lima, Peru, this book highlights how two groups of working young people, all living in Lima and whom I first met in 2007 when they were ages 7 to 18, provide key insights into the working of state power.[6] They reveal a state that is maintained by the promulgation of disparity and imbued with multiple forms of violence. Since the 1990s, the state has done this largely through a neoliberal discourse that declares children's rights and children's individual voices a priority, while at the same time deepening inequality and structural systems of harm. That is, young people in both of these contexts expose a range of ways that state violence in Peru reproduces itself through sustained disparity, while at the same time relying on a logic that imagines children as actors located first and foremost in families and "far from politics."

The first group of children the book looks at, discussed in Part I, lives in Lomas, and it includes Elena and her siblings. Many of the young people in this group come from families who migrated during the 1990s from the highlands.[7] The second group of young people, discussed in Part II, are members of a political activist working children's movement in Lima named the Movement of Working Children and Adolescents from Working-Class Christian Families (Movimiento de Adolescentes y Niños Trabajadores Hijos de Obreros Cristianos or MANTHOC). MANTHOC, founded in 1971, was one of the first organized children's workers' groups in Peru. The organization, which is dedicated to advancing children's rights as citizens and workers, has led many high-profile political campaigns in Peru and internationally.

Critical race, gender, and decolonial theorists, as well as activists, have long argued that those closest to injustice, and with lived experience of it, have access to understanding and epistemic knowledge that others may not.[8] This book's methods and findings builds on, strongly affirms, and is shaped by this scholarship and analysis. Attending to the words, hopes, fears, and commentary by these particular young people—who have been directly impacted by austerity and various forms of state violence, whose lives and labor are depended upon by the state, even as they are simultaneously "made marginal" by the state—provides an important lens on (re) considering what "the state" itself is in Peru and how state power and state violence play out in everyday life.[9]

In Lomas, for example, when Elena discusses what makes up daily life, what she underscores most are details about her longings, fantasies, and everyday observations.[10] As discussed in the first three chapters, other comments by the young people in Lomas provide similar insights: They speak of the regular burning of trash that hurts their lungs; the poison in the streets that kills their beloved dogs; and the kicked up dirt, dust, and pollution on the unpaved roads that interrupts their ability to play. These examples, at first, don't seem to be about the state at all, but rather about place. Yet all of these comments point to the way environmental degradation is a central mechanism of state power and injustice. Through their descriptions of daily life, labor, and environment, young people help explain how Peru's recent political, economic, and policy models maintain not just disparity but also a form of violence. For them, state violence includes not just hyper-localized experiences of life in the shantytown of Lomas, but something wrapped up in, and necessarily dependent on, translocal patterns of both capital and environmental inequity that manifest in their bodies and lives, as well as those of their family members.[11] Their voices are influenced by their direct relationship with state power, both in terms of their spatial marginalization and by the historical and contextual factors shaping the very place of Lomas, and Peru.

Peru's internal armed conflict in the 1980s and 1990s, which killed and displaced tens of thousands, is known for how it both reflected and reproduced patterns of social hierarchy and exclusion, according to the Truth and Reconciliation Commission (Comisión de la Verdad y Reconciliación or CVR) that was charged with investigating the conflict. They found that over 70,000 women, men, and children were killed or disappeared during the conflict.[12] In 2003, Salomón Lerner, the president of the CVR, noted Peru's deeply entrenched inequality when he remarked that Peru is "a country where exclusion is so absolute that tens of thousands of citizens can disappear without anyone in integrated society, in the society of the non-excluded, noticing a thing" (as quoted in Drinot 2014: 3). Since then, conflict, inequality, and exclusion have continued, albeit in different ways. Even with a newly established middle class in Peru, there remain many young people living in dangerous environmental and deeply unequal economic conditions.[13] Feminist scholars of Latin America have long argued that the failure of the state to guarantee a life free from violence is itself a

6   Introduction

human rights violation.[14] In Peru today, this failure, as the young people discussed in this book make clear, is manifest in interlocking forms of environmental, structural, historical, and political violence.[15]

Although they do not always name it as such, the young people featured in this book provide unique insight into how violence and state power coalesce in their lives. Listening to the particular ways they narrate their experiences—sharing their knowledge and affect and even fantasies for the future, or, on the other hand, discussing political campaigns, children's rights, and workers' rights—provides important commentary into the ways the state in Peru operates as a purveyor of inequality and disparity among the country's children. But to be able to hear their comments as particular insights about state power in Peru, it is also necessary to move past conceptualizations of childhood that frame them as without subjecthood or political agency.

Reconceptualizing Childhood in the Context of the State

In recent years, important scholarship on Peru and Latin America explored how best to listen to young people, especially those in Lomas and the members of MANTHOC, who in multiple ways have been made marginal by the state. This book draws inspiration from this scholarship, while also suggesting some new approaches. Recent works on this subject could be said to fit into two main categories. One of these categories, which includes a number of compelling and moving accounts, many from across Latin America, emphasize children's individual stories and voices and how their perspectives can shed light on key issues in our understanding of politics and society (see Bellino 2017; Crivello 2015; Taft 2019). There are also important historical and legal writings on the institutional and structural context of place, through the perspective of adults, that frame how children's voices are heard and that help explain the dominant spatial scheme in which children are contextualized, understood, and often erased (see Albarrán 2014; Han 2021; Katz 2004; Leinaweaver 2008; Premo 2005; Simmons 2015; Webster 2021). Many of these books have helped provide a shift toward a reconceptualization of childhood in both scholarship, NGOs and human rights organizations, and in public policy. This impetus matters for decolonial approaches particularly because dominant understandings about childhood and child development grow out of a Western developmental-psychological view of children.

Over the last three decades, Peru's government has instituted a number of new laws and policies aimed at children and children's rights. These policies, like in many Western countries, have been partly grounded in an understanding of childhood as a time to be protected. Often credited to scholarship by Talcott Parsons or Jean Piaget in much of this dominant understanding, children are seen as sites of future investment and in terms of who they will become, rather than who they are now.[16] From this point of view, childhood is something to be protected, and ultimately, as a time viewed as apolitical.[17]

The 1990 Convention on the Rights of the Child (CRC) is the most ratified human rights treaty in the world, which is likely due in part to the neutral ways childhood tends to be viewed by state actors.[18] Indeed, the overwhelming global consensus about children's rights is arguably a reflection of the ways politicians paternalistically rally around vulnerable subjects to protect. Almost every country in the globe has ratified the CRC, which, unlike women's rights or Indigenous and Native peoples' rights, is arguably due to the ways that children's rights are largely seen as a neutral issue. Put differently, because of how children are widely dismissed, infantilized, and treated as apolitical subjects, nearly all state actors see children's rights as an automatic good.[19] The categories of children and childhood are often subsumed in the public imagination under the umbrella term "the family."[20] Such erasure contributes to why "children are largely absent from our texts, missing from our studies of human life and cultural production" (Theidon 2013: 303). Yet all erasures are not equal, and recent scholarship highlights the politics and power of ways that certain children, and bodies, have been largely, and intentionally, written out of historical and social accounts.[21]

Part of the erasure of particular kinds of children in social life as political subjects is not just about how children are imagined or understood in public policy, but also because of a certain doctrinal reading of the state and state power. In numerous academic fields, scholars have documented how the state and state processes are often seen by policymakers as somehow "outside" of society and social processes. Socio-legal, critical race theorists, and feminist scholars have collectively disputed this framing and have made clear in recent decades the non-monolithic nature of "the state," as well as

8   Introduction

the need to question what constitutes state power.[22] Relatedly, rather than imagining law and legality primarily in terms of rules and norms as dictated from "above," a number of scholars have demonstrated the need to understand law as expressed through the consciousness embedded in everyday lives and practices.[23] Together, this work sheds light on a problem in the very spatial imagining of "above" and "below" language of rights—both by uncovering that lived experiences of law (i.e., law "from below") is often just as formative in legal consciousness and by showing that the very binary framing itself can be limiting.[24]

Rather than a state working as a static, coherent, cohesive entity—with a set purpose to undermine children's rights—the story of children's rights in Peru is much more nuanced and complex. Commentary about state power by the young people most affected by state violence is reflected through imagined absences, definitive logics, and affective longings. That is, in their discussions of everyday life in Lima, two groups of working young people featured in this book put forward specific new insights and political knowledge about the state and state power in Peru. But these insights were only able to come about over time, and through what I term "relational listening" practices.

Listening to Children Speak of Disparity of the State

What does it mean to genuinely listen to working young people, and those most affected by state and political violence, as narrators on relevant issues in their lives and as political subjects? What would be demanded by taking their subjectivity seriously, and what does such listening entail? Drawing on the work of multiple critical scholars, I define the type of listening in this book as a "relational approach" to listening.[25] Such an approach allows for the surfacing of multiple types of interrelated, historical, and routine experiences.[26]

Relational listening overlaps with other established research techniques that scholars commonly use with young people (such as qualitative interviewing and narrative driven approaches). But it has key differences, particularly in the amount of time over which this listening occurred, the degree of self-reflexivity with regard to interpretative methods, and an overt grounding in multiple types of critical theory and praxis. For the research for this book, this relational approach consisted of a long-term engagement;

it was not a one-off act. Nor was it only focused on the words the young people spoke. Instead, it involved understanding these children, and myself, as situated in time and space, which was reflexive of both my own positionality and theirs and was attentive to the knowledge that power, and history, would necessarily shape not just what these young people would say, but also how I would hear it.[27] Such an approach thus required being attentive to histories of colonialism, imperialism, sexism, and racism, knowing that each of our (the young people's and also my own) experiences and insights are shaped by processes seen and unseen, and these are grounded in the past and in the present.[28] It is a type of listening that pays attention to silences and narration about law and violence in context and relationship, as well to "historical and political conjuncture" (Santos 2005: 7).[29] A relational model turns toward the complex and intricate ways people are implicated in each other's lives, how knowledge is often co-constituted, and is attentive to the everyday impacts of long histories of colonization, global violence, and systems of domination.

I raise the question of this relational approach, because a core challenge I faced in the writing of this book, and one that is not often discussed enough with regard to children, is the question of partial and shared knowledges. Because of children's particular (dependent) standpoint, their expressions and views will always be in some ways mediated by adults. Children are not, and cannot be, fully self-autonomous; they are dependent, as are all beings. Research for this book therefore demanded participatory approaches to learning and knowing that draw from the counter-hegemonic traditions of activist research and that seeks to be non-extractive as a key goal of its practices. As Aída Hernández Castillo notes, such "research based on 'dialogues of knowledges' (*diálogos de saberes*) recognizes the partial nature of our perspective, the multiplicity of the subject positions characterizing the identities of social actors (including their relations of subordination), and the limitations of our situated knowledges" (2016: 35). This form of dialogue attends not only to what those most impacted by violence *add* to a broader understanding of political structures and political subjectivity, but also reveals the need for a relational commitment that is able to self-reflexively recognize what the co-formation of such knowledges can and does reveal.[30] In many ways, such an approach demands being able to break free from the myth of the "pure" or solo subject or self.[31]

10   Learning How to Describe the State

I first began the research for this book over a decade ago, curious about the meaning of Peru's particular commitment, on paper, to children's rights and the emergence in the 1990s of a wide number of laws in the country that accompany the discourse of child participation. In 1990, against a landscape of internal armed conflict, corruption, and violence, Peru was among the first twenty countries in the world to sign the international Convention on the Rights of the Child (CRC). Since the ratification of the CRC in 1990, the Peruvian government introduced numerous plans, including the National Plan for Children and Adolescents (Plan Nacional de Acción por la Infancia y la Adolescencia), National System of Integrated Attention for Children and Adolescents (Sistema Nacional de Atención Integral al Niño y el Adolescente), National Child Rights Code (Código de los Niños y Adolescentes), and Advisory Board of Girls, Boys, and Adolescents (Consejo Consultivo de Niñas, Niños, y Adolescentes, CCONNA).[32] Together, these legal instruments contributed to Peru having some of the most robust and notable children's rights policies in Latin America.

Starting in 2008, as I began research on the policies and laws that were emerging in the years following the ratification of the CRC, I conducted extensive interviews with policymakers, people working in nongovernmental organizations, scholars of Latin America, and workers in multilateral institutions, along with doing archival research and textual analysis. The aim of this research was to discern the imagined child that these laws and policies were identifying and to understand what had prompted the Peruvian government to enact notable numbers of legal mandates as compared to other neighboring countries. In addition, I was interested in understanding how the larger state architecture intersected with these laws and the motivations behind them, the historical emergence of children's rights in Peru, and an analysis of the discourse of the policies themselves.

Over time, however, after many years of studying the dominate official state narrative about children and children's policy in Peru—listening to adult policymakers talk about the "gap" of policy and practice and being immersed in the largely legalistic language of children's rights—this background ultimately hindered, or at least influenced, what I could and couldn't hear when I first met the children presented in this book. That is, being adult-centric and state-centric shaped much of the book's early years of research in that I inadvertently set up a mental dichotomy of children's

The Everyday Lives of Young People in Lima   11

perspective versus policy perspective, children's realities versus children's rights, the "local" voices of the children versus the "global" legalities of (state) policies.

I began to see that these adult-centric, state-centric approaches to issues were limiting my ability to fully hear the actual children at whom these laws and policies were supposedly aimed. In Peru, both children and adults are situated within numerous forms of intersecting violence—poverty, legacies of war, economic inequality, gendered and racialized violence, and environmental violence. The government's move to ratify the CRC and embrace children's rights policies in the 1990s emerged during widespread fear and violence. These policies, I came to understand, were shaped by a strong logic of dichotomy and difference. The imagined child subject was an individual child, a rational (yet dependent) being, a moral and innocent subject. What I was only able to realize after a number of years of research is the relationship between such an imagined rights-bearing child and longstanding logics of European colonial thought.[33] In many ways, it depends on a paradigm that obscures intersectional forms of violence, champions and privileges certain forms of knowledge over others, and relies on hierarchy as a key orientation. In the case of Peru, Spanish colonialism was particularly litigious, depending on law, bureaucracies, and institutions to lay foundations of domination and slavery.[34]

As such, what was demanded for this project was a frame that was able to hold the historical legacies, the contextual legal and structural frameworks, while also centering the particularities of what was both being said and not said by those most directly living through violence. It has not just been about the content of what children or adults say, but the relational context in which they say it and a specific critical interpretative analysis that is able to be both distinctive and specific about power relations. Put another way, it took me over a decade to shed a state-centric orientation that remains so dominant in most disciplines and to, instead, begin with what was emerging from the young people themselves, as political commentators and agentic subjects.

In practice, this approach meant doing field visits over many years, getting to know the young people's families, drawing pictures with them, playing soccer and jumping rope. It meant individual interviews and group interviews. It involved talking about what the young people themselves

12   Introduction

most wanted to talk about, rather than what I deemed important. Additionally, it was critical to the project that I wasn't just an outsider dropping in. Rather, the familiar relationship I was able to form with the young people in these pages was mediated through my research collaborator for this project, Enrique, someone who lived and worked with the community for years. At the time, Enrique—called *Profe* (short for teacher) by the young people of Lomas—was a Peruvian fieldworker, and he facilitated the trust and insights that these young people and their families so generously shared.

But genuine relational listening in this project also demanded humility and a recognition of one's own partial knowledge that extends far beyond the voices of just individual children. This was particularly evident from the members of MANTHOC—the second group of young people that I followed during those same years, living in a range of places across the city.

When Children Lobby the State for Rights:
Collective Organizing in Peru

MANTHOC was one of the first organized children's workers' groups in Peru. It is part of a larger unified working children's movement throughout Latin America, with vibrant regional chapters in multiple countries. MANTHOC emerged at the beginning of the turbulent era of political violence and internal armed conflict in Peru. I first witnessed some of the ways the organization worked when, in 2008, I attended several meetings at MANTHOC's base sites in Lima. The first meeting I went to took place in a large room, and the presenters, who were no older than 10, spoke about the importance of using rights-based language to realize their protagonism. For them, being a protagonist meant a recognition of their collective rights and their collective subjecthood, a concept discussed in Chapter 4. The meeting was part of their campaign at the time to change the national children's legal code, which they wanted to include clauses about the need for "dignified work."

Initially mobilized around the "foundation and consolidation of organizational and social identity" (MANTHOC 2016: 18), the movement used the language of rights they acquired as sons and daughters of union organizers, almost thirteen years before Peru ratified the Convention on the Rights of the Child. They argued that children should not be treated only as vulnerable objects to be primarily protected, but that they should be treated as people, and in their case, workers in their own right who deserve dignity and respect. In turn, the core values mobilized by MANTHOC calls attention to the widespread overemphasis on imagined solo voices in politics and raises the possibility that not enough attention is spent on what is being said collectively, or by movements.[35]

Unlike the young people in Lomas, whose embodied commentary on the state—including their anxieties, fears, fantasies, and hopes that helped shine light on the ways the state enacts violence in their lives through disparity—MANTHOC members, who are discussed in detail in Chapters 4 and 5, make another important contribution. By showing the fluid and expansive nature of the state, the young people of MANTHOC demonstrate how the state in Peru presents itself as a space for children to conceptualize their positions as state subjects, and as rights holders, while also shedding light on the particular logics needed to do so.

MANTHOC has chapter "bases" all around Peru, with multiple sites in Lima. I attended meetings and political events (public rallies, speeches, and campaigns) and did multiple interviews periodically over a span of ten years. In each encounter with members of MANTHOC, they always made clear that their sentiments and ideas were grounded in collective understandings of larger principals. Whereas in Lomas the young people identified key patterns of state violence without consciously engaging in "politics," MANTHOC members expressly engaged in political commentary, lobbying politicians, presenting at political events, and participating in policy debates with adults and other young people. By doing so, even if state policy largely imagines children as subjects through a lens of protection, MANTHOC members powerfully affirm the ways that children can, and do, engage in self-conscious political activity. But the complexity of this point is not to be overlooked.

For this project, embracing the ethos of this relational approach has meant questioning my own subjectivity, research decisions, and interpretations of the words and knowledges of the young people.[36] In particular, my position as a white, Western woman doing research with, and about, young people of the Global South, necessitates concerns over what Linda Martín Alcoff rightly calls "the problem with speaking for others." Alcoff notes that "we need to become clearer on the epistemological and metaphysical

14   Introduction

issues that are involved in the articulation of the problem of speaking for others, issues that most often remain implicit" (1991: 7). Part of the reason researchers often do not make such issues explicit, perhaps particularly with young people in the Global South, are the inherently parochial interpretations of children as not serious actors or political thinkers. But it is often equally grounded in the dominant categories used in research and policy to describe and understand children largely as individual (albeit dependent) actors, rather than as also embedded in historical, racial, gendered, political, and environmental economies. This book grapples to do both.

Defining Terms: Violence, Colonialism, and the Spatial Logics of Children's Rights

For the purpose of this book, I define violence as beyond only physical acts. The working young people in this book are all affected by extreme inequity and what Rob Nixon calls "slow violence": This is "a violence that occurs gradually and out of sight, a violence of delayed destruction that is dispersed over time and space, an attritional violence that is typically not viewed as violence at all" (Nixon 2011: 2).[37] I include in my definition structural violence, gross unequal access to resources, multiple forms of extractive practices, and the actions or lack of actions by governmental entities that block particular people from access to basic essentials of their lives—making a living, breathing clean air, health care, adequate food, clean water, and shelter (Gupta 2012: 5). As discussed throughout the following chapters, violence is both material and sometimes invisible, and plays out daily in the lives and bodies of those made marginal.

Such violence is also not just located in the present or the immediate. Peru's history of colonialism and colonial dispossession has meant there is a long, complex legacy of multiple scales of violence (discussed in Chapters 1–3) that influences how children and adults alike give insight into violence's multiple and intersecting forms. Historian Bianca Premo's scholarship about children in colonial Peru maps out a fuller picture of this. She notes how in colonial Spanish America, the ideal type of authority, in colonial practices, was "based on the belief that multiple individuals—male and female, young and old—were naturally subordinate to an authority figure, usually a male, who held superiority based on the hierarchal model of the Western family"

(Premo 2005: 9). A specific feature of colonial Spanish America, in other words, which was so dominant to the workings of colonialism in Peru, was that which naturalized, and normalized, a hierarchal relation between ruler and ruled, often through law and everyday customs. Premo's work documents how this ideal-typical model of subordination within a family was "replicated in political ideology at the level of the Spanish empire, with the King taking the role of father and colonial subjects conceived of as children" (Premo 2005: 10). To Spain, Lima, in particular, was one of the most important cities in colonial Latin America for trade, commercial activity, and slave labor.

This colonial history remains prevalent today. When I began this research, Peru was one of the most unequal countries in Latin America. Its history of dispossession, colonialization, and immense social and economic disparity directly inform the insights children offer about their lives there. Their knowledge shed light on what I term "spatial logics" used by the state, which, I argue, has been central to the employment of public policies about children in absolving the state of responsibility of injustice. When I use the term "spatial logics," I am referring to the ways policymakers and state actors tend to imagine children as nested first and foremost within families, rather than in states or as part of global processes of transnational exchange. It is a relational ordering that largely presents the state as neutral or benevolent and views politics as far from young people's lives (Hart 2008; Bernstein 2011).[38] The dominant orientation of politics as imagined as either "close to" or "far from" the lives of children is particularly prominent in Peru because of the state's strong discursive commitment by politicians and governmental actors for legal and political investment in children and children's voices.

Through the continual updating of national plans and laws related to children's rights and child participation over the last thirty years, the Peruvian government continues to elevate a seemingly child-centered approach, which influences all aspects of policy relating to children. For example, the National System of Integrated Attention for Children and Adolescents (Sistema Nacional de Atención Integral al Niño y al Adolescente *or* SNAINA) was conceptualized as the coordination of different institutions and public services aimed towards the enactment of children's rights. Legally speaking, SNAINA was enacted through law 26518, which offers general principles as well as specific articles outlining its scope. The first general

16   Introduction

principle is that it must act as the overarching framework for all "policies, plans and programs in the area of child and adolescent well-being." The second article states that "integrated attention should be directed towards the development of the child and adolescent in all aspects physical, moral, mental, and other dimensions of life in order to achieve the full incorporation and responsibility to the society and allow for the fulfilment of individual development." Finally, the law states that there should be coordination of national services (law 26518, article 4). Specifically, it states that SNAINA has the responsibility "to orient, integrate, structure, coordinate, supervise, and evaluate the policies, plans, programmes, and actions at the national level designated to the integrated attention of children and adolescents." This language of coordination and integration guides other laws and policies regarding children's rights in Peru. A "systems" approach, in this legal sense, is one that is about promoting consensus and integration with regard to children and child policy in Peru.

At the same time as the state has sought to demonstrate its engagement in children's welfare through these coordinated policies, legacies of economic, environmental, ethnic, and gendered violence in the country shape current realties. In Lima, a city of nearly 8 million people, more than 60 percent of the population live in "urban slums,"[39] and, as of 2015, incidents of gender-based violence against women and girls in Peru were among the highest in Latin America.[40] As such, the history of the Peruvian state's legal and political investment in children, and the elevation of children's voices, reads alongside high levels of disparity and is arguably even upheld by the very structures that maintain such inequality. Children are the assumed recipients of a dominant trickle-down economic orthodoxy and are imagined to be beneficiaries of the country's recent years of economic development.[41] But those made most marginal still suffer in direct and everyday ways. Children's rights policies in Peru have embraced child subjectivity but have largely done so in ways that uphold structures that enable and sustain state violence and economic marginalization.

The insights that young people in both Lomas and the members of MANTHOC discussed throughout this book underscore that it is a disservice to children, and particularly those who have inherited and experienced legacies of state violence, to present politics and violence as far from their lives, with children imagined as nested first and foremost within families.

A technocratic read is one that sees policy as about action, coherence, and easily distinguishable spheres of influence. But as the case of Peru makes clear, this conceptualization depends on a spatial schema in which children are rarely treated as political subjects. Said another way, it is a spatial order and conceptual schema that depoliticize and distance the role of state power in young people's lives, while simultaneously creating conditions of state and structural violence.

Unstable Comparisons: A Note on Methods and Organization

This book draws on two distinct groups of young people in one national context, while purposely trying to challenge false binaries. A danger with focusing on distinct case studies, particularly when set up as a comparison, is that it can seem to encourage a reading based on difference and distance (Abu-Lughod 2013). In this book, I use examples from two groups of young people not to oppose them against each other, but rather to show their connectedness. While these two groups of young Peruvians may seem, on the surface, to share stable terms and universal units of comparison—age, nationhood, conditions of poverty—the basis of their comparison is actually unstable in that one group understands their work in terms of the ways they have been made marginal by the state (having to work to help their families economically) while the other group understands their work in terms of an organizational orientation and shared ideology.[42] Despite the fundamental differences, therefore, in their comparison, what connects these young people is their shared experience of disparity and state violence. The history of colonialism in Peru and the lived effects of that legacy make the representation of these two groups particularly important and yet also unsettle the very basis of comparison itself (Kazanjian 2016).

Although an unstable comparison originally seemed to be a methodological challenge for this study, it ended up providing an important insight into this book's core analytical questions. The two groups of young people live in distinct contexts, yet they each ultimately offer valuable commentary on their experiences of state power, even if the texture and evidence of these lessons are quite diverse. This was something that became clear early in the research. With the young people in Lomas, for example, our time together was spent drawing pictures, playing soccer, and talking about everyday life.

18   Introduction

I got to know their families, their life histories, their individual aspirations. The conversations were not about an overarching collective or shared consciousness, but rather a located, geographic neighborhood experience: what they noticed and didn't notice about their everyday lives as children in their particular shantytown settlement. In contrast, the young people of MANTHOC were focused on their ideas and collective experiences as part of the movement. These young people wanted to talk about their lives as workers, and they were notably consistent in their understandings of the aims and values of MANTHOC, and also its mission. They spoke, first and foremost, as representatives of the organization, as a union. For MANTHOC, I went to public marches and organizational meetings, and I held focus groups and individual meetings. I took my cues from them about what they most wanted to speak about. Over the years, my "data" with both groups began to look increasingly unalike.[43]

In their differences, however, the legibility and illegibility of the young people's critiques about state violence reveal that young people's voices can and do speak of injustice—underscoring that the sound of critique doesn't take just one pitch. Indeed, because of the wide range of ways state power and state processes present themselves, in order to gain a fuller understanding of that power it is necessary and useful to listen to a host of young people who have been (differently) marginalized by the state.

For this book, part of the ethics of listening to both groups of young people demanded taking cues about how they *themselves* wanted to be represented and what core issues *they* wanted to discuss.[44] While the young people of MANTHOC spoke as representatives of a highly organized movement, the young people of Lomas spoke as individual children living in a poor, marginalized neighborhood. Although my methodological commitment allowed the two groups of young people to drive the subject matter of their interviews, which shapes what I do and don't know about them, both groups reveal different and important insights about the working of state power as located beyond only place or embedded in institutions and point to new ways to conceptualize children's subjecthood as political commentators about global capitalism's piercing inequalities.

This book is organized into three parts. In an effort to avoid centering the state and state policy as the driving lens for contemplating the children and their communities, I purposely begin the book with the children themselves. The first three chapters focus on a small group of young people living and working in Lomas de Carabayllo, an urban shantytown on the northern outskirts of Lima.[45] These chapters describe multiple types of historical and everyday violence that the young people and their families face, including the legacies of colonialism in Peru, internal armed conflict in the country, their parents' experiences of migration to Lima in response to such violence, and current day-to-day environmental and "slow" violence. The chapters grapple with the complexities of finding adequate ways to capture how the young people speak both directly and indirectly about global and historical forces affecting them, while also staying attuned to the particular experiences they describe about their lives.

Part II focuses on members of MANTHOC, whose home neighborhoods are primarily in the center of Lima. Chapters 4 and 5 provide a social history and overview of MANTHOC as a movement and discuss some of the political stakes in a rights-based organization. For MANTHOC members, enacting children's rights is about pushing for fair labor conditions and arguing for what they term "dignified work." These chapters discuss the history of the MANTHOC movement and the influence of the children's rights theorist Alejandro Cussiánovich, specifically the theories in his 2007 book, *Aprender la Condición Humana. Ensayo Sobre Pedagogía de la Ternura*. The young people of MANTHOC, influenced by Cussiánovich's work, understand participation and citizenship in ways that are directly related to the history of state formation in Peru and internal armed conflict. These chapters focus on the ways these young people employ rights language to describe state violence, a language that is largely deductive of a philosophy that they have been taught and that they make their own. In this way, listening to MANTHOC young people necessitates a questioning as to what *kind* of state is centered and showcased for everyday life in Peru.

The final chapter of the book, Chapter 6, expands several key analytical threads from the prior chapters and discusses how, with regard to contestations with state power, it is not just children like the ones living in Lomas and the members of MANTHOC who are enveloped in the paradoxes of grappling with the logics of state power. Rather, this chapter argues it is also state and non-state actors, normative legal documents, and everyday public discourse that reflect such logics. Drawing on examples from children's rights policy in Peru, the practices of participatory budgeting, government children advisory boards, and Peru's National System for Children's Rights, this chapter demonstrates a range of ways the Peruvian state uses a discourse of children's rights and children's participation to elude certain forms of critique, while at the same time furthering unjust conditions and material realities. Paying attention to these issues today is particularly timely: Since beginning to write this book over a decade ago, legal and economic inequality has only grown more pronounced, and many governments across the world have taken a wider turn to the political right and have explicitly taken steps to shift away from rights-based discourse for both children and women. My argument, therefore, is focused not just on the need to reimagine the very categories of *who* we turn to as experts in order to reveal the everyday workings of state power, but also, the importance of reexamining the means and methods of doing so.

The political insights and ideas about state power presented by the children and young people in this book challenge key questions about children's subjectivity, and also complicate the spatial frame of state violence itself. Since many of the insights about state violence have remained dominantly narrated and generated by adults, the questions (both asked and left unasked) about daily workings of state power have been skewed.[46] In particular, when children who have been made marginal, especially those whose daily work and lives are most directly implicated in economic systems of inequality, aren't taken seriously as commentators of state violence, it becomes easy to fundamentally miss key insights about the working of state power. In the case of Peru, such gaps in knowledge have had as much to do with a technocratic "systems" understanding of (modern) childhood as about doctrinal and colonial conceptions of statehood and law.

PART I

I

Listening Between Generations

Past and Present Violence in Lomas

IN THE WINTER OF 2008, I met Eva and Clara, two girls living in Lomas de Carabayllo. At the time, Eva was 7 years old, and Clara was 9. They loved to draw pictures of flowers, and during long drawing sessions, they would tell stories about their father, whom they admired and loved. Their father, they told me, was the center of their universe. Their father Julian worked at the landfill not far from where they lived in Lomas, an area in the northern cone of Lima. Julian had been working there for almost ten years, but, by the spring of 2008, he was sick with tuberculosis and could not work at the landfill anymore.

When I first met Eva and Clara, several local NGOs were doing public health campaigns and programs in Lomas to educate the community about the heavy leads and pollution in the area. Eva and Clara believed their father became ill because of "unclean water." They told me there were diseases in the water that were the cause of their father's illness. Local NGOs increased public health programs in the neighborhood partly as a response to an outbreak of serious illnesses associated with the water some years before. State officials had declared the neighborhood *contaminada*, and this language was made very public.

Initially Eva and Clara's father was the only one in the family who had tuberculosis. Both girls expressed worry about their father, and they were concerned about contaminated water and the toxic land on which they lived. Within a year of when their father first became sick, Eva, Clara, and their mother Andrea all tested positive for tuberculosis. During that time, Julian's sickness worsened, and he was now too sick to work. In addition to Eva and Clara, there was Luana to care for, their 2-year-old little sister. And the three girls saw the effects of their father's illness in an intimate way—the whole family shared a bedroom. Both Andrea and Clara had to get paying jobs outside of their home to cover what Julian alone had made before becoming too sick to work. Clara, then aged 10½, began paid factory work, cutting glass bottles in the landfill near their house. Andrea, who was pregnant, took a job as a maid. Eva, then 8½, was responsible for cooking, cleaning, and caring for her younger sister and a neighboring child while Clara and their mother were out working. Despite the hardships of working, Clara told me multiple times how much she enjoyed her job at the factory because it was social, and she got to be with her friends. She liked contributing to the household as well. However, one day Clara cut herself on a machine in an accident at the factory. While she recovered and could still work, she recognized that, as one of the primary breadwinners in the family, the accident could have changed her life, and the life of her family, forever.[1] These experiences would impact how Clara understood her life in Lomas and how she describes the environmental violence that she and others in Lomas faced in their daily lives and work, particularly from living so close to one of the largest former landfills in Lima.

Clara's description of the injustice she faced, including needing to work to support her family as a result of her father's sickness from what she saw and described as toxic land, was similar to the ways other young people in Lomas discussed the injustices they encountered. Like Clara, other young people in Lomas would describe the regular burning of trash in their neighborhood that made their lungs hurt and the poison in the streets that killed their beloved dogs. Their play time was interrupted by the kicked-up dirt, dust, and pollution on the unpaved roads. They often worried about their parents, mainly because of their difficult labor conditions, and told anecdotes of how their work directly impacts their bodies. In doing so, through their descriptions of daily life, labor, and environmental degradation, the young people of Lomas pointed to the kinds of state violence they experience in Peru. Although they did not use conceptual or legal language when speaking of the state, their descriptions highlighted the state (and its absence) by speaking of the piercing injustices they saw in their lives, such as Clara's identification of the environmental conditions that prompted her need to work and the unclean water she believed made her father sick.

Current structural, everyday violence in Peru shapes the way young people like Clara discuss the injustice and environmental violence they witness.[2] This type of everyday, often invisible violence transforms the lives of young people like Clara and Eva and informs specific ways of how they think about, and describe, rights, law, and politics. Scholarship, media, and international organizations frequently suggest that what counts as "violence" is physical and immediate, often leaving out temporality and intergenerational effects.[3] That is, violence that occurs over time—such as the slow effects of pollution—or the ways colonial settlement redefines people's relationship with the land not only obscures the toll that this kind of violence inflicts on people, but it can also overlook the role of the state, obscuring the state as a violent actor and presenting the state as a neutral site.

This downplaying of state violence is often made through legal frameworks that depoliticize the state itself and that remove it as a source for this kind of violence.[4] When "the state" is discussed in relation to these kinds of slow violence, however, it is largely presented as monolithic and static, as a moral entity or agent.[5] But these representations, as children like Eva and Clara make clear, overlook key ways that the state expresses itself in people's lives. For example, when the young people of Lomas spoke of state processes and state violence, they did not speak of physical threats, domestic violence, or militarism. They spoke instead about the daily effects of environmental violence, about moments of unequal or unfair treatment, or about inadequate services in their neighborhood. Rather than inferring to an "entity," the young people of Lomas regularly described the state through relational terms, desires, and affect.[6]

José was 11 years old when we first met and lives and works in Lomas. He lives in a small lodging not far from Clara and Eva's family, and he works to help pay the bills by doing commercial work selling items in a

26   Listening Between Generations

small store. Also, like Clara and Eva, he regularly speaks of environmental injustice he faces in his life, but in a tone and tenor that is one of longing and feeling. For example, as discussed more in Chapter 3, he notes the ways he feels "forgotten" by the state.

The language that José and Clara use to portray state processes in their lives is different than the way politicians, policymakers, or scholars describe the impact or methods of government or the state. The young people living in Lomas depict state violence and state processes largely through a language of absence. They used descriptions of their physical landscapes and daily experiences, grounded in their relationships and longings. They list elements of their everyday lives—no running water, polluted air, an inadequate sewage system—as factors that affect their health and development, while at the same time being some of the reasons why they work. By describing the issues in this way, Clara, like other young people from Lomas discussed in this chapter, point to the state not as an abstract force, but as a dynamic located in their bodies and kinship, played out and bound up in the everyday. The environmental examples the young people give—their lack of access to clean water, the ways the pollution burns in their lungs, and the lack of trees—may not all be classified as acts of physical violence, but they are still violations.[7] And they shape how the young people in Lomas come to understand and speak of justice and injustice.[8]

These comments from young people like Clara and José on such everyday experiences shed light on broader structural disparity. But they also reveal the nature of political commentary itself. For example, their insights on structural violence are not just discernible in what they say; they are also made apparent by what they don't say. This can be heard most clearly when considering their words and thoughts in the context of Peru's political and colonial history.[9] While the children of Lomas themselves don't remember the recent history of political and colonial violence in Peru, that legacy still reverberates in the landscape and in the stories and memories their families and teachers pass on to them. It is a legacy that shapes how the young people living in Lomas see and understand the world around them, as well as the key institutions with which they interact.[10] The phenomenon of looking both to silence, as well as words, to understand forms of violence is hardly specific to Peru, and scholars have identified its importance in numerous other national contexts. Anthropologist Clara Han, for example, recalling her childhood as a Korean American and what her parents did or did not say about the Korean War, writes about the notion of the "inheritance" of violence that young people of families who have lived through war, genocide, and multiple forms of violence experience. Han notes the challenge of being able to hold what children are saying as they are "piecing together a world" (Han and Brandel 2020). In her book *Seeing Like a Child*, Han urges a specific kind of curiosity, and in turning to this inheritance of violence, she suggests that we not "overwrite it with stable adult categories" (Han 2021: 22). She distinctly doesn't label this type of violence as trauma, for example, or even assert that such articulations are entirely conscious. Rather, Han points to what it would mean to not assume categories and place them on children. In this same way, the young people who live in Lomas "piece together" in their words and silences multiple types of interrelated, historical, and everyday experiences of violence. Their ideas and commentary consistently reflect this quotidian violence and the structural conditions of inequality, even if not always in overt or marked terms.

Centering the young people of Lomas's commentary about everyday life and their interpretations of the world helps uncover the violence that they encounter while also revealing the wider context of injustice that the many young people in Lomas like Clara, José, and Eva face in their daily lives. Later in this chapter, I discuss how multiple sources of inheritances of violence have come to shape the ways the children discuss their lives in Lomas and with the state. But to do so requires a careful attention to identify and understand key sources of material inequality impacting their lives.

Living in a Peruvian Urban Periphery

Lomas de Carabayllo lies in the northern outskirts of sprawling Lima and is deemed by the city to be the fourth poorest district in the capital. Reaching Lomas from Lima city center takes at least two hours by bus. It is one of nine districts that comprise the northern cone of Lima and is often described as a marginalized area, in both the spatial and the socioeconomic sense, in relation to the city center. Yet, its history is one of immense importance for the city, dating back to colonial times, in that it has been an area of tremendous production and export, including wheat during the sixteenth and seventeenth centuries, and sugarcane in the eighteenth and early

28   Listening Between Generations

nineteenth centuries. The district was also at one point a major producer of cotton. The 1920 census noted that 70 percent of land dedicated to agriculture in Lima was located in the district of Carabayllo.[11]

Despite this early focus on production and export of goods and agriculture, Lomas de Carabayllo was only formally recognized as one of Lima's residential zones in the early 1990s.[12] Before then, Lomas was designated by Lima officials as first an agricultural zone and then as a garbage industrial zone—rather than a residential area. This meant that although people lived there, much of the infrastructure necessary for habitation was not provided by the state, nor were public services.

The history of how Lomas de Carabayllo became inhabited, after being the city's largest landfill for fifty years, is a story of slow violence against the people who came to live there. It was largely uninhabited from the 1920s to the 1960s; then governmental agrarian reform policies led a group of poor workers to move there. These families settled on the land to work and later became legally recognized as residents, a contested process that, even until recently, was explained by the government as a story of "invasions" by the people.[13] Agrarian reform began in Peru in 1969, and the declared aim was to replace large estates of land and subsistence farms with a more just and equal property system. The reform gave a framework for the expropriation of landholdings and permitted small tracts of land to be owned by individuals, peasant communities, and fragmented cooperatives. However, as Enrique Mayer notes, the ways that "land ended up predominately in the hands of smallholders was not by design of the reformers, but by the autonomous actions of its beneficiaries" (Mayer 2009: 231). In 1998, based on organizing by the community of Lomas, the owners of the landfill extended a passageway from one of the major roads through Lomas and allowed many more people (primarily poor workers) to live in the area, prompting the official recognition of the district as residential.[14]

During the late 1990s, Peru was still in the midst of a twenty-year internal armed conflict between a communist-Maoist insurgency named *Sendero Luminoso* (Shining Path), armed governmental military forces, and the Túpac Amaru Revolutionary Movement (Movimiento Revolucionario Túpac Amaru *or* MRTA). This conflict had devastating consequences that played out in material ways across the country. On top of increased urban migration from rural areas to Lima due to the conflict, the country experienced what is now known as "*fujishock*"—a term that refers to the neoliberal restructuring and dramatic limiting of the state during the presidency of Albert Fujimori that lasted from 1990 to 2000. Between 1990 and 2000 alone, living expenses in Lima increased by nearly 400 percent, resulting in the deepening of poverty and stark inequality.[15] Public expenditures were dramatically reduced, and taxes increased, transforming the geographic and socioeconomic makeup of the city, particularly in terms of further disenfranchisement of poor people living and working in the informal outskirts of the city, such as Lomas.

Today, Lomas de Carabayllo consists of eighty-two smaller informal settlements, which are commonly termed *pueblos jóvenes*. These settlements began to become formally recognized by the state between 1998 and 2014. The legacy of the years of families living and working in what was once deemed an "inhabitable" space by the government, and was only recently deemed "habitable," remains alive today. State services—such as schooling, health centers, electricity, and so on—have been slow to come to the area. While the majority of the neighborhood residents' wages depend on trash and recycling, Lomas has slowly developed infrastructure over the past eighteen years, including the building of a state-run school, electrification, and, in January of 2009, a much-celebrated small health center (*la posta*).[16] Despite this, even the local municipal government recognizes the high levels of structural and infrastructural inequality that exist, especially in comparison to Lima's city center. A 2015 local municipal government report highlighted how a considerable portion of the inhabitants of Carabayllo don't have access to drinking water, a sewage system, and electricity. It noted the inadequate infrastructure and the lack of equipment needed for educational institutions, as well as how "malnutrition among children remains a problem" ("*Plan de Desarrollo Concertado de Lomas de Carabayllo 2004–2015*": 23).

While the garbage landfill in Lomas, which is called El Zapallal, contributes enormously to the environmental degradation of the area, it also provides a primary way for many families to earn a living, as most of the men of Lomas sort and recycle different trash materials.[17] While there are other landfills in Lima that are much bigger now, El Zapallal remained for many years one of the largest sites for the sorting of recycling materials in the city.

When I first met the young people in Lomas in 2008, for many of the working young people there were two main avenues for them to earn money at the landfill. The first was from finding or picking up recyclables in nearby areas. A 2006 report done by a local NGO noted that the common pay for this type of work was 10 soles (US $2.89) for twelve hours of work, contingent on the young worker collecting at least 20 kilos of recyclables. The second way was from entering the garbage trucks and separating the various materials (cardboard, plastic, glass, cans, etc.) and selling the recyclable items. The report noted that more boys than girls performed this type of work, and they typically earned an average of 20 soles (US $5.78) in a twelve-hour period. While there has not been enough research regarding this particular zone and rates of pay, 20 soles was overall low compared to the national pay average for people scavenging and selling recyclables.

Families in Lomas live daily with contradiction. Living next to a landfill means living with environmental pollution, poverty, and marginalization—but the land, specifically the landfill, serves as a key means for people to earn money and make a life. This paradox represents the material precariousness for the families living in a place like Lomas. Kathleen Millar, writing about

Figure 1: A main road in Lomas de Carabayllo. Photo taken by author, 2008.

Figure 2: View of a valley of Lomas de Carabayllo. Photo taken by author, 2008.

families living and working in a city garbage dump in Rio, Brazil, notes that one of the dangers of focusing on labor largely in terms of production is a glossing over of the deep yet often elusive contradictions of global capitalism. "What the celebration of labor and production ignores is wage labor's enduring history as a form of violence and technique of governance" (2018: 9). Living in Lomas embodies this kind of everyday contradiction: People's labor allows their participation in the economy, and to provide for their families, while at the same it exposes them to violence and toxicity. The Lomas young people describe and pick up on these complexities and dialectics.[18]

Defining State Violence Through Materiality and Everyday Life

Navigating the contradictions of labor, financial needs, and inequality in Lomas is daily life for the young people who live there. Much of their description of their neighborhood emphasizes this disparity, highlighting through their accounts of place, desire, and affect. But it is also described through relationships and play and emotions. When children in Lomas talk about what they like about their neighborhood, they emphasize the phys-

32 Listening Between Generations

ical environment. "I like the animals, the nature, the air," Monica, age 12, stated. Monica lives with her brother and sister and parents in Lomas. She was among the larger group of children that I first met in 2009. She likes to jump rope with her friends and has a wide and glowing smile.

Like Monica, the other children in Lomas also emphasized the physical environment when they described things they liked about their neighborhood. Some talked about the flowers, their dogs, and the parks. Although they consistently named things in the physical environment when describing what they liked about their neighborhood, it was also the physical environment that they described when identifying what they didn't like: with a particular focus on the contamination and pollution of the air. In this conversation, excerpted from an exchange that took place during a focus group of young people ages 7–12, they transitioned seamlessly between these topics:

> Enrique (interviewer): What do you like about your neighborhood?
> Janita: Nature.
> Enrique: What else do you like about your neighborhood?
> Monica: The animals.
> Enrique: Which animals?
> Monica: The dogs.
> Dina: Yea, the dogs.
> Enrique: What else? What else do you like about your neighborhood?
> Katy: The plants.
> Monica: The air.
> José: I like my house.
> Katy: I don't like the air in my house because it is contaminated.
> Enrique: Ah, we have arrived at the second question. What don't you like about your neighborhood?
> Katy: The air.
> José: That the mayor says he was going to give us parks and he didn't do it.
> Enrique: And this is something you don't like. What else?
> Janita: That they burn the garbage.[19]

Past and Present Violence in Lomas   33

For Janita, Monica, Dina, José, and Katy, the issues of the "burning of the garbage" and the everyday surroundings were not abstract or theoretical but played out in their bodies and the lives of their families. One local NGO who has worked in Lomas since 1976 conducted a study and found that negative health effects and illness were common for young people who work with recycling in the landfill in Lomas. The CESIP report notes some common symptoms among Lomas children and young people:

> suffering from acute respiratory infections, frequent headaches, parasites and diseases of the stomach and skin, as well as to being exposed to accidents related to the activity they perform (cuts, punctures, burns and abuses). More than half of those who reported having been ill in the last six months reported respiratory problems. Also, 35% mentioned various conditions such as dizziness, headaches, body (spine, legs), diarrheal, intestinal parasites, skin problems, and other diseases.

While the physical symptoms are one aspect of everyday life in Lomas, another is that of perceived connections. That is, Clara and Eva, like the other young people of Lomas, believed their everyday working conditions were linked to their health. It was not uncommon for the young people to speak about "contamination"—and reflections about the land and the air would often come up when discussing their neighborhood or surroundings. Lela was an only child. She would sometimes go to help her father who works in recycling, and sometimes she would help her mother sell bread at the market. She was 13 when we had this discussion about Lomas:

> Mikaela: What do you like about your neighborhood?
> Lela: That there is light and the church I go to on Sundays.
> Mikaela: And what don't you like about your neighborhood?
> Lela: That it is contaminated. That there is so much scattered trash.
> Mikaela: So there is trash, but there are also many plants? [*referring to the plants in the picture Lela had drawn*]
> Lela: Yea, there are, but it can contaminate the plants too, and then they can't grow, and this happens too.

34   Listening Between Generations

Mikaela: And what else? How do you know there is contamination?
Lela: When they burn the garbage. The smoke. [*el humo*]
Mikaela: What is *el humo*?
Lela: When a candle burns something and it comes up black, that is the
smoke. That is smoke. And that's what does damage to your lungs.
Mikaela: Ahh. And when do they do that?
Lela: When they burn the garbage.
Mikaela: Do they do it in the day, or in the night?
Lela: Sometimes they burn it in the day and sometimes at night . . . then
smoke comes out and then when you breathe it hurts your lungs.[20]

The image of the contamination hurting the young people's lungs when they breathe is something that may not be marked as spectacular violence or even as immediately linked to illness or disease. Yet, the relationship between health and the embodiment of living in Lomas was something the young people strongly emphasized; the language of contamination and toxins often came up in our conversations when speaking about everyday life in Lomas. The young people of Lomas spoke of their own precarity not in terms of crisis, or even something overt or remarkable, but rather through descriptions of everyday life and place.[21]

The young people of Lomas became most animated when speaking about their neighborhoods and about the importance of their daily physical environments (trash, trees, flowers, pollution). Until recently, children's rights discourses, used on behalf of children, have traditionally omitted environmental justice as central to the realization of other rights.[22] As Cindi Katz notes in her ethnographic study of young people both in New York and South Sudan, "the widespread and serious environmental problems that are symptomatic of capitalist relations of production have received plenty of public attention, but not necessarily as problems of social reproduction" (Katz 2004: 21).[23]

What was striking about the young people's commentary about everyday life and the environment in Lomas was the ways their descriptions were also observations of (state) injustice. For example, Camila, age 14, works by sewing clothes with her sister, as well as doing daily chores at home such as cooking and cleaning in the house. When I asked what she likes and does not like about Lomas, Camila noted:

Here in my neighborhood, there isn't anything—no water, no sewage. Sometimes we fill water in our containers, but they get dirty. Then comes the *dengues* [mosquitoes carrying dengue fever]. One time there was an invasion of *dengues* and they were in all of my water. I had no water to drink or to use for anything. It got so bad that there was a little worm that showed up in my water—I had to dump it all out. On top of that, they say that there was a meeting about the water and sewage system for my neighborhood and that they were going to change the public faucet. They had to change it because the person who had been taking care of the water tank would charge us all the time. So, they were going to change the keys to the tank and change the piping, but they haven't done it. They say that all the water has rust in it now, that we're drinking rusted water.[24]

Camila's physical everyday experiences, including the water she drinks, help constitute what she describes as the neighborhood and, as will be discussed in the next two chapters, what she sees as the (absent) workings of the state. What she describes may not read as overt or physical violence. But, in this case, a narrow focus on individual physical violence would miss or occlude larger structural elements of which Camila speaks so clearly.

Camila's observations about the lack of access to clean water in Lomas provide specific insight into the workings of state power in Lomas. A 2015 study by Oxfam found that in Lima water for poor people cost ten times more than for those living in affluent residential areas.[25] Such structural inequality is evident to the young people when they carry the physical weight of the large blue plastic water jugs on unpaved roads, when they fear their water is not clean and carries disease, and when they hear from their parents about the burden of water costs. As such, to listen to the young people of Lomas is to listen both to moments of care and relationship, of interdependence with the people and environment around them, and how such narratives of place are linked to larger systems of dispossession. More specifically, it is about listening to the contradictions to which the young people of Lomas are attuned: that their physical everyday lives are predicated on a basic disparity. And that disparity is tied to the very source of their labor and livelihood. It is not just that the water they drink costs ten times more than water in other parts of Lima; it is also the hardship involved for their families to earn money to drink such water, the burden involved in physically carrying such water, and the mental weight and worry that such water will bring illness to their families. All of these factors carry a great cost.

But listening to young people in this way is not just to pay attention to scarcity or lack.[26] Rather, a relational approach brings forward specific insights these young people offer on both geopolitical inequality and daily contradictions, as presented through mundane stories of environmental injustice and everyday life. This includes stories of slow violence enacted by the Peruvian state (for example, about lack of access to clean water) but, importantly, also descriptions of wider systems of exclusion and hierarchy. It is these systems of violence, circulating both beyond and within the margins of the (nation) state, that could be easily missed in the young people's narratives and that require paying attention to more than just the words they spoke.

Drawing a Story of Life on the Margins

The political commentary that the young people in Lomas offered as observations about the centrality of their environment and everyday life was not just through speech. We often spent time drawing and playing soccer or jumping rope together. Through play or nonverbal exchanges, insights sometimes emerged about how they view and experience Lomas. For example, near the beginning of my time in Lomas while I was still getting to know the young people, I asked them to draw pictures of their neighborhood. Many of the children drew similar images of roads, flowers, and houses, but they frequently presented them in what were more like visual maps than pictures. There were few people in their drawings, but there was a notable consistency in their use of what looked like aerial views to depict their neighborhood. Cynthia Enloe writes about what she refers to as a "feminist curiosity"—an instinct to pay attention to silence and margins as a method to form conceptual links (2004). When I first saw the young people's drawings, I drew on Enloe's concept of feminist curiosity. Instead of just asking what was in their pictures, I asked what, for them, was just off the edge of the page in their drawings? They often responded to this question by describing things they said they did not like (the trash, the contamination, the mines).

The young people's recognition that these environmental and physical elements of their neighborhood might be considered part of the narratives in their pictures, even if they are not included in the images they chose to draw, served as a prompt for deeper conversation.[27] José, for example, would come shyly at first to these drawing sessions, which often consisted of mostly girls. He would stand at the doorway listening and adding to the conversation, but not sitting down. The girls would try to convince him to stop standing in the doorway and to join. During one of the drawing sessions at a community hall in Lomas, Jose decided to participate and make a drawing of his neighborhood. Afterwards, when I asked him about it, he described the margins of his page as the site of the pollution. The following is an exchange with José about his neighborhood drawing when he was 11:

> Mikaela: What do you like about your neighborhood?
> José: That the people are so nice, really funny, that there are [soccer] fields, that there is a school, a school where they teach well and where the hills are very beautiful.
> Mikaela: And what don't you like?
> José: I don't like that there is garbage.

Figure 3: Neighborhood drawing by José, age 11. Photo taken by author, 2008.

38   Listening Between Generations

> Mikaela: And what is behind here? [*points to just off the top of the page*]
> José: That's where the garbage is.
> Mikaela: Ah, the garbage.
> José: And the mine is in this space. [*points off the page*]

José was very clear that the mine and the garbage were part of his neighborhood. They were part of his description. However, he did not draw them. José loves to ride his bike and to play soccer, and although the spaces in the drawings where José drew soccer fields are indeed some of the spaces where he and his friends play soccer, there are no actual formal soccer fields in Lomas. Rather, José and his friends play soccer in large, sandy areas on the edge of the unpaved roads near their school. But in José's picture, three large soccer fields were front and center. Map drawings done by the young people of Lomas served as prompts for them to be interpreters, curators, and narrators of the neighborhood, and they did not see them as solely visual representations of their everyday realties.[28] Part of what came through in their interpretations, through talking about their drawings, was that what was on the actual page—what they deemed visual—was only one piece of a whole array of insights they had about their sense of place and the neighborhood.

In 2008, Ana, who was 9 years old at the time, described her neighborhood picture in this way:

> Mikaela: What do you like most about your neighborhood?
> Ana: Ahhh, the little dogs! I have a little dog. I didn't draw many, I
>   missed them, but there are several dogs here. Here the neighbor also
>   has a dog and here is a shop, I don't know which one it is here . . .
> Mikaela: Ah! Many dogs!
> Ana: Yes! So many dogs!
> Mikaela: Yes. And what are the things you don't like?
> Ana: I don't like it when they burn the garbage that comes here. Like
>   when the woman burns her garbage then there is smoke, and it gets
>   into us and makes us feel bad in our lungs.
> Mikaela: Which neighbor? Here? [*indicating the drawing*]
> Ana: Yes, sometimes here, here, here and all of the houses that make
>   smoke. I mean, if we burn garbage then we make smoke, right? It goes

into our noses . . . and this goes to our lungs and makes us feel ill . . . it's better to throw the trash away.

Mikaela: But there is no garbage in your drawing.

Ana: A car comes. A giant car comes there. [*points to area off of drawing*] But actually, not many cars pass through there, because there are walls, and behind there is a mountain that is like a mine. Yes, there also is the mine here [*points to area off of drawing*] and there are several that are higher up, over there, but behind here there are more houses, there's a block, and there are more houses. Over there. Behind my house there are some houses and behind there are bricks but that is a mine behind these bricks, there is a mine behind the wall.

Mikaela: What type of mine?

Ana: Mines, not of gold, not much in the hills, but they work, they make dirt and there are so many that we complain because it gets into our noses.

Ana, like José, did not draw some of the elements she described—in her case, the mines, garbage, and dogs. She showed me with hand motions where they were located, as if they were spatially part of her imagined picture of her neighborhood, but not physically on the page. There were also no people, no neighbors, in Ana's picture. Rather there were the blue water jugs of water and brightly colored, neatly lined, adjoined houses. Listening to Ana in a way that allowed her to narrate and make visual where the margins for her neighborhood begin and end (whether or not on the actual page) facilitated hearing some of the contradictions the children saw in Lomas, particularly in terms of environmental injustice. That is, Ana's beloved dog, her neighbors, and her friends were not captured visually in her picture, but such relationships and people were indeed part of how she described her neighborhood, as well as the toxicity and description of what "makes us feel ill."[29]

These map drawings, and our related conversations, reveal the centrality of the environment for the young people of Lomas. The children imagined and described their neighborhoods in terms of the materiality of their daily lives, and the scenery and landscapes that surround them. Their drawings reinforced this. While the prompt from me was to draw a picture of their neighborhood, nearly all of them drew what could be seen instead as maps, scenes without people, without interactions of daily life. It was as if they had zoomed out and were looking at their neighborhoods from above. Noticing the ways they left images of trash, toxicity, and landfills off their drawings but still included such descriptions when discussing these drawings, was made possible by a type of listening that took place over time, and over many meetings. By engaging with the young people over time through drawing, playing soccer, and talking, I came to see how representation for them was not just concerned with rationality or "fact" in the way an adult or researcher might look for facts. Instead, what the young people were offering in their descriptions of daily life in Lomas, and seen in their drawings of their neighborhood, was fundamentally a notation about the linkages between their sense of place and contradictory systems of inequality.[30]

Hearing the "quiet" of the Lomas young people's images—what was included in their narratives of their pictures but imagined by them as just off the borders of the pages—meant attending to not just what was drawn but also how they used such visual representations as prompts to say more. More specifically, listening to the young people required being attentive to the historical and geopolitical dynamics, which, even if the young people weren't directly aware of them, served as a backdrop through which they both drew, and described, their pictures.[31] Environmental degradation, colonialism, and capitalist production are part of the contextual histories that

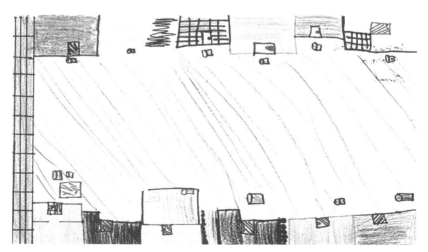

Figure 4: Neighborhood drawing by Ana, age 9. Photo taken by author, 2008.

Figure 5: Neighborhood drawing by Clara, age 10. Photo taken by author, 2008.

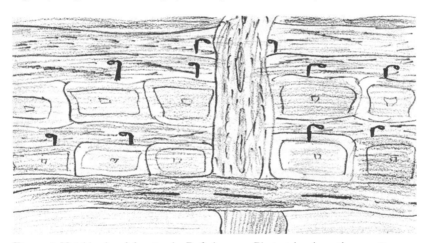

Figure 6: Neighborhood drawing by Rafael, age 11. Photo taken by author, 2008.

shape the place of Lomas, all of which, in some ways, informed and organized what the young people drew.[32] Asking questions to understand more broadly their many perceptions of their communities and everyday lives, as well as the complexities involved, was grounded in the ways these young people spoke of their experiences as anchored in place. And, like all places, the "locality" of it is embedded within the larger contexts of history, power, and relationships (Smith 2012; Eslava 2015).[33]

42 Listening Between Generations

Being able to hear both the present as well as the historical and contextual, proved crucial given that the place of Lomas, which came through the young people's descriptions, was not able to be separated from the global and longitudinal forces that shape that place, nor the historical violence and legacies of struggle that gave rise to its inhabitancy.[34] At the same time, there is danger in overreading that history of place and reducing these young people to being only vulnerable subjects.[35] Being able to find a relational method to hear both the young people's concrete and everyday examples of their experiences of Lomas, as well as the ways historical and slow violence has shaped their experiences, meant being comfortable with the friction and contradiction of both narrative and experience (Van Vleet 2020).

Scholars studying children in different contexts have noted a similar finding about how drawings and visual methods can prompt discussions of issues in children's lives that might have otherwise remained undiscussed. For example, anthropologist Nancy Scheper-Hughes (2008) found during her work with street children in Brazil a notable contrast between the sunny and bright drawings and the young people's daily lives. Scheper-Hughes highlighted these upbeat drawings as altering the narratives about their "violent" lives, demonstrating the children's resiliency and coping methods. In the case of Lomas, what shone through in terms of commentary against the structural and environmental violence in which they were living was not just what was on the page, but rather what was just beyond the margins. That is, the young people's abilities to represent, speak about, and critique what they saw in their everyday spaces was not always fully expressed on the page itself. But such complexities, and even contradictions, were often expressed in layers through their narratives. Everyday violence organizes and influences the ways the young people experience their neighborhood, and their drawings reflected a broad array of feelings they had about their lives as residents in Lomas, as well as the daily contradictions, inequality, and toxicity they see.

In some ways, the Lomas young people's drawings seemed to serve as aspirational images, representations of what they *thought* made a good drawing: sunshine, animals, brightly colored houses. Yet because of our longitudinal relationship and the normalcy of drawing pictures, they also were ready to share the larger context of the narrative and the pieces of their neighborhood that they did not draw.[36] One potential explanation as to why the young people of Lomas did not include the physical sources of toxicity in the drawings of their neighborhoods—but discussed them as being present in the undrawn, surrounding areas—could be because of the way other histories of interrelated violence also circulate at the edges of life in Lomas; environmental violence is only part of the larger contexts of violence in which the young people are living. The particular enduring legacies of colonialism in Peru, for example, as well as the violence from years of internal armed conflict and uncertainty, remain a constant yet in some cases undiscussed influence.

Legacies of Violence and Displacement

Lomas de Carabayllo is a place shaped by multiple and overlapping forms of violence—both past and contemporary. The colonial history of Peru provides one foundational source of the violence. Lima was one of the very early Spanish colonial cities, founded by Francisco Pizarro in 1535. It was a significant colonial settlement for Spanish domination of Indigenous people who lived there and migrated there. Early after the city was founded, Spaniards killed and removed the original Indigenous people of Lima Valley (Graubart 2007).[37] Lima became populated with Indigenous immigrants either from other parts of Peru or from the Iberian Peninsula and African coasts, as well as Spaniards. Because of its geographic placement as a port city near the sea, in the sixteenth and seventeenth centuries one of Lima's major features was its multiethnic diversity, as well as its importance for colonial Spain. Indeed, Lima grew to become one of the major hubs in Latin America—both for the commodification and enslavement of people, as well as the commodification of goods and materials, and was dubbed far and wide as the City of Kings. It became "one of Spain's most significant imperial footholds" and by 1700, "slaves compromised more than a third of the city's population and were almost equal in number to American- and Iberian-born Spaniards" (Walker 2017b: 3). Economic systems of domination and enslavement altered the emergence of the city, as well as patterns of migration and social relations. And they also transformed, and depended on, law. Bianca Premo notes: "At the close of the sixteenth century, the category of minor was reconceptualized to include native inhabitants of Americas, and offices were established for the legal representation of Indians in

Spanish courts" (Premo 2005: 31). The colonial history of Peru, and the ways domination and racial subordination shaped three centuries of Spanish colonial rule, transformed all parts of social and domestic life in Lima.[38] And it also gave form to legal and conceptual racial paternalism of "Spanish fathers ruling infantile Indians" (Premo 2005: 33).

The violence of colonial subjecthood, although legally ended in the eighteenth century, provided both the roots and critical social context for political violence that would play out in the country two centuries later. A twenty-year internal conflict between government forces and armed groups that occurred between 1980 and 2000 inflicted enormous suffering, death, and fear on the people of Peru, particularly Indigenous and Quechua-speaking peoples.

Much of the political violence in Peru began in the rural highlands, under the leadership of Abimael Guzmán, with Sendero Luminoso. Sendero Luminoso embraced a vision of terror as a means to usher in a communist utopia and sought to break down the current order of state and society through violence. The highly structured party hierarchy meted out discipline that extended to execution for criminal behavior, ranging from snitching to homosexual acts to adultery to stealing.[39] One of the core principles of Sendero Luminoso was an imagined "moral" society, not moralism straight from a communist manifesto, but rather a communist-Maoist blend of ideas and beliefs that placed moralism and punishment as a key feature of the Sendero Luminoso mission. Organizers focused on recruiting people whom the state had marginalized, particularly those in poor, rural, and Indigenous areas.

Because of the number of people Sendero Luminoso killed and disappeared, as well as their particularly gruesome and violent methods of doing so, anthropologists and historians typically compare Sendero Luminoso to Pol Pot's Khmer Rouge (McClintock 1984). The Peruvian military responded to the growth of the Sendero Luminoso with its own mass violence and murders. Scholars Lisa Laplante and Kimberly Theidon described the initial governmental response as "a brutal counter-insurgency war in which 'Andean peasant' became conflated with 'terrorists'" (2007: 232). Part of the technique was government supported and expanded local peasant self-defense militias (*rondas campesinas*).[40] Additional armed actors included the MRTA.

Sendero Luminoso's growth emerged out of an everyday rage at the inequality, marginalization, and imperialism in the country. Alan García, Peru's president from 1985–1990 (he would later be reelected in 2006), led the country into severe economic instability during the 1980s. By the late 1980s and early 1990s, the violence was not contained to the rural areas of Peru: In Lima, car bombings, murders, power outages, and water shortages were common occurrences.[41] Corruption, high levels of inflation, and racial hierarchy contributed to increased and widespread violence across the country during the twenty years of conflict. Although the area of Lomas in the early 1990s was not inhabited as much as it is now, the people who would eventually move to Lomas largely consisted of migrants from the highlands, places where whole communities were affected by fear and violence from the brutal and nationwide conflict.

Alberto Fujimori, running on a populist ticket, defeated García in 1990 by promising to end hyperinflation and also to stop the growing guerrilla movements and widespread political violence. He sought to repress Sendero Luminoso through aggressive military and authoritarian policies. In 1992 he staged and executed an *autogolpe*, a self-coup of Congress, disbanding the legislative branch, suspending the constitution, and implementing direct control of the judiciary with the assistance of former army captain Vladimiro Montesinos.[42] Fujimori's government captured the leader of the Sendero Luminoso, Abimael Guzmán, and a number of its high-ranking armed leaders. He rewrote the constitution and established authoritarian rule.

Fujimori used a discourse of terrorism and guerrilla violence as a rationale for his actions. The new constitution included thirteen new laws in 1992, all of which he termed the "anti-terrorist" legislation (law 25475). Under these new laws, the Peruvian state could detain people accused of terrorism for twenty years to life, without due process. Vague language described what constituted terrorism. The Inter-American Commission of Human Rights 2000 Report noted, for example, "By not linking the proscribed conduct to the subjective element of terrorist intent, this [anti-terrorist] decree law can be interpreted to permit law enforcement officials to regard almost any act of violence as a crime of terrorism."[43] Thousands of innocent people were falsely arrested, prosecuted, and sentenced to prison for terrorist activity.[44]

Fujimori was ousted from office in November of 2000.[45] However, his

46 Listening Between Generations

"anti-terror" tactics—of using strict "law and order" to incarcerate people based on fears of terrorist activity but without regard for due process or other standards of justice—has shaped many contemporary Peruvians' national imagination and perception of the legal system.[46] And it has also shaped national discourses and public framings of the very notion of terrorism. While Fujimori was sentenced to twenty-five years in prison for human rights violations,[47] his legacy of narratives of violence and ideas of terrorism remains firmly rooted in the minds of Peruvians, particularly those who were coming of age during that time—a generation that includes most of the parents of the children now living in Lomas.

In 2001, the interim president, Valentín Paniagua, established the Truth and Reconciliation Commission (Comisión de la Verdad y Reconciliación or CVR). A public campaign entitled "In the Name of the Innocent" gained national attention, and in 2002 the CVR held a public hearing regarding the anti-terrorist laws Fujimori had created and how they fit into the larger picture of the general political turmoil, unrest, and violence during that time.[48] The mandate of the Truth and Reconciliation Commission was to uncover what had caused the conflict and who could be held criminally accountable. Human rights organizations had estimated that some 30,000 people died or were disappeared in the course of the conflict. Based on testimony of 17,000 people, the final nine-volume report of the CVR in 2003 doubled that figure, finding that nearly 70,000 women, men, and children had lost their lives or had been disappeared, and hundreds of thousands were displaced. The CVR attributed 54 percent of the deaths and disappearances to actions by Sendero Luminoso and 37 percent to Peruvian state forces. Peruvians who spoke *Quechua* were vastly overrepresented among the dead and missing, as were rural people; 79 percent of the victims killed came from rural areas, and 75 percent spoke *Quechua* (CVR 2003).[49] State armed forces commonly recruited girls and boys between the ages of 15 and 17, according to the CVR report, for violence as a "systematic and widespread practice." The report identified long-term, damaging, and traumatic effects of the conflict on families and communities.[50]

The commissioners of the CVR concluded that the conflict had inflicted psychosocial disorders that "weigh like a serious mortgage on our future and decisively affect the construction of a national community of free and equal citizens in a plural democracy on the path to development and equity."[51]

They pointed out the deeply entrenched class and ethnic divides that led to the conflict, advocating for measures to prevent a recurrence.[52] The CVR report exposed the role of the state in the conflict—both its immediate violence (i.e., the use of the military and state orders for the killing of innocent people) but also in terms of ongoing structural violence (i.e., how starkly class and ethnic inequality played a role in creating the conflict).

This history and legacy of political violence in Peru, as well as the direct ways many of the families in Lomas experienced it and were displaced because of it, shapes part of the historical context of how the young people of Lomas narrate and understand their lives. While very few of the young people of Lomas with whom I spoke were even born in 1990, many of the parents of the children lived through and experienced firsthand that political violence. Many of the Lomas parents were migrants from rural areas where most of the political violence took place, and while most had direct experience with this violence, most also choose not to talk about it with their children. For example, José's father, Simon, came to Lima at the age of 12, fleeing violence in the mountains of Ayacucho. Multiple members of his family were killed in the violence, including an uncle he was close to whose framed portrait hangs in their living room. Simon told me there was no simple polarization of "victims and terrorists" but, rather, "all kinds of violence"—violence from the army and the police and the "terrorists." He described the experience like this:

> There was nobody to believe in. For example, if you knew something and told someone, the police would make you tell them. They would interrogate you and beat you if you didn't want to say anything. But after the police would leave, the others [Sendero Luminoso] would come and they would kill you immediately. They called you "snitch or gossip." It was horrible.[53]

Simon depicted how the nights were especially frightening, because it was particularly at night when Sendero Luminoso "came to rob houses, and if there were young people, they would take them. It was an obligation that you belonged to them and that you fought alongside them." Loyalty, allegiance, and obedience were demanded through fear and violence because, as Simon recounted, "if you didn't want to join them, they simply

48   Listening Between Generations

killed you." As Simon and others began to see the realities of this up close, a coping mechanism was to hide during the night hours. In anticipation of nightfall, after 5 p.m. Simon and his neighbors would leave their houses and hide, knowing restful sleep would not be possible. But such constant fear and worry weren't sustainable, and Simon recounted one particular massacre in detail, in which it wasn't Sendero Luminoso but the Peruvian police who killed an entire village near where Simon lived. After that, he fled and moved to Lima, eventually settling in Lomas because it provided a place to work and create a livelihood.

Andrea, Clara and Eva's mother, told her girls considerably less about her experiences than Simon told José. She fled her hometown in Huancavelica, in the mountains of Peru, with her parents at a much younger age than Simon. She recounted having "to escape because if they were to encounter us in our houses, they would kill us. . . . These terrorists had come from Ayacucho and were coming for Huancavelica. So, we slept hidden in caves."[54] Andrea was only 5 or 6 when her family fled. When I asked Clara and Eva what they knew about Peru's political history of violence, they said they didn't know anything. Clara did not enroll in fifth grade when she would have been taught about it in school, but instead she was working full time as a housekeeper and going to school one day a week.[55] Nevertheless, the narratives of fear, social isolation, and not knowing whom to trust is sharply present in the Lomas parents' stories of that time period and of their own youth. Therefore, Clara and other children like her inevitably confront the effects of this. Moreover, the history of the two-decade-long armed struggle and widespread violence among the state, Sendero Luminoso, and the peasant communities largely represents the backdrop against which the young people know and understand the state.[56]

When asked what she wishes for her children Clara and Eva, Andrea said,

> I want my children to study, to go forward in life, not like me, I don't want them to suffer like me, I want them to study and to finish their studies and then become something. They could be a doctor or a professor or a secretary. That is what I hope for my daughters.[57]

There is a lot spoken, and unspoken, in Andrea's statement about how she wants her children not to "suffer" like she did.

The histories of the Lomas parents as having been displaced because of past political violence, forced to leave their homes and migrate to Lima to work in an uninhabitable landfill, creates a context for the children's observations about the current place and space in terms of environmental violence. Yael Navaro-Yashin writes of "affective geography" of postwar northern Cyprus and how "there is a phantasmatic element to all state practices" (2012: 28).[58] The slow violence Lomas as a place experienced, the current structural and environmental violence the young people still experience, as well as the memories and legacies of violence their parents experienced all influence the affective geographic landscape that the Lomas young people depicted in their drawings. The inheritance of these intergenerational encounters and the history of colonial and structural violence has perhaps taught the Lomas young people about the importance of looking to silence as a place for clues about how to read state power and violence. It does not come through in stable, static categories. Yet, their understanding of the workings of state power is not just informed by what has been passed down to them from their families. Rather, their knowledge is also informed by their direct observations and lived experiences of present-day place of Lomas—and all the contradictions they see play out through environmental, socioeconomic, and structural injustice.

The ways that Clara, Monica, José, and the other young people in Lomas spoke of their neighborhood and its environmental toxins—including the ways they saw themselves as being neglected by the state—underscores how "place" cannot be understood as dislocated from larger structures and histories of power (Quijano 1972; Quijano 2000). The colonial and violent history of Lomas was embedded in the daily stories the young people told, yet could have been easily overlooked if one just reduced their stories to "the local" and immediate place of Lomas or even intergenerational "trauma" of war.[59] By privileging a kind of listening that is able to hear both—a centering of the young people's experiences and an acknowledgment of the ways this is linked to both global and local violence—the tensions and contradictions that come through in the young people's narratives are not treated as something to be resolved, but rather are core to their political insights.[60]

A relational approach to the young people of Lomas offers insight into how to listen for state violence both in terms of current material realties and in terms of histories and legacies of violence. Their observations of their physical surroundings as linked to their emotions and well-being highlight how violence is not just about public and private acts (by government or governmental officials) but also about the need for understanding young people's contributions as curators and readers of state power—both in what is included in their narrations but also in what they leave out. If one takes historical, geopolitical, and structural legacies of violence as contextual factors to understand young people's experiences, then the actual "local" and concrete quotidian experiences they speak of offer important insight into these larger forces, whether the young people are conscious of them or not.

The perspectives and narrations of the young people of Lomas, many of whose families were displaced because of Peru's political violence, are grounded both in their family's particular histories and in their specific and everyday sense of place. Their perspectives, which have been structured by both capitalism and colonialism, are also intertwined with experiences of sexism, racism, and inequality. The young people of Lomas—both in their words and drawings—consistently point to the complex and multiple ways state power operates. These voices underscore that in order to hear how violence, hierarchy, and systems of domination present themselves in their community, one must listen beyond only the immediate. In some cases, the history and legacy of violence lies just beyond young people's imaginations, just like state power is right off the pages of their drawings.

2

Deferred Promises

How Young People Describe Injustice in Lomas

THE CHILDREN TRIED TO COMFORT Lela. It was 2014, and six children had gathered around a small table at a community room in Lomas. Laid out on the table was a large bottle of Inca Cola, individually wrapped packages of Casino cookies, and crayons and paper for drawing. A small black Sony cassette player had been brought by one of the kids to play music. But Lela, who was 9 at the time, and the other children were not interested in eating, or listening to music, or drawing. Instead, they were agitated and sad. Lela's dog had been found dead—poisoned, they believed. Lela was close to tears as she spoke about it. She described feeling a mix of anger and sadness. As an only child, she loved that dog, even if she hadn't had it very long.

One of the other kids shared how the same thing had happened to him. "They killed my dog, too. They kill the dogs in our neighborhood."

José said that he believes neighbors leave out poison and kill other people's dogs, especially ones that bark. Lela said that she blamed the "contamination" and "toxins" in Lomas for her dog's death. The other children tried to attribute it to specific people, neighbors they thought who may have

52 Deferred Promises

done it. Dogs make up part of the daily landscape of Lomas and regularly come up in conversations about everyday life. The children described their beloved animals as central relationships constituting their neighborhood. The uncertainty of how it happened, along with the finality of the dog's death, hung heavy in the air.

Development agencies, United Nations entities, and international policy actors dominantly understand state policies to be about what states do.[1] Policy by these actors is framed primarily in terms of law and legality and is largely understood as located within national and international sites and organizations. Built into this dominant framing is often an assumption about the state and statehood, as enacted through clearly defined entities and actions, and through institutions and sites (schools, police, global markets, and so forth). Indeed, when describing Peru, scholars and policymakers have long categorized the Peruvian state largely in terms of either institutional weakness (what the state does or doesn't do) or as a site of exclusion (where and for whom state services are or are not).[2] As demonstrated by the field of international development, on one self-evident level the state is fundamentally about the material conditions of everyday life. The kinds of descriptions that one finds in the literature of international development are heavily focused on institutions and physical infrastructure: "It is about the construction of roads, of hydroelectric and irrigation projects, of mines and oil fields, of schools, hospitals and factories" (White 202: 412).[3] But while the outcomes of these means and transformations are material, they are not solely technical.[4]

This description of the state as primarily about the material conditions of everyday life leaves out other relational ways of comprehending how states and statehood are integrated into people's everyday lives. Immaterial and affective expressions of state power are fundamental in state processes, something that the young people living in Lomas made clear in their conversations. When they described violence and state power, they did not just speak of action. Instead, what they spoke about most often was of apparent absence, loss, affect, and care.[5] In our time together, they told stories of multiple, daily experiences of material exclusion and marginalization, juxtaposed and paired alongside stories of relationships, kinship, friendships, and everyday life. The young people in Lomas narrate state presence not just in terms of institutions or sites or locations, but rather through descriptions of their daily experiences, observations, memories, and longings. Depictions are grounded in affect and contextualized by a history both known and unknown to these young people.

For some of the younger kids, there were stories of contamination, toxicity, and—like Lela shared—dead dogs. As they tell these stories, they struggled to know to whom or what to assign blame. For the older young people (ages 12–14), these relational descriptions were more located around specific people: mayors and politicians who haven't fulfilled their promises, presidents who the young people described as "corrupt." Regardless of age, all the young people I met in Lomas became most animated and descriptive when they would speak more generally about their everyday lives, their normal routines, and their daily experiences—accounts that were filled with parents, sisters, cousins, teachers, and also pets. These relational stories even if not named as such, were packed with political actors, insights, and theories.

Although the children referenced individuals or ideas that may easily be considered political, the children themselves made clear that they saw themselves as far from "politics." In 2008, for example, when Maria, age 14, was describing her neighborhood, I asked her what word or image came to mind when she heard the word "politics." She quickly replied, "there are no politics here." She then went on to speak in great detail about injustice in Lomas and police corruption. For Maria, like many other young people in Lomas, when asked about politics, they were dismissive, answering with one-word answers such as "elections" or "government." And like Maria, they explained that their short answers about politics were because they didn't see it as enacted in Lomas. Yet their descriptions of an "absence" of politics, and even of state services, reflects a political observation. That is, through their relational, daily stories of life in Lomas, there were rich accounts of imagined state interventions, albeit in ways that were fluid, heterogenous, and affective.

Listening to the young people's conversations through a relational lens allows for hearing how they describe and understand not just inequality, but also everyday violence. These young Peruvians speak to how state structures in their lives present not just through contemporary (state) institutions and policies, but also daily relationships, historical injustices, and wider patterns of disparity. The ideas and fantasies of the state that they put forward are both ideological and material.[6] And in the context of Peru, their insights offer a reassessment of some of the very mechanisms of how state power reproduces and presents itself.

For the young people of Lomas, the "absence" of politics they describe in their neighborhood is connected to its visible presence that they encounter every day: places that they pass daily on their way to school, on their way home, and where they see and imagine the state "should be." Each of these examples often highlights where the state is *not*. Instead, they describe environmental degradation, corruption, and what they see to be ineffective policing, inadequate support for education, lack of roads and running water, a physical landfill, and toxins in the air. But they also see and describe places to play, places to work, churches, a small health center, and so on. Their descriptions of the everyday place of Lomas in terms of absences are shaped by normative statements and discursive language that the young people hear from politicians, other state actors, and adult workers of NGOs that surround them on a daily basis. And, as described in the last chapter, such observations are shaped by relationships, longings, and histories of (intersecting) violence, grounded in the place they live and work. The young people's longings, anxieties, and descriptions about life are formed both by their daily experiences, their imagining of possibilities and expectations, and also by the local and the global frictions that they both witness and contribute to.

The method of relational listening, which I discussed in the last chapter, demands suspension of an immediate judgment (i.e., how right or not they are). It is a way of listening that is not just focused on the "facts" the young people observed (if there is literally a police presence in Lomas or not, if there are politicians present or not) but rather is interested in the young people's interpretations. That is, it attends to the observations they make, the relationships they highlight, the futures and present they imagine. When Maria says "there are no politics here," an orientation towards relational listening moves beyond solely content and attends to affect, word choice, and sentiment. It centers an attention to care, complexity, and context, as well as a commitment to seeing the young people as knowers based on their experience (Brown 2013; Collins 2000; Fujii 2018). At the same time, like adults, young people's insights are partial, incomplete, grounded in historical and cultural norms, and reflective of larger geopolitical contradictions and tensions.[7] As such, relational listening, which necessitates a carefulness that does not confuse adult versions of children's analyses and which instead situates their perspectives within cultural and historical contexts, brings into view ways state power in Peru maintains everyday and environmental violence among people who have been made marginal, while neutralizing and distancing the state's role in such violence and inequality.

This chapter looks closely at how young people of Lomas describe many of these daily contradictions of the state in their lives, specifically institutional sites such as their schools, policing, and in discussions of security in their community. Their descriptions, communicated through stories of daily life and relationships, vividly portray the *processes of state power* rather than just sites or places of state intervention.[8] Their expressions of longing, hope, contradiction, desire, and even distrust all constitute core features of their political knowledge.

Education and the "Myth of Progress"

"I like school because when you finish your studies you can be somebody in life" said Clara who was 10 years old at the time.[9] This description of school, where you can "*ser alguien en la vida*" was a common sentiment among Lomas children. Like Clara, many describe key parts of their identities through recognition that attending and completing school was to "become someone in life." School, in other words, was described as far more than just a location; it was also an imagined vehicle toward progress.

When Clara was 15, she temporarily moved away from Lomas, and from her family, in order to work and, as she put it, to "help" her family. She moved to a district closer to the center of Lima, that takes two hours by bus from Lomas. She found the job through an employment agency, which had previously found similar work for her mother, and went to live and work as a maid for a family with two children. While her father's drug-resistant tuberculosis improved, as did her own symptoms, her family never regained the relative financial stability they had had before his illness, requiring Clara to make more money than was possible in the factory work she did

56 Deferred Promises

in Lomas. A year later, at age 16, Clara reflected, "I saw my mom killing herself trying to pay for all the bills, the school uniforms, and utility bills and I decided I needed to help her to bring in more."[10]

Clara describes what a shock it was to have to leave Lomas and move away from her family, especially her younger sisters, and to go to work as a live-in maid. "I cried a lot. But I did it so that my family could get ahead."[11] In her job as a live-in domestic worker her daily routine consisted of getting up at 6 a.m. to cook for the young children, cleaning the house while they were at school, and feeding and caring for them when they arrived home. Clara's employers—immigrants to Peru from Spain, would arrive late in the evening from their jobs, often leaving Clara to be responsible for putting the little children to bed.

For two years, every Friday Clara left late in the evening to take a number of *combis* (a small van shared with others) to arrive back to her own family in Lomas. She then rose early every Saturday and left to study at a private institute on the main highway near Lomas, from 9 a.m. to 1 p.m. She made this weekly journey not only to see her family, but also because she was determined to finish secondary school. As she told her father, she wants to go to university. And when he "gets a little better he should work too, but he needs to be strong to help support me to study."[12] Clara believes in the power of education as a way "to advance" (*para avanzar*).

Clara's relationship with schooling and work is tied to her physical well-being and environmental surroundings. She describes the medicines she took for tuberculosis as making her too sick and weak to concentrate and that her classmates gossiped that she was pregnant because of how bloated and engorged her normally small frame and belly appeared. She recounted how dizzy she would get and the fainting during school hours. The gossiping, paired with her exhaustion, made her stop school at age 15. Yet, school still is a place of hope and ambition for Clara—so much so that even working full-time she still traveled to Lomas every weekend to study and be in her own family's home.[13]

In their interviews, Lomas young people talked about their dreams, with education as a pathway to a future that would be different from their present lives. And they looked to their teachers as authorities for truth. They expressed an unwavering view about the value of the Peruvian education system and of education itself as a ticket out of individualized poverty. At the same time, they also reported about absent teachers who did not show up for class, classrooms without books, shame about not being able to afford uniforms, and even some examples of physical violence and corporal punishment within the classroom.

In Peru, scholars have noted the trend of an often idealized view, or even ideology, of education among young people and their parents and other caregivers.[14] This trend has grown alongside the global rise of citizenship discourse in schools, where there seems to be an increased focus on individual agency and personhood, as well as the country's recent neoliberal turn, which began in the early 1990s.[15] Between 1990 and 2000, former president Alberto Fujimori instituted a series of political and economic legislative reforms, including the bolstering of children's rights, which he claimed as an opportunity for bringing the country more centrally into the global economy. On the surface, his reforms focused on radically reducing the presence of the state in all areas of economic and social policy and were largely grounded in neoliberal logics of self-autonomy.[16] Many of these reforms led to notable economic growth, and also to vast economic disparity. Education in Peru is one of the biggest examples of this, in that it sits at the heart of the everyday (lived) contradictions of neoliberalism, both in terms of unequal access but also in the ways it serves as a source of what educational scholar Patricia Ames calls the site of both "desire and distrust" (Ames 2002).

The ways the young people in Lomas expressed this tension was often to stress schooling as encompassing a space of ambition, an imagined site of modernity and progress, even if also a source of longing and lack. Peruvian anthropologist Carlos Iván Degregori, describing shifting aspirations among Andean peasants in Peru, has identified this tension within a wider historic and social context: a shift from the "Myth of Inkarri" (an Indigenous myth of conquest) to the "Myth of Progress," which captures the elevation of the promises of modernity and the devaluing of Indigenous knowledge and identity (Degregori 2007). Through schooling, ideas of modernity and the "Myth of Progress" promise Andean peasants "freedom" from ignorance through education (Degregori 2007: 4–5). Degregori's description of school as an imagined source of both conquest and modernity rings true when listening to the young people of Lomas where, particularly in terms of education, their interviews capture and reflect schooling as a site of both longing and aspiration, but also of shame, anxiety, and inequality.[17]

58   Deferred Promises

Like Maria, Clara also gave one-word answers about politics in Lomas. In her conversations, she too imagined politics as something happening "far away." Yet, like many of the other young people of Lomas, even while Clara names structural inequality in terms of the absence of the state, she expressed great faith in the Peruvian state educational system and a belief that education would alleviate their (individual) poverty. In other words, the young people frame education as key to their individual success, rather than as a community right and benefit. They present the state, in these reflections, as neutral, not a hindrance. Indeed, in their narrations, the bulk of responsibility to "be someone" lay at the feet of individual citizens. This was true despite Peru's recent history of having low learning standards in Latin America and a notable level of inequality in the education system (Ames 2013).

Education was coded by the young people as the avenue toward development and a way to become "somebody." Anthropologist Jessaca Leinaweaver's important historical scholarship about Indigenous Andean childhood in Peru offers context for this insight by the young people in Lomas. Leinaweaver describes how ideologies of self-improvement in Peru are not only internalized commentaries about modernity but also about race:

> [O]vercoming poverty—*superando*—means sloughing off the markers that might make others define you as indigenous. . . . To *superarese* means to acquire some traits and shed others. This is an active reframing and a deliberate use of context—race in Peru is situational, a point that has been bolstered by recent scholarship on the location of race in the Andean landscape from the Enlightenment into the present. (Leinaweaver 2008: 110)

Ideas about progress, and modernity, as linked to education, not only grow out of but also are centrally related to a long, racialized history in Peru, by which Indigenous "culture" is contrasted with formal educational institutions.

Indeed, even the evolution of Peru's education system, is, in and of itself, a history of statehood, citizenship, and the making of a child citizen. The history of centralized education in Peru, or the establishment of the Teaching State (Estado Docente), was closely tied to ideas of progress and modernity.[18] Primary schooling in Peru was understood as critical to the process of state formation since independence from Spain in 1821, and, according to historian Antonio Espinoza, largely established as a means "to reproduce social hierarchies, encourage authoritarianism and intolerance, rather than promoting egalitarianism and democratic republican values" (2013: 3). Espinoza describes the establishment of the Estado Docente, which he dates as materializing in 1904 in Peru, as growing out of the centrality of institutional arrangements for education. Before then, education was "intended to correct the moral vices of young children, making them into 'useful' adults who would assume social positions appropriate to their ethnic and cultural status. There was almost no state oversight for school curriculum, and teachers gained and lost employment based on personal relationships" (Soule 2015: 306, discussing Espinoza). The Estado Docente offered wider access and consistency for young people, and also remained racked with contradictions, patronage, and exclusions. It wasn't until the 1950s and 1960s that public schooling in Peru became more fully institutionally cemented, which was reflected not only by the number of schools and structures put in place, but also by the very textbooks used. School was a vehicle, like in so many places, for the Peruvian state to deliver and underwrite messages about nationhood, sovereignty, and what it meant to be a citizen.[19]

This legacy of both exclusion and possibility remains. Clara longs for and hopes that schooling and education will serve as a pathway to better her family's situation. Yet the financial stress of having to pay for her uniform, the environmental toxins of Lomas, and the global structures of inequity that make her family more vulnerable to live under poverty all serve as part of the same fundamental system that contributed to her not finishing secondary school in the first place. In terms of schooling, the range of "modalities of power" (Mitchell 1990) in Lomas, therefore, are not only about state action or even state institutions, but as the young people so vividly describe, also about the symbolic and contradictory meaning that the idea of education holds. The tensions present in the ways the young people of Lomas speak about schooling, and their relationships and longings about school, is necessarily situated within a larger context of the wider contradictory system of global capitalism, and also Peru's history of a colonial scheme that equates being Indigenous with being less than a person.[20] The dreams of schooling, and "being somebody" in the eyes of the state, described by Clara

60   Deferred Promises

and other young people reveal such histories. If listened to in a relational way, these tensions and conflicted feelings by the young people exemplify where state power reproduces and presents itself in Peru.

Massacres, Terrorists, and the Lawful State

Because of the legacy of violence in Peru, questions of how history is taught to new generations remains a central concern both for the state and for public and private institutions (see Paulson 2011; Paulson 2015; Teillier and Uccelli Labarthe 2018). In Lomas, the young people reported developing knowledge of Peru's history of internal armed conflict through snippets of stories from family members, or media, or sometimes in school.[21] For example, when I asked Raquel, age 14, if and how they were taught about Peru's history of armed conflict, she told me she knew she was supposed to study about it in school, that there is a chapter about it in their social studies book, but she said the civics teacher who was supposed to teach it rarely shows up for class. Instead, Raquel noted that she learned about the country's past conflict directly from her father:

> My father was in the army and he went to kill the terrorists and all those things. There were massacres. The [terrorists] went from town to town and they killed people and he saw how they killed people. I think the killing was with an ax or machete. They placed their head on a log and cut them off.[22]

Other children's answers contained similar graphic and vague images of violent terrorists. We were sitting in José's living room when he was age 13 when he reflected:

> Sometimes my father explains to me. I didn't know who the person in the picture [hanging in our living room] was. I asked my father and he told me it was Huambaraca, and that he was my uncle. He was a professor, and he said that he advanced his career to be mayor of the village. He was the general councilor and the terrorists said: this guy advanced in his position in too short of time. And so they killed him.[23]

Mario, age 11, who made money busking in the center of Lima by juggling fire, spoke about learning from his teachers that there was a time when "terrorists were very strict, and if they found a robber they would simply kill them."[24] Mario described the state as having an important role in creating laws and regulations to stop the violence and terrorists from committing these kinds of killings. This presentation of the state as benevolent, quelling violence, and enforcing democracy and rule of law was common among other young people as well. This account aligns with the state's official version of conflict. Sendero Luminoso, in the dominant state narrative, was lawless whereas the state and military were lawful. Lela framed it this way:

> [Teachers in school] told us about Sendero Luminoso. We all heard that they killed people and there were a lot of terrorists. All of this finished because [the state] spread laws and rules that didn't exist before. Now there shouldn't be more massacres. That's what they taught us.[25]

Terrorism in Peru ended, according to the Lomas young people like Lela, because of "laws and rules." It was common for the young people to describe "terrorists" as the primary perpetrators of violence in Peru's conflict. When they did speak of the role of the state or military in the history of the conflict, they spoke of them in upstanding or glorified ways. Raquel recognized that the Peruvian army was active in the armed conflicts, but she focused on the violence of the terrorists. This juxtaposition of innocent and guilty underlines and drives a reading of political violence that largely drops state actors from the frame. "Laws and rules" in this formulation, serve in heroic terms, and legality becomes a shorthand for describing the role of the state. This depoliticization and clean-cut narrative of political violence is rooted in dominant presentations of law, sovereign authority, and presentations of statehood.[26] And it is also shaped by education, and the ways these narrations of violence are both taught and not taught.

The ways this history is narrated in Peruvian national textbooks has been highly contested, as well as highly politicized.[27] Critics have argued that the narration of the internal armed conflict, as put forward by the state-approved curriculum, largely ignores the violence and corruption en-

62   Deferred Promises

acted by the state police, the Peruvian military, and other state agents. They argue it has also largely erased the role of armed civilians in Movimiento Revolucionario Túpac Amaru *(MRTA)* and instead keeps a pretty narrow focus on crimes and violence committed by Sendero Luminoso. The result, as comparative education scholar Julia Paulson documents, is a portrayal of past violence in Peru as temporally unique and that instead focuses on "fanatical terrorists and a Peruvian armed forces operating under now non-existent and never-to-be-replicated conditions" (Paulson 2010: 142). That is, "it creates an explanation of conflict as exceptional and disconnected from the structural inequalities and racism that other historical accounts, including Peru's truth commission, identify as causes of the conflict in Peru, and that persist into the present" (Paulson 2015: 28).

While transitional justice processes often argue for the role education can and must play in the aftermath of mass violence, educational scholars of multiple post-conflict contexts have commented on the tendency towards linear narratives of internal armed conflicts, particular as translated in state-sanctioned history textbooks. Edited out are often the complexities of inequality that lead to and foster such violence, embodied through institutional, structural, and even systemic ways.[28]

The (state's) telling of Peru's internal armed conflict through its history and civics textbooks for young people is an important contribution to these current debates. The internal armed conflict in Peru is particularly known for the ways it both reflected and reproduced patterns of hierarchy and exclusion.[29] Lela's quote that the Peruvian state enacted "laws and rules" to put an end to the conflict speaks to an important yet insufficiently discussed part of this entrenched exclusion—the deep association with statehood and "lawfare," which is an elevation of, and anxiety about, the law and the legal citizen in contexts of conflict. Dominant and polarizing framings of state power, often depending on the language of law and order, influence and organize popular narratives of individual human rights as well as humanitarian discourses of need (Malkki 2010). But, as the young people of Lomas show, and as other recent studies with young people within Peru confirm, such a narrative, steeped in contradiction, also depicts a particular presentation of the moralizing Peruvian state.[30]

State Narrations of (State) Violence

National discourses and public framings of the notion of terrorism and lawfare has a particular history relating to Peru's state-building project. The ways the state textbooks and government reports discuss Sendero Luminoso provides an important illustration of this. In the early 1990s, under the leadership of Abimael Guzmán, Sendero Luminoso emerged in the rural highlands in Peru, embracing a vision of terror as a means to usher in a communist utopia. At this point, Peru was already ten years into what would be twenty years of internal armed conflict.[31]

Earlier, in the 1980s, during Alan García's first period as president (1985–1990), the country faced major economic instability, and the corruption, high levels of inflation, and racial hierarchy stemming from that era contributed to increased and widespread violence across the country. As Carlos Iván Degregori notes in his description of that time:

> In the closing days of Alan García's government (1985–90), 32 percent of the territory and 49 percent of the population of the country was under military control (Senado de la República del Perú 1992). Hyperinflation bordered on 60 percent monthly, the economic crisis brought havoc to the population and was destroying the state and the social fabric with as much or more efficiency than in the insurgency itself." (2012: 24)

Sendero Luminoso's growth emerged out of an everyday rage at the inequality, marginalization, and imperialism in the country (Stern 1998).

In 2003, the Comisión de la Verdad y Reconciliación (CVR) recommended that the political and social violence over the twenty-year period from 1980–2000 must be part of what Peruvian young people learn in school, as featured in the national curriculum, to promote democracy and the realization of human rights. The evidence from the Peruvian Truth Commission was that education played a crucial role in creating the conditions for and the maintenance of the conflict in Peru. In their final report, the CVR noted the role that inequality played in fueling the violence, both in terms of Sendero Luminoso's influence through the national teacher's union but

64   Deferred Promises

also, importantly, in terms of the Peruvian state's lack of quality education for young people, particularly in poor and rural areas (CVR 2003).

In Peru's 2009 National Curriculum Design (NCD), Peruvian educational state policymakers upheld the CVR's recommendation, instructing teachers and textbook publishers to teach Peruvian children about the armed conflict in Peru. As mandated by the state, all national social studies textbooks reference the violent conflict. Earlier, in the NCD from 2006, the state mandate said that children in year five of secondary school (ages 16–17) must learn about the construction of civic culture, which explicitly included learning about Peru's "history of internal conflict" (Ministerio de Educación 2006). In the 2009 NCD, the educational ministry added "collective memory and national reconciliation" and the directive to teach "about the important role of the armed forces, national police, and national security."

Though mandated to teach this contested history of the internal armed conflict, teachers were not provided training on *how* to teach it, nor were they given tools for processing their own feelings about what may come up when teaching the subject (Paulson 2010; Teillier and Uccelli Labarthe 2018; Uccelli et al. 2017). Contested politics about how to narrate to the next generation about the conflict at the national level was evident in classrooms across the country. These debates would have a felt impression on the ways the youth in Lomas (like Clara, Maria, and Raquel) would learn about this history. Their descriptions of the state as absent or invisible—the violent history they know hangs in the background of their family experiences, or the way they draw the pollution in their communities off the margins of the pages of their drawings—point not only to the way the state's actions impact populations but also to an expression of state power itself, processes that become realized in the bodies, understandings, and silences of young people like those in Lomas.

For example, a common phrase "apology for terrorism" was regularly used in media headlines in Peru following the internal armed conflict and since the printing of national textbooks. The CVR report itself was called an "apology for terrorism" by politicians and media commentators, and there were educational controversies about how to best teach this history at the exact historical moment when the public was engaging with the CVR report.[32] Indeed, in 1990, under Fujimori's presidency, it became mandated by law that anyone who was offering a "apology for terrorism" be sentenced to jail. Peru's law

25475, article 7, punishes anyone who offers an "apology for terrorism." Still in effect today, the law calls for six to twelve years of jail, if proven guilty.

The lingering consequences of this law still take many shapes. For example, in 2012, there was media and public outcry targeting a fourth-year social studies textbook's offering an "apology for terrorism." One particular critique was about a textbook page that shows a picture of Sendero Luminoso's leader Abimael Guzmán smiling and wearing glasses. Critics suggested that the picture portrayed Guzmán as an elite "intellectual," which, in Peru, has positive associations because of how education is held in high esteem and viewed as the path to progress.[33] Critics argued that any photograph of Guzmán should not portray him as a professor, but rather as a "terrorist"—and behind bars. Others also claimed that the text presented Sendero Luminoso in ways that were too kind—namely, that the text noted how they were "providing protection to farmers" and "providing food aid."

A 2014 civics textbook, which the children in Lomas showed me, included an image of Guzmán as a prisoner behind bars, in a prison uniform. The relevant chapter is entitled "A Painful Past: The Crisis of Violence in Peru." There is a photo in the chapter with the caption: "The photo shows the moment when Abimael Guzmán, the head of the terrorist group Sen-

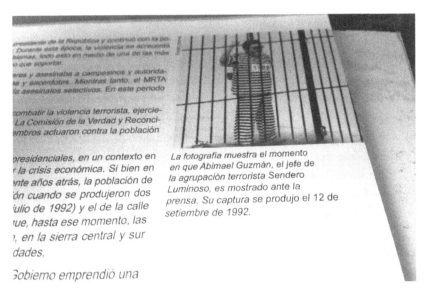

Figure 7: Passage from a Peruvian civics textbook, published in 2014. Photo taken by author, 2014.

dero Luminoso, was shown to the press. He was captured on September 12, 1992."

Various iterations of the Peruvian textbook debate have arisen periodically, demonstrating the difficulty in fulfilling the CVR report's mandate to capture the complexities of the history of political violence in Peru in the national curriculum. In 2017, a member of Peru's congress argued there needed to be a narrower focus on the terrorism that gripped the country. The articulation of the law (laws 02243, 02124, 01953) occurred in 2018, but popular outcry, as well as protests from the minister of education, declared that the rewriting of textbooks was not a congressional responsibility. Current textbooks depend on decipherable notions of time and space and present conflict as something contained (in the past) and/or something able to be contained (through law).[34] The choice to update the image of Abimael Guzmán, from plainclothes with glasses to prison garb behind bars, captures this duality and helps explain the importance of law and order in the descriptions of the young people of Lomas when talking about the armed conflict.

The narratives presented in Peru's state-approved textbooks exemplify how education itself performs narrations about statehood. By centering "terrorists" as the focus of violence and largely erasing the state's role, these texts perpetuate a type of impunity for state actors and portray them as fundamentally depoliticized and benevolent. These logics are reflected by the young people in Lomas and confirmed through recent educational research around the country.[35] This dichotomous presentation in the textbooks maintains a presentation of violence in only one dominant form (for example, physical violence from distant terrorists) and makes other forms of violence (colonialism, imperialism, environmental degradation, or even gendered violence) less visible.[36]

Legacies of economic, environmental, ethnic, and gendered violence in Peru—what Jelke Boesten (2010) has called "intersecting inequalities"—shape present-day realties. The young people in Lomas understand such inequalities in ways that shed new light on the sources of that inequality. Listening in relational ways helps to hear how they see, grapple with, and describe the daily world around them. And it also allows for a better understanding of the multiple narratives of state processes of power, put forward by both state and non-state actors.

Policing and (In)Security in Lomas

Besides schooling, another way the young people in Lomas highlighted the state's role in the inequalities in their lives was in their conversations about police and insecurity in the neighborhood. Much of the young people's discussions about the police followed a similar pattern as that of schooling: an imagined desire for what should be, marked with a tension of what actually is. When discussing the police, this tension was even more vivid, with a common perspective among the young people that framed the police specifically within a context of lack or absence.

One group of girls, for example, in answering what they thought of the police, said they all agreed that they didn't know because "there is not one single police here," but then gave detailed descriptions of what police "should do."[37] Others said the police are in Lomas, but they are just *un adorno* (an ornament). Many told stories of corrupt police, or of police taking bribes. The Lomas young people's descriptions of police contained a shared presentation and collective imagination of what police "should do" in their neighborhood, alongside the dominant portrayal of the Lomas neighborhood as one that lacks police presence.[38] Maria, age 17, said, "The police don't do anything. They don't come, they don't do anything."[39]

The state the young people of Lomas describe is marked by both a longing and abandoning presence. José, at age 12, stated: "The police should be better than [they are] because they are police. They should help the people when there is something, when something happens or there's an accident, but you can't find them." Two years after making this comment, José (now 14) recounted a vivid example of the kind of everyday violence and police he was likely referring to:

> Yesterday, my neighbor she has a baby and the father of the baby he was fighting her with a knife while the baby was in his arms. The kid had one of his arms with his mother and one with the father. They were pulling him. My neighbor she went to the police station for help. But since her brother is in a gang, they didn't listen to her. The police said they [the couple] should just kill each other and that it was her fault. The woman said she was going to denounce the police because they didn't do anything in this emergency. But they don't

68   Deferred Promises

do anything. Sometimes they do nothing. Even after that, another police officer came outside, maybe he was sleeping inside, and they were angry with her. He yelled at the woman to go away. He yelled that she came just to bother them [the police]. What happens if the couple kills each other? Here it doesn't matter for the police. Because that couple was fighting, even with a knife and smashing glass bottles, but the police don't care.[40]

José's description in this story of a police force that comes but doesn't "care," illustrates a similar affect that many of his peers in Lomas also describe. His understanding, and observations as expressed in this story, reveal how he has come to understand the state in Peru as a consistent absence.[41] As José tells it, it is not just about having the police respond, but rather, how they respond with contempt.[42] The problem is not only about the physical absence of police or about the police not responding to victims of domestic violence, but rather watching as they arrive and do nothing or only worsen the situation. When the young people describe the state as absent or of being "forgotten," they are not just describing lack.[43] They are also talking about condemnation.[44]

While the sense of abandonment, as Vanessa described, or what José called contempt by the police, was one clear narrative of state intervention in Lomas, the other obvious pattern was that of reported bribes and corruption they see from the police. For example, in more than one focus group, the children (Laurita age 10, Isabel age 11, and Maya age 10) described how the police "help" the robbers:

> Laurita: In my opinion they [the police] don't help Lomas. Because one day there was a robbing of the cables there down below and they [the police] didn't do anything.
> Isabel: I agree.
> Mikaela: Really? Why?
> Isabel: The police help rob the cable.
> Laurita: That's right.
> Mikaela: Why?
> Maya: They give them [the robbers] help, they help them.
> Laurita: They don't help us.[45]

The children explained that the loss of cables means there is no electricity for their neighborhood. In this exchange, "helping to rob the cables" appeared to be grounded in the people's sense of the police's indifference and not doing enough to stop them. Another group with adolescents (ages 12–17) stated it this way:

Mikaela: What do you think of the police in your neighborhood?

Vanessa: There aren't many around here, at least not where I live. Only in this one area there are some, but not that many police. When there is anything—no, actually, not that much happens, like robberies or anything.

Marissa: Many problems?

José: No, not many problems here, and if something happens all the residents leave, but the police don't come.

Vanessa: Around here, it's just like everyone says, that when there are problems, robbing or something, they say that they grab all the robbers, the delinquents, but [the police] say that they just have to pay, they give the police money and with that the police just let them go. There isn't a lot of justice around here. Because of that the community is really tired of it all and just want to take it on themselves. If they find a robber, they'd want to grab him, hit him, put him out in the public to beat him up. More than anything, when the police do show up, they can take him away all beaten up. We have to take justice into our own hands. . . . There isn't much justice in this zone.

. . .

Mikaela: And so why do you think that it is like this? That the community helps the people more than the police?

Vanessa: Because there isn't much justice here is the main reason. No one abides by the laws. More than anything it's about the bribes. Sometimes this is required of the youth, too. More than anything they have to earn money, right, and sometimes they get themselves into this and sometimes leave losing.

Marissa: I've seen this too! Because, look, the community doesn't call the police when there are problems because they know that the police are just going to take bribes, so the community has to make justice with our own hands.[46]

70   Deferred Promises

This pattern was frequently mentioned in the descriptions of the young people speaking about corruption in relation to the police. These descriptions revolved around bribes and injustice in Lomas.

The framing of state "corruption" is prominent in daily newspapers in Lima and in the news more broadly in Peru. As of 2021, news outlets have widely noted that six former Peruvian presidents have either served jail time for corruption (Alberto Fujimori) or were under investigation for it (Martín Vizcarra, Alan García, Alejandro Toledo, Ollanta Humala, and Pedro Pablo Kuczynski). A dominant phrase in both the popular news media and in the people's civil protest is the need to defend the nation (*en defensa de la nación*), a phrase that draws not just on nationalistic teachings, but also on a need to protect a common good (Milton 2018).

The correlation of popular discord about corruption and the comments on corruption by the young people of Lomas, no matter how superficial their knowledge of it might be, nevertheless places these youth in direct dialogue with key societal issues and debates. Even if they otherwise have limited ability to express these ideas within a broader rights or political discourse (such as the kind that members of MANTHOC employ, discussed in later chapters), they pick up, adopt, and make their own discourses on key issues related to the state and the nation, and they reveal their insights through an affective language of everyday materiality.

For the young people of Lomas, the state is expressed as a source of contradiction, wrapped up in longing, disappointment, and abandonment. Paired with these expressions are also the young people's hopes and desires for better conditions and/or for the individuals themselves to be different or better. As José, at age 12, noted, "they are police, and they should be better."[47] The young people were animated in their descriptions of yearning for the police to be better, while also demonstrating a shared fundamental belief about who and what the police are in Lomas. The police were not written off as merely state actors—instead, the young people's descriptions point to, in anthropologist Akhil Gupta's words, "the violence enacted at the very scene of care" (2012: 24). For the young people in Lomas, this "violence at the scene of care" was not just grounded in past and present actions, but also in the way such violence is narrated within the community, both by adult state and non-state actors, and in reaction to the broadly shared (but imagined) idea of the state actors as enforcers of rule of law—the defenders of the nation.[48]

Participatory Security and Local Justice in Lomas

While the girls and boys of Lomas are adamant about the absence of police protection in their neighborhood, they were not saying Lomas was devoid of neighborhood enactments of justice. To the contrary, the young people often spoke with pride of the role community members play as informal enforcers of the law and the need for the community to "take justice" into their own hands. The very hill that frames their neighborhood has a large sign that has "community action" written into it, symbolizing that this is an area protected, patrolled, and watched over by the community members themselves.

Numerous scholars of Latin America have written about what happens when local actors are forced to step in when the state (overtly and inadvertently) disappears. Boaventura de Sousa Santos, for example, has long argued that looking at the informal legal processes in a squatter settlement in Rio de Janeiro revealed how the community created a kind of internal or unofficial justice system. He termed this a type of "parallel law" (Santos 1977: 9). In recent years, many other scholars have pursued studies into the ways marginalized communities in Latin America have formed extrajudicial policing mechanisms. Santos's notion of legal plurality remains relevant in Lomas, and the logics of community responses to injustice featured prominently in the young people's discussions. For example, Maria, at age 14, described to me the need for the Lomas community to "create justice with our own hands."[49] She reflected: "The community doesn't advise the police of problems because they know the police take bribes. Because of this the community creates justice with their own hands" (*con sus propias manos*).[50]

This relational way of conceiving of community action was highly visible in Lomas. For example, in August 2008, during my second year of fieldwork in Lomas, I witnessed a dynamic of community action that Maria and the other young people described. I was observing and spending time in Lomas one afternoon, meeting a group of fifteen children who were participating in afterschool programs run by Enrique, who was with CESIP, a local NGO. They were particularly energetic and excited because it was the beginning of school vacation: two weeks free of school. Enrique gave the children crayons and paper to draw. About twenty minutes into the drawing session, however, a mother came up to the door and asked to speak to Enrique outside. His face instantly dropped as he spoke to her. He quickly said to the kids through the windowpanes that he would be away for a few minutes but would be back. We continued coloring. We began to hear commotion, and one of the girls ran outside, telling her friends she heard something about a missing child. All the other children followed. Enrique was at the bottom of the hill, surrounded by a group of about twenty women and children. One little girl came up and grabbed my hand. The children told me that Ana, age 9, the youngest girl in the afterschool program, was missing. She was supposed to meet up with the other children after school, and she never arrived. I told the group we should go back inside and wait.

When Enrique eventually returned, he said that he was frustrated. They had gone to the local police, and they said there was nothing they could do. He had asked the police officers to call the district police, and they told him they didn't have the number. He asked the police officers to put it out on their radios, and they said the radio system was broken. He said this indifferent response from the police made the mothers angry and concerned. They didn't believe the radio was broken. Enrique got on the phone and began making calls. He called his boss at the center of Lima, and she said she would call the district police herself. She called back to say a child had been found in the next district over, and she was working to verify if it was Ana. They were hopeful.

By then the sun was beginning to set. The kids started saying goodbye and going home. Neighborhood women now gathered in the street looking worried. They were surrounding one woman who was speaking on the phone. She was trying to call the police for updates on Ana. It was nightfall by the time we finished speaking to the mothers and watching the concerns and anxieties grow. Enrique received a call from his boss saying they spoke to the authorities in the next district, and the child they found was not Ana. Enrique said he needed to go to Ana's house and tell her mother directly.

We started walking up the hill in silence. I kept picturing Ana and the hundreds of possibilities of what could have happened to her.

Enrique finally crossed to the other side of the street to a small, one-room store made out of wood and tin. Potatoes lined the counter. Enrique called out to see if anyone was there. Ana popped out from under the counter. "Ana!" Enrique exclaimed. "What are you doing here? Where were you?" he asked. "Here," she reported tentatively. "I was sleeping." Her father emerged from across the street to speak to us. Enrique was already on the phone calling his boss. The father approached us, and I greeted him and exclaimed how great it was she was okay. He nodded silently. Enrique was less pleased and asked what happened. The father said Ana must have come home after school and curled up and gone to sleep unnoticed. He thanked us for coming and said he was sorry for the trouble. We all said goodnight and Enrique and I started to walk down the hill. As we got to the bottom, the group of neighborhood women were still in the middle of the street. This time there were more than there had been earlier, thirty-five women altogether. Enrique approached them and told them everything was okay. Ana had been asleep in her home.

Some of the women starting yelling in frustration, raising their arms because they spent all afternoon worried. Others started questioning if this news was really true: How did Enrique know it was true and not rumor? He assured them he had seen and spoken to Ana. Some just left and started walking home. Others exclaimed how great it was she had been found. Others started talking about their own experiences of their child being in the bed and not seeing them. We stayed twenty-five more minutes as the crowd slowly dispersed.

The incident confirmed in multiple ways what the young people reported. According to them, when a problem arose in Lomas, it wasn't just that the police were unhelpful, but that a lack of infrastructure and political will conspired to drive the police ineptitude. Yet, even with state inaction, the community, and more specifically in this case, Enrique and the women in the neighborhood, spontaneously became a collective neighborhood community force.[51] This kind of informality and absence of state action cannot be dismissed, nor does its absence mean a void. As it turned out, this was not a case that required further state action, but there were

74   Deferred Promises

other incidents like this one and the ones José and the other young people described above. In such situations, it was made clear that the mechanisms in place for mobilizing in response to a crisis were largely taken up by the community members, and not necessarily the police or other state actors.

Many scholars have written both what is termed "participatory security" and "community policing" in Latin America—where because of the absence of the state, local residents, particularly in rural or poor areas, maintain and oversee residential social needs ranging from community policing to systems of governance.[52] Peru has a long and expansive history of the use of the informal economy and the ways where community members relied on themselves, and one another, to "take justice" in their own hands: for example, the creation of communal soup kitchens run by rural women in the 1980s (the model of *Vaso de Leche*) to local security patrol units and informal community watch groups.[53] Popular justice mechanisms, such as collective economic arrangements at the community level, are practiced in Peru and throughout Latin America. Such systems have arguably grown out of community members' perceptions of the state's absence and should be understood as the "products of concrete encounters and distinct historical processes" (Rasmussen 2017: 331). Indeed, the ways the young people in Lomas convey knowledge about the state is not flat or static, but rather through multiple, relational, fluid avenues: the absences they observe, the community actions they see, and also the justice they long for and seek. While there may not be "politics" in Lomas, as expressed by the young people, that doesn't mean it is void of justice mechanisms.

What the Lomas young people understand about politics and legality in their everyday lives is not just about what they see and bear witness to in their neighborhoods regarding the materiality of everyday inequality but also a relational dynamic: the many scales of deferred promises that silence, absence, and injustices sometimes embody. For the young people of Lomas, both dynamics—the daily experience of what they categorize as absence as well as their hopes, desires, and fantasies—contribute to how they characterize the workings of the state and (lack of) politics.[54] But, as this chapter also showed, such hopes are in many ways *also* shaped by the state—through national textbooks, the absence or presence of police, and instances of visible inequality as experienced through the material everyday. In this way, listening to the young people of Lomas demands a theorizing of the state that moves beyond only a story of weak institutions, or even exclusion, but rather also as a source of deep contradiction. It is not just about public (visible) actions and policies that center around the state, but also about silences, absence, and even desires that are related to a paradoxical state: a relational dynamic where the young people identify friction, feel ambivalence, and express both a sense of loss and possibility.[55]

While discussing both schooling and the police, the young people of Lomas speak to a shared articulation of change as possible. They imagine individual schooling as a ticket out of poverty and describe a police force, and military for that matter, that "should be." Contradiction and friction lie at the center of the Lomas people's political consciousness and articulation and reading of the Peruvian state. This point lies in contrast to other young people who have developed specific (legal and rights-based) language and ways of contemplating the state, such as the children in MANTHOC in the center of Lima. As will be discussed in Chapters 4 and 5, MANTHOC conceptualizes the state largely in terms of legality, public recognition, and governmental structures. Further, the young people of MANTHOC describe a state politics in which they feel marginalized yet visible, and they seek to be even more visible. For the young people of Lomas, on the other hand, their reading of state intervention is both embodied and symbolic. It is riddled with stories that require looking at their physical landscape and environmental conditions, at the (lack) of green spaces to play soccer, at poor air quality, and at scenes of gendered violence. At the same time, the young people speak of the state through historical and symbolic contexts, which are inevitably shaped by a Peruvian legacy of both past and present violence.

The Lomas children express frustration about crime, but also that the police are absent and "you can't find them." They are tired of not having clean water and also weary of the unfulfilled promises of state actors about providing clean water. They are sad about dogs who have been poisoned and the mystery of why this may be so. They are frustrated about the trash and the burning of that trash in the neighborhood, but also that a specific state program is charged with cleaning up the trash, and they "haven't cleaned anything here." These unfulfilled promises from the state inform the children's material everyday experiences and also their expectations. Their descriptions of daily life are threaded with their hopes for state action, but also with their honest assessments about the state's failings. For the Lomas young people, embodiments of the state are present not just in the institutions, but rather in their hopes, dreams, desires, and fantasies of what these institutions, and relationships, symbolize.

3

Stories of a Visual Landscape

Murals, Slogans, and Margins in Lomas

"ABANDONO" WAS A COMMON WORD the young people of Lomas used in our conversations, frequently in a reference to their neighborhood as a place "forgotten" or "abandoned." When I asked what word or image came to her mind when she hears the word "politics," Vanessa, age 17, replied:

Figure 8: Billboard in Lomas de Carabayllo settlement stating "Welcome to Lomas de Carabayllo. The Promised Land" (*Bienvenidos a Las Lomas de Carabayllo. Villa Las Lomas de Carabayllo. Tierra Prometida*). Photo taken by author, 2008.

78   Stories of a Visual Landscape

I don't really like politics much because there is none of this. There is no justice, there is a lot of injustice, there are many things but there is no order inside the government. The people who live around here, we are very forgotten. They concentrate more on the people who live in the center of Lima, but not here. Around here, we are abandoned. They rob the money of the population more than anything.[1]

Vanessa's phrase "we are very forgotten" stood out to me—both because it was shared by many of the young people in Lomas, but also because, as I would learn years later, the refrain *pueblo olvidado* (forgotten town) is commonly used in the Peruvian Andes and is born out of a specific racialized and colonial history.[2] Being "forgotten" implies a sense of neglect from the government—a personalized and intimate term—one that may seem to imagine or conjure up an image of a parent, rather than state officials.

It is also a relational term—with the young people imagining themselves in relationship to, and with, other towns or municipals. Often such comparisons would happen when the young people were describing the municipal government and what other neighboring areas have or don't have in comparison to Lomas. A group of 11-year-old boys in Lomas described it this way:

Elena (interviewer): When I say the word "politics" what do you think of?

José: What should be.

Andres: In the elections.

José: What should be.

Andres: A just president.

Rafael: Yea, that there should be a just president!

José: In politics it's not like that. The president wants to be president so he can make wars and all that but the government fails this and makes changes only where people vote. What should be justice, and what doesn't change, is that the people elect the president but what happens is that the president doesn't carry it out . . .

Andres: And also he doesn't achieve the promises that he said he would fulfill.

Rafael: Yea, carry out.

Murals, Slogans, and Margins in Lomas   79

Elena: Do you have examples?

Rafael: They said there is no poverty.

José: And there is so much poverty!

Andres: They say we would be able to see progress and nothing . . . also they say there would be more work and there is nothing.

Rafael: None!

Andres: Now there is worse unemployment.

Elena: And why do you think that is?

José: Because they give the money to the district mayors, and the mayors spend the money on other things instead, in other districts of their community.

José: They pay for other districts.

Rafael: In other districts in his group.

Elena: Like which other district for example?

Rafael: Over there!

José: This is the district of Lomas.

Andres: And there is no work here.

José: The mayor does more work for the community in the district Santa Patricia de Retama.[3]

Andres: In the water and drain that should be in the middle, they don't sort the water and the sewage.[4]

José, Andres, and Rafael, in this exchange, became full of conviction when they spoke of politics and governmental officials. They used comparative logics—picturing families in Lomas as juxtaposed to those living in other nearby districts. They imagined there was work available in other parts of Lima, but not in Lomas. They imagined there was running water and running sewage systems in other parts of the city, but not in Lomas. Their impassioned statements were animated from a place of feeling forgotten by the state, versus acknowledged. But they were also driven by what they imagined was happening elsewhere versus their immediate experience of place and their everyday landscape.

Early in my fieldwork, in 2008, I took a picture of a billboard at the entrance to a main road in Lomas that read in simple, bold lettering "Welcome to Lomas de Carabayllo. The Promised Land" (*Bienvenidos a Las Lomas de Carabayllo. Villa Las Lomas de Carabayllo. Tierra Prometida*). At the bottom

80   Stories of a Visual Landscape

of the billboard, smaller letters state, "Mayor's resolution no. 1155 2003," citing with precision and accuracy the law that brought this particular settlement zone of Lomas into legal, bureaucratic existence.[5]

Formally inhabitable (by law) and now inhabited (by law), the billboard marked a moment of transformation at the municipal level. In front of the billboard there were several homes of Lomas residents, all with freestanding containers of water, lining an unpaved road. Set against the dusty hills of the adjoining landfill, the site where most of the Lomas young people worked or had worked for a time, the sign conveyed a double meaning: It invoked the biblical promised land but also publicly cited the exact legal instrument through which the state constituted the land into being as a new kind of space. The inclusion of the legal code signified a moment of supposed transformation: from being unseen by the state to being seen and legally recognized. The significance of this messaging of being "seen" by the state was obviously important not just to the young people of Lomas, but to all its residents. The history of land rights and belonging, as discussed in Chapter 1, is important to the place of Lomas, and is grounded in the history of colonial dispossession, agrarian reform, and the ways the state used law, and legality, as a tool for reinscribing power.[6] Dating back to Spain's colonization, the use of law and dispossession was particularly prominent in Peru, where "the Spanish conquest challenged and redefined land ownership as a central imperial strategy" (Graubart 2017: 68). This billboard, announcing that the land of Lomas now deserves visible pronouncement of pride and "promise," relates to a specific historical and colonial context. Through legal codification by the mayor and governmental officials, this particular settlement zone of Lomas was now, by declaration, a new kind of livable space.[7]

Murals for political campaigns and slogans adorning public walls and even, over time, on private residential walls were a common feature throughout my ten-year period of going to Lomas. The continuous presence of these murals and slogans became an important element to the relational ways young people frame and understand politics. That is, as discussed in the last two chapters, the young people of Lomas speak about politics and law not just in terms of enactment and state presence, but also importantly in terms of state absence. Their daily experiences are narrated, in part, in terms of what they describe to be disparity and abandonment: in school, by the police, and in their daily physical environment. And, as also highlighted in the last two chapters, the young people's political insights about the Peruvian state are constituted not just by the material realities, people, animals, and experiences that they observe. They are also shaped by visual and symbolic messaging, and by the everyday landscape.[8]

This chapter looks at the murals and images that appear throughout the neighborhood streets and on the Lomas schoolyard. These murals seem, on the surface, to be part of the landscape—the backdrop to which the young people live, play, and interact. But in that landscape they also take on specific meaning, particularly through what might be called Lomas's "visual economy"—to use Deborah Poole's term—and the messages they present, like those in the billboard in the image at the start of this chapter (Figure 8), offer specific articulations of state and government possibility, and of legality.[9] Rather than just descriptive landmarks, these murals convey meaning as to how the state represents itself to the young people. They communicate messages of the young people being "seen" and recognized, while also depending on logics that draw on a long history of colonialism, colonial power, and legality.[10] The specific visual economy of rights and legality that these murals communicate is an important context for how the young people in Lomas read everyday state violence through the lens of inaction and invisibility. The ways the young people interpret these murals in their community sheds light on how they understand, make meaning, and challenge everyday messages of statehood in Peru.

The young people of Lomas, as discussed in the last chapter, describe their relationship to the state largely in terms of feelings of marginalization and invisibility. They describe state inaction as just as formative as state action. The constant presence of visual political messaging paired with their sense of the state's unkept promises and absence has helped to inform their material and everyday experience. That is, the murals and billboards of discursive political promises, coupled with the absence of actual services—including running water, operating sewage system, parks, and responsive police—and enactments of those promises reveal not a binary effect of justice as an object, but rather a dynamic of injustice and a cultivation of articulated disparity. The historical and particular nature of these images, exemplified by a series of ideologically explicit public murals, party political slogans, and NGO public discourse about (children's) rights, intersect

82   Stories of a Visual Landscape

directly with larger historical and social contexts in Peru, and in particular the racialized and classed meanings such images have held in the cultural imaginary.

Taken together, the context of Lomas, including the visual landscape, reveals a political dimension of these children's subjecthood. A key element of their sense of both aspirations and injustice comes from their direct experience and observations: of the land, of the water, of the promises made to them by the state through everyday murals and political slogans. This element of children's political knowledge is not always recognized and is certainly less discussed in research. As children living within families on the edge of a shantytown in Lima, descendants of families who nearly all moved from the highlands of Peru, they are both part of and commentators on longstanding histories of state violence and economy disparity. This chapter helps situate the young people's descriptions of "being forgotten" by looking to everyday artifacts and the material messaging in Lomas that appear in a variety of ways. Political tactics employed by mayoral candidates, murals of political and electoral slogans, and human rights discourse on the local schoolyard all contribute to the young people's sense of, as 11-year-old José put it, "what should be justice, but what doesn't change."

Visual Political Propaganda in Peru in Context

Peru has a long history of politicians using visual materials to circulate messages of nation building and statehood in its political messaging, most notably through clear, concise slogans.[11] During the military presidency of Velasco (1976–1978), the Peruvian government used two famous slogans to promote its policies of agrarian reform: *"Campesino, el patrón ya no comerá más de tu pobreza"* and *"La tierra para quien la trabaja"* ("Peasant, the landowner will not feed off your poverty anymore" and "The land is for those who work it").[12] These political slogans were intended to advance a vision for a wide-scale policy shift backed by the Revolutionary Government of the Armed Forces (Gobierno Revolucionario de las Fuerzas Armadas or GRFA). To circulate these slogans, the government relied on visual culture and public posters, ones that were specifically geared towards the country's large population of agrarian workers.[13] These posters had an explicit political narrative dimension and were accompanied by messages underscoring national class reform and symbolic progress. The state used populist language of the people, but some argue that "the reform's ultimate purpose was to lay the foundation for a more capitalist, efficient system of agriculture production" (Kamphuis 2010: 6). There are similarities between the kind of images and slogans used during agrarian reform (employing visual and participatory messages for political purposes) and the kinds of slogans and visual discourse that politicians use in Lomas.

For example, in 1970 the state created a specific system, the National System of Support for Social Mobilization (Sistema Nacional de Apoyo a la Movilización Social, SINAMOS). Its aim was to "achieve the conscious and active participation of the national population in the tasks demanded by economic and social development" (Cant 2012: 10). Specifically, its objectives were, "the training, orientation and organization of the population; the development of social interest organizations; and communication, particularly dialogue between the government and the population." Historian Anna Cant notes how SINAMOS "combined a rigid, military-style command structure with an important discourse on social mobilization" (Cant 2012: 10). Its main job, in blunt terms, was for the mobilization of the people to align with militarized ideals and political reforms.[14]

Notably, SINAMOS targeted Peruvian children in its public campaigns and messages. In 1970, for example, one account describes a puppet show, directed at children and organized and performed by SINAMOS in 1970, where the children in the audience were described as seeing "the advent of a more beautiful world and a more lasting fraternity" (Cant 2012: 10). Children as central subjects of both state building and messaging was not happenstance, but rather central to the undertaking of cementing new forms of militarized capitalism at the time. Giorgio Alberti and Julio Cotler, two prominent Peruvian academics, wrote a series of papers in the 1960s about the increased reach of formal education in rural areas under Velasco's military rule and gave a nuanced picture of how education, and hence children, became important subjects used for the fracturing of the oligarchic regime.[15] Many historical accounts of overt nation-building projects often write children out of the historical picture, and if children are discussed, it is largely done through discussions of schooling and education reform. Rarely are children discussed as beneficiaries of these kinds of political campaigns, or, for that matter, as targeted consumers.[16] Yet, in Peru and

84   Stories of a Visual Landscape

elsewhere, children's specific gendered, racialized, and/or classed positions are a source of their direct knowledge about the state and nation, even if written out or erased in historical accounts (Webster 2021).[17]

State reforms in Peru have historically made use of romanticized and idealized portrayals of children as both symbolic and substantive vessels for the nation and nationhood.[18] Christina Ewig writes of Peru's history of the state using racialized and gendered messages in visual representation of political messaging.[19] More specifically, she writes about the state's instrumental use of women, where official policy language conjures up the image of global women's rights and reproductive justice while simultaneously undermining those rights and running mass-sterilization campaigns (Ewig 2006). Family planning murals were often targeted at poor, rural, and Indigenous women with messages about family planning and infant health (Ballón 2014).[20] One family planning campaign, under the presidency of Alberto Fujimori, read "Only you can decide how many children to have." Two images, side by side, are portrayed—two contrasting images of families—one with a girl, a boy, a mother, and a father outside a house with windows and plants, and the other image with ten children crowded around a shell-shocked father and angry-looking mother in a chaotic interior space. Ewig writes how this family planning campaign, "telescopes a racialized message. By controlling one's fertility, one will 'live happily' . . . and apparently simultaneously become white and lose indigenous cultural traditions" (Ewig 2006: 645). Peru's state campaign for family planning instrumentalized and politicized not only women, but children. And it was done so not just through slogans but also through images. Children's bodies in these campaigns become visual messages and symbols for ideals of nationhood and citizenship, as well as questions of morality, nationalism, and reconciliation.[21]

In 2003, Peru's Truth and Reconciliation Commission delivered its final report on a grand stage built in Ayacucho, the site where the internal armed conflict began. The report told the story of the internal armed conflict, based on testimony of 17,000 people. As noted in Chapter 1, the final nine-volume report found that nearly 70,000 women, men, and children died or were disappeared and that hundreds of thousands were displaced. On August 29, 2003, the physical stage in Ayacucho that was created for the presentation of this report to the public was set as a symbolic *retablo*, which, in its traditional setting, is a type of folk art popular in Peru, particularly in the highlands.[22]

The theatrical stage setting and dramatic visual imagery for the final report signified the dynamism for the story they hoped to convey. And it also portrayed its grand and imposing scale. In her description of the event, Peruvian anthropologist Maria Eugenia Ulfe took note of the commission's choice to use a chorus of children, almost as a framing for the event, singing on the stage as the backdrop for the reading of the final report. "This chorus of children sang the anthems of both the nation and the city, their voices joined by those of the commissioners and the people of Ayacucho in the central plaza" (Ulfe 2014: 117). Ulfe writes:

> The *retablo* stage was divided into two levels, with two condors placed between them, flying with their heads looking down at the commissioners, who stood on the first level, and two enormous plants of maize were set up on each side. Two doors decorated with Andean flowers, combined with the *escarapela* (the redandwhite insignia that symbolizes the Peruvian flag), further flanked the main box. Lerner and other CVR commissioners addressed the people of Ayacucho in the foreground, and schoolchildren sat in the background. (Ulfe 2014: 117)

The setting was intended to provide a dramatic metaphor for the nation-state that was now shaping the recounting of the country's violent recent past. Within this metaphor, the use of children's bodies and voices to frame the message was not accidental. Childhood signified teleology, progress, future, a nod towards new possibilities of nation building. Indeed, the use of children in this important historical juncture fits into global patterns of how children are often used as crucial symbols of both modernism and state development projects (Stephens 1995). While the children of Lomas and also of MANTHOC were neither audience nor participants in this tableau, they are familiar with and knowers of the nation and nation building, based on everyday political messages that surround them.

The Presence of the Absent State in Lomas

Along the exterior wall of a concrete building near the center of Lomas, there is a slogan that reads in bold red letters: "Constructing Peru 2007" (Figure 9). The message was written by the government to generate support for a state program initiated under the second term of then-president Alan García (2006–2011). The program's aim was to generate temporary job creation in particularly poor and marginalized areas of Peru.[23] The promise of job construction and investment through a simple and straightforward message was read daily by the community because of the centrality of its placement, in the middle of Lomas on the wall of a main building. Construction, in this messaging, reads as shorthand for modernity.[24]

Slogans like this are painted on walls and buildings throughout Lomas. Some were painted by politicians looking for votes before campaigns. Others, like the one pictured here, were painted by the government to generate public support for specific initiatives. Given that Lomas is a shantytown set against sandy hills, these painted words and images provide bold color to an overall gray landscape. However, they also could be read starkly, given that the majority of the people in the neighborhood are physically and socially marginalized. Given the context, these kinds of catchy political slogans may also be read as ironic: Despite the minimal local infrastructure,

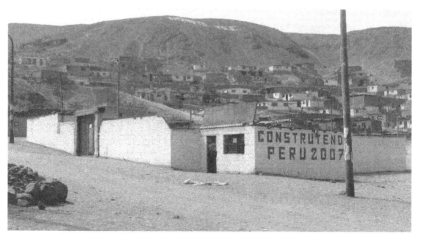

Figure 9: "Constructing Peru 2007" slogan painted on a wall. Photo taken by author, 2008.

whole walls of the community are taken up with political slogans calling for action and development.

The "Constructing Peru" mural was painted in 2007, seven years before running water or sewage was introduced into the community, and even then it was for only some homes, not all. Such images give additional context for why the young people of the area might articulate governmental interventions as largely in the realm of the aspirational and ideological. For example, one political message that took up an entire wall in the center of the neighborhood stated, "We are neighborhood action" (*Somos accion vecina*). Another one promised: "Yes, complete action" (*Si, cumple*). Another one: "We are always united" (*Siempre unidos*). These murals were painted by various mayoral campaigns. Even after the elections were over, the slogans remained on the walls, providing vacuous sentiments of political solidarity in a region where people live with unrelenting environmental injustice, while being taught neoliberal logics of personal responsibility. These messages, in the context of the impoverished material conditions of Lomas, illuminate the discursive promises to which the young people frequently allude. The young people's common description of police as an abandoning presence is contextualized by constant messaging that governmental elections are about "action." But rather than reading these words as indicative of everyday action, the words, which are literally hand-painted onto walls

Figure 10: "We are neighborhood action" slogan painted on a wall. Photo taken by author, 2011.

Figure 11: "Yes, complete action" slogan painted on a wall. Photo taken by author, 2011.

Figure 12: "We are always united" slogan painted on a wall. Photo taken by author, 2011.

that surround the community and which the people pass every day, instead read as unfulfilled political promises.[25]

There are several features of these political murals in Lomas that serve as context for how young people interpret politics in their lives. The first is the way the images have a timeless or atemporal nature. If it was not for the dates painted onto the actual murals, it would be difficult to determine when they were painted. This quality gives them the feeling that they are part of the community and its history, rather than just a slogan for any particular election. Another striking feature of the murals is that many are hand-painted, rather than mass produced. This serves as a visual reminder that these images are purposely not mass replicas. They are not plastered posters that have been hung and left. Rather, the choice by the politicians to hand paint these images and slogans, seemingly by a member

Murals, Slogans, and Margins in Lomas   89

of the community, and with words and slogans that, while generalizable, are grounded in the needs and wishes of the community, is intentional. The hand painting symbolizes, and enacts, a permanence, an investment, and an intimate quality.

Many of the murals are painted onto half-constructed walls, walls that, despite years passing, were not built up—the construction was not completed. Politicians chose to use walls that already existed, but then left them half constructed for years. I noticed the placement of these murals while going through pictures of Lomas year after year. While the walls the murals were painted on didn't change or become buildings or other structures, what did begin to change was the location of where these images would appear. Slowly, it wasn't just walls that were adorned. Figure 13, for example, shows the side of a small *tienda* run out of a resident's home. The image stands out because it states both the mayor's name for Lima and also the political party (Somos Perú). Next to the slogan it states: "Put your heart in your district. Mark both hearts." (*Ponle corazon a tu districto. Marco los 2 corazones*).

Figure 13: "Put your heart in your district" slogan painted on a wall on the side of a store. Photo taken by author, 2014.

For the politicians, these visual descriptions are meant to be instructional. The goal of telling the reader to "marco" indicates which political party the adults should choose when they vote. The "x" marks that are painted through the slogans and images (in Figures 11 and 12, for example) are not defiant graffiti, but rather a directive from the political parties for the community to know which symbol they should select when voting. In the mural in Figure 10, where the words "*Somos accion vecinal*" appear, the mural creators included the number 8 because that is the symbol voters should use to choose that candidate. This could partly be a literacy tactic (i.e., attempting to influence voters who are not literate so they choose the party's symbol on voting day), but it also underscores the ways the particular political messaging of the murals in Lomas work: Instead of painting the actual names of candidates or plastering up images of their faces on every wall, the murals depict slogans about politicians' concern for the place itself—their investment in place—and the use of hand-painted symbols and slogans of community and unity depict this.

In addition to these kinds of slogans of community investment, other murals present texts and images that suggest voting for a particular party or candidate will improve the police and education systems in the area. One mural, from the political party *Somos Perú* (We are Peru), takes up a wall

Figure 14: "For security and education, vote like this" slogan painted on a wall. Photo taken by author, 2014.

in the center of Lomas. It reads: "For security and education, vote like this" (*Por seguridad y educacion marca asi*), and it has an arrow pointing to their political slogan.[26] This particular mural is from a mayoral campaign in 2014, and although the campaign managers for Somos Perú who painted this mural seem to have had adult voters of Lomas in mind when they painted it, the children and young people of Lomas pass the mural daily. Even though they would know it is directed to their parents, the messaging clearly intersects with the young people's longings and their beliefs in the transformative power of education. Through these murals, politicians instrumentalize the promise of quality education (and in turn the investment in children) in their efforts to get votes.[27]

The political murals of Lomas offer a daily backdrop of political and social exchange, illustrating the kind of everyday context where the young people identify politics as "absent" or as José notes, "what should be." Yet, by virtue of the hand-painted murals, ever present in their lives, political aspirations are literally inscribed into their visual landscapes as normative aspirations. These political slogans help form their sense of absence and remind them that services and infrastructure are instead: aspirational.

Hand-painted murals with slogans in Lomas of political messages are not solely one-sided. In 2014, one of these murals addressed President

Figure 15: "We want roads and sidewalks" demand. Photo taken by author, 2014.

92   Stories of a Visual Landscape

Ollanta Humala by his first name. It stated: "Ollanta!! We want roads and sidewalks" (*Ollanta!! Queremos pistas y veredas*). While it is not evident who the "we" is who painted this statement (Do adults in Lomas equally want roads? Women? Men? Children?), what is clear is that community members feel empowered to write messages to the then-president (using his first name) in the everyday spaces of Lomas. Since promises of education, security, and neighborhood unity are being made on everyday wall spaces, residents in Lomas also utilize these same spaces to demand basic material infrastructure.[28]

These exchanges, both by the state through political murals, and presumably by the adults in response, underline the way these wall murals and their images and texts represent a prominent and interactive site for discursive reflection of state presence in their community. That is, rather than through action and enactment of these promises, what the young people see instead is the visual formation of the state's absent presence. The slogans themselves are the political investment. This is true not just in the walls they pass every day in their neighborhood, but also on the walls that make up their school.

Murals of Morality in the Schoolyard

In 2011, on the inside wall of the courtyard of the school in Lomas, a mural painted as part of an environmental campaign by the local municipal government and a Peruvian NGO read: "Save energy and save millions of trees. The future is in your hands. Recycle: Fulfill your role." Since Lomas is primarily a desert, all that borders the school for miles are gray, sandy hills and a landfill with trash. The area that encloses the school is barren of trees. Most of the children who attend the school, like siblings Clara and Eva who were described in Chapter 1, work in sorting and scavenging of recyclables. They sort glass and plastic bottles at an adjacent landfill as a way to help their parents pay the bills, work that was prompted by their father becoming ill with tuberculosis. One could certainly say that "fulfilling their role" in the family depends on their recycling work, but for child workers to pay for the hospital bills of a sick parent does not seem to be the intended message of the NGO that painted the school mural.

Context transforms these slogans. The mural is placed within the courtyard of a school in the sandy foothills of the margins of Lima, where the main audience is comprised of children who work or have worked in recycling. In its literal context—that recycling is the key to the future and children have a role to play—the image hinges on irony and absence. In the same way the young people note the police are *un adorno* (an ornament), the trees painted in their schoolyard read in this context as ornamental as well. The directive to "save millions of trees" addressed to the Lomas children who are living on a sandy desert gives context to the young people's sense of the state as a source of contradiction. Adding "fulfill your role" calls forth an individualistic politic in which the state drops out of sight, and the imagined children (citizens) are those called on.

A mural on the adjacent wall shows two young, white-hued children cheerfully recycling bottles. The boy wears a backwards yellow baseball cap, the androgynous girl helps him lift bottles out of a brown bag. Endorsed by the local municipal government, the mural notes that there is a school education committee devoted to environmental growth. The children in the image appear to be recycling happily, as if recycling is simply what it means to be environmentally friendly and part of the community. The intended race and ethnicities of the children are hard to discern, but the painter did

Figure 16: "Recycle: Fulfill your role" mural in school courtyard. Photo taken by author, 2011.

not seem to have an Indigenous child in mind. The decision by the municipal government and the NGO who painted the mural to choose nondescript white (Peruvian?) children as the protagonists for "good recycling" holds meaning. Not only did the painter ignore indigeneity, but the painter actively reproduced the moral responsibility of citizenship as a function of whiteness, where whiteness and dutiful behavior are rendered synonymous (Harris 1993, Walker 2017a).[29] Such messaging fits into the pattern of Peru's history of discriminatory state policies and the ways these policies have depended on visual messaging, which is gendered and racialized.

In 2014, in the schoolyard of Lomas, a local NGO painted over these murals and replaced them with a mural supporting a campaign against child labor (Figure 18). Next to an image of children entering a school, the 2014 mural reads: "No child labor" (*No trabajo infantil*), "With the gentleness of a child and the sweat of an adult, the comparison is 100% visible" (*Con la delicadeza de un nino y con la sudor de un adulto, la comparación es 100% visible*).

When speaking about their daily activities and how they spend their time, the children in Lomas commonly referred to "helping" their families. The younger ones in particular did not refer explicitly to their daily activities as work or "child labor." Yet child labor is the discursive language that surrounds them on murals in their schoolyard. The main consumers of this messaging are the young girls and boys of Lomas, many of whom, at the time these pictures were taken, were working in addition to attending

Figure 17: Recycling mural in a school courtyard. Photo taken by author, 2011.

school. This message conveys meaning to the young people not only about work, but about gender. By using male pronouns, the message teaches the girls and boys of Lomas that work, in this framing, is about sweat, and is what male adults do. Childhood (and presumably femaleness) are about protection and non-work. Additionally, as stated in the mural, equating work as about something "100% visible" implicitly assumes work as something public and associated with the market, versus much of the domestic work the young people do, which is supposedly invisible and private.

Even though the text of the mural appears to be in the young people's interests, the lack of correlation between its messaging and the lived experiences of the young people erases the work the young people of Lomas perform. Many of them do work, or have worked, in recycling and also go to school—the two actions are not necessarily exclusive. Yet, the message relies on dichotomous language and assumptions built into much of dominant children's rights language—namely the binaries of schooling versus work, adult versus child, visible versus invisible, and delicateness versus sweat—and conveys messages many of the young people don't experience. Saying no to child labor and the delicacy of childhood are adopted language from the Children's Rights Convention (CRC) and international rights organizations. It is a framing of protection that positions childhood and work in particular (visible, public) ways, and that does not necessarily align with the lived experiences of the girls and boys in Lomas.[30] But it is the language and imagery that surrounds them. The messages from these school murals reveal how global rights language, and child protection slogans, shape the ways young people think about and understand state power as partly about what is absent.

The binary slogans of these school murals, using the international language of human rights, point to an important part of this particular group's political subjectivity and political knowledge. The state, in this case, invokes their participation as rights holders and rights consumers, but does so devoid of actual fulfillment of many of those rights. It calls forth their right to clean water and green trees, in a context where they do not exist. These particular children's experience of violence, therefore, is grounded not just by their daily experiences, but also through visible reminders and manifestations—murals and slogans of the state's abandoning, and as they name it, a "corrupt" presence.

José's phrasing that "we are forgotten" or Clara's phrasing that "there are no politics here" are given new meaning when contextualized with the daily state slogans that surround them. NGO workers, taking up the language of the state, and through visual slogans and murals, reflect a refusal to see fully the children's everyday lives, their daily experiences, and certainly their material realities. As such, these constant visual cues through political slogans and murals inside the schoolyard in Lomas work to remind the children of messages about the state (and its presence as absence), but also gendered and racialized messages about law, rights, and statehood.

One could argue that having the visual presence of a discourse of human and children's rights is better than having none at all. The images and murals themselves are painted with bright colors, in an otherwise mostly gray landscape. And the messages themselves seem, on some level, not only harmless but arguably even positive and important in that they promote a global discourse of democracy and global human rights. For example, directly outside the Lomas schoolyard, there is another mural using rights language that is painted in a vibrant and cheery way. At a nearby empty lot that is used as a playground and common play space for the children, a mural reads, "Girls and boys, we have the right to art and culture" (*Las niñas, los niños tenemos derecho al arte y cultura*). Rights language in this case serves as a moral and

Figure 18: "With the gentleness of a child and the sweat of an adult, the comparison is 100% visible." Mural against child labor in a Lomas schoolyard. Photo taken by author, 2014.

Figure 19: "Girls and boys, we have the right to art and culture." Mural at an empty lot in Lomas. Photo taken by author, 2015.

aspirational message. And, in this global moment of the shrinking of rights and rights language across the world, I want to be cautious that I do not mean to deny the potential of this message.

At the same time, the "we" in this sentence stands out, meaning to convey that the statement is written by the children themselves. The style of lettering and the colors suggest it might have been written by children (rather than adults)—similar to the way political murals throughout Lomas are presented as having been written by community members, rather than outside campaign experts. In this case, the "right" to art and culture draws on the largely aspirational history of cultural rights and rights entitlements for children in Peru. This mural, written by local NGO workers, employs the same tactic as that of the political murals in Lomas, attempting to portray a (politicized) message as being de-political. It serves to contextualize how the children describe legality and rights as ideological, rather than felt or present in Lomas. In these murals, which are found throughout Lomas, children are not necessarily treated as sophisticated receivers or political commentators, but rather are arguably used as (political) props.

The use of children as symbolic props shows up in other ways besides in relation to rights or work. For example, a mural from 2011 in the Lomas schoolyard reads "To treat your family with love ... is as easy as listening to music" (*Tratar a tu familia con amor ... es tan fácil como escuchar una canción*). It shows an apparent nuclear family consisting of father, mother, daughter,

Figure 20: "To treat your family with love . . . is as easy as listening to music." Mural against domestic violence in a Lomas schoolyard. Photo taken by author, 2011.

and son. All members of the family are smiling. Musical notes are coming out of a small stereo to their right, next to a table with a tablecloth on which sits a glass of milk and a cookie. It stands out as a supposedly apolitical presentation based on a prototype of a happy, heterosexual, nonviolent family. The mural is part of a campaign against domestic violence, organized by a local NGO. It is one of the few examples in Lomas where domestic violence is overtly engaged, but it presents as fiction by implying that preventing domestic violence is "easy." Although the intentions are to address social ills, the lack of engagement with the community's concerns only furthers a perception of distance between state-affiliated political actors and the people in the community. Like the other schoolyard murals, however, in obscuring reality it reveals a larger truth.[31] Indeed, the mural's presentation of nonviolence as "easy" is itself a reflection of the state's treatment of the problem.

The messages of these murals, both within the schoolyard and also on their playground, contribute to the young people's ideas about material injustice in their lives, as well as their commentaries about state violence. The political slogans and murals are not read by the young people ironically—an insight I gained by noting that they rarely deface or even critique these messages. Over the ten years visiting Lomas, there was rarely graffiti. Rather, these slogans and murals provide the daily backdrop and context for why the young people understand "politics" as largely ideological and absent. The language of rights and of child work is positioned as something aspirational but divorced from daily realities. For these young people of Lomas, the messages don't read as the presence of state intervention (of the state attending or listening to them as future voters, for example), but rather serve to underscore the constant failing of the state to fulfill such ideological promises.

These messages and murals provide greater context for a relational way to hear young people's observations of the reach of the enactment of the state: available to be prescriptive but unavailable to change conditions that would make the enactment of "rights" a reality. And even in the state's apparent material absence, community and local NGO groups step in to deliver similar neoliberal messaging.[32] Put another way: It is difficult to fully understand the young people's sense of justice and "what should be" without this contextual history. Similarly, it would be hard to look at these murals on their own, devoid of knowing the place and history, and how such political and legal messages themselves reflect a logic in Peru that has historically used racialized and gendered messaging for nation building. More specifically, it comes after a long history of law and legality being used by Spanish colonizers in Peru as a key colonial strategy for emphasizing difference. This history, as the young people so aptly pick up on, builds on core sets of contradictions and lived tensions.

Failed (Political) Promises

The disjunction between the promises by actors of the state in the political slogans and the lack of concrete action in the community helps explain the young people's articulation and sense of "abandonment" by the state. Seeing the visual (politicized) landscape of hand-painted murals in Lomas, and pairing it with the articulations that opened this chapter of feeling "forgotten," reveals the ways the young people's political subjectivity is constituted not just by their relationships but also by the messaging from the state. The discursive promises (the purposeful use of rights language) from a range of state and non-state actors help inform the descriptions from the young people of state inaction, deferred promises, and the sense of being abandoned. It is not just about the words on the murals throughout their district,

100   Stories of a Visual Landscape

but also the context in which those murals are painted, the substance of the messages within those contexts, and the normative and aspirational ideas about the particular kinds of "politics" they promote. These messages make visible a defined sense of inequality and highlight multiple forms of slow violence in Lomas. In naming their perception that "there are no politics here," the young people, whether conscious of it or not, point to a daily landscape of local, global, and translocal politics at play.[33]

Christopher Krupa and David Nugent have written about understandings of statehood in the Peruvian Andes and note how "one of the most enduring conventions of state realism is a centrifocal imaginary. That is, state power is regarded as something that is concentrated in various bureaucratic-administrative centers, from which it radiates outward across national-territorial space" (2015: 10). Relational listening to the young people in Lomas problematizes this cenrifocal imaginary of state power and reveals how such narratives divorce state power from the very places in which it is experienced as structural violence. The young people show how material absences fundamentally constitute an important part of what is deemed "political" and that one should not only consider what states do, but also what states do *not* do and what promises they do not fulfill.

In the opening exchange of the 11-year-old boys—José, Andres, and Rafael—when speaking about what words or images come to mind when they hear the word "politics," they noted that the president just wants to "make wars and all that, but the government fails, and makes changes only where people vote. *What should be justice, and what doesn't change is that the people elect the president, but what happens is that the president doesn't carry it out.*" These boys identify politics as the potential for what "should be," and they also identify it as what is missing in their own neighborhood. They name the government's unfulfilled promises as part of what they understand politics to be but also describe it in terms of what they claim is lacking. Given that they are 11 years old, it makes sense that they are more apt to assign this dissatisfaction to one or two political officials and not to larger structures of inequality. Even in a mural they pass on their way to school, only the president is the target for material requests of roads and sidewalks. But José, Andres, and Rafael also identify key ways community members are being instrumentalized for their votes, and the clientelism at play. Their focus on the individual politician failures, on deferred promises, rather than wider system inequality may well be a political tactic in and of itself.

Sociologist Javier Auyero argues that poor people living in shanty-towns in Argentina become "patients of the state" through their encounters with politicians, bureaucrats, and state officials. He makes a temporal argument—that through the mundane and everyday process of waiting for state services, residents begin to learn to "remain temporarily neglected, unattended to, or postponed" (Auyero 2012: 9). In his work in an Argentine neighborhood, with many environmental and impoverished features similar to Lomas, he notes that, for the residents, "politics is not understood as an activity that they do or as a motor of collective change, but rather as an alien, distant practice that renders them powerless" (Auyero 2012: 28).

For the children of Lomas, Auyero's argument both resonates and doesn't. The murals the young people pass every day, either in the school-yard, or on their way to work, occlude the actual experience of their lives: There is no running water; sometimes there is no electricity in police station when women go to report domestic violence; there is no operating sewage system; and there is not always a choice about whether to work or not. The state's presence in this way participates in the manufacturing of a sense of abandonment that the young people articulate quite clearly, and that aligns with Auyero's findings about the creation of a shared understanding "among the oppressed concerning their own situation, their expectations, and their rights" (Auyero 2012: 155).

But the visual landscape of political murals in Lomas, paired with the slow environmental violence discussed in Chapter 1, promotes a shared understanding by the young people of democracy as a veil in Lomas. That is, they see daily the state's deeply contradictory nature and unfair political order. The deferred promises on the murals, paired with the environmental degradation and everyday violence that they witness day in and day out, form the context that creates a particular consciousness, and immediate sources of political knowledge, for these young people. Their sense of having been wronged by the state, their descriptions of being "abandoned" in many ways, derives from the ways the state itself makes them political subjects. That is, it is the pairing of the visual and the daily landscape of hand-painted promises by the state, with the everyday experience of unfulfilled promises, that has prompted an articulation among the young people and that makes them not just passive consumers of these murals, but important commentators, and knowers, of everyday state injustice.

The children in the marginalized shantytown of Lomas, therefore, offer an interesting puzzle that is distinct from Auyero's findings in Argentina: In Lomas, commitments by the state remain largely abstract and visual, and the idealized language of political participation and political slogans (*"Siempre unidos"*) actually works to obscure the underlying conditions and economic interests at play that keep those material conditions stagnant. At the same time, these political promises by state and non-state actors, and the ways the children of Lomas have come to understand politics, have promoted an articulation in them as to how inequity, state violence, and even organized abandonment works (Gilmore 2008).[34]

The young people of Lomas provide important observations of the material (and embodied) effects of inequality around them, though they rarely code these insights in terms of the presence of "politics." In their rich descriptions of everyday life, they are clear about the political implications of the slow and everyday violence they see around them and that it is a temporal dynamic. Their descriptions include both material actions by the state, but also the *absence* of such actions, actors, and services. While dominant discourses of what constitutes state intervention often are imagined in terms of located, technical action, the voices of the young people disrupt this idea. They point to the need to conceptualize violence not just in terms of visible or spectacular acts, but also what is treated as invisible and out of sight. Just because the state treats something as invisible or marginalized does not mean it is state-less. The pairing of the young people's statements that there are "no politics" in Lomas, along with their damning descriptions of police absence and everyday material inequality, points to an implicit (and sometimes explicit) expanded conception of the state both in terms of its ghostliness, and also its presence. It is a reading of the state's constant absence/presence for these young people that shows the importance of understanding the workings of state power as a constitutive tension in Peru, rather than just as a located site.

Together, the insights and observations of the young people of Lomas challenge key assumptions about children's subjectivity. They speak directly to the myth of childhood as a protected space, far and separate from institutional sites of state power, and they challenge dominant discourses that imagine children first and foremost in families. Instead, the Lomas young people show how, in many ways, they are political actors of a different order. They are dissidents of a political order that invokes their participation while rendering them non-participatory subjects.

PART II

4

Young People Together

Children, Protagonism, and Organized Labor

ON INTERNATIONAL WORKERS' DAY, May 1, 2014, the members of MANTHOC (Movement of Working Children and Adolescents from Working-Class Christian Families, Movimiento de Adolescentes y Niños Trabajadores Hijos de Obreros Cristianos), a youth-led children's rights movement founded in 1976 in Peru, marched through the streets of Lima. Both adults and young people from all points of Lima streamed through the city center to make their presence known within a larger demonstration of the Workers' Union of Lima. Earlier that day before the march, roughly 1,000 adults from various factions of the Workers' Union of Lima gathered in the central plaza alongside members of MANTHOC and many other young people from a broader coalition of child and adolescent workers, known as MNNATSOP (National Movement of Organized Working Children and Adolescents of Peru, Movimiento Naccional de Niños y Adolescentes Trabajadores Organizados del Peru). For one of the first times, representatives from MNNATSOP, of which MANTHOC is a participating movement, were asked by the leaders of the Workers' Union of Lima to

107

publicly address the May 1 workers' rally.[1] The members of this coalition of child and adolescent workers gathered early at a nearby plaza—arriving by foot, by shared *collectivos*, or by buses. They planned to meet a few blocks from the main plaza so they could enter together as a collective unit. In preparation for the May Day rally, the children had drawn colorful signs with political slogans, and that day the children neatly lined up with their signs around a statue in the center of the plaza. The signs proclaimed, "Value and respect my work" and "Celebrate my work, respect my rights" and "Long live workers!"

Adult *colaboradores* (allies of the youth activists) were in the crowd too, speaking with the children, coordinating chants, setting up a portable sound system, handing out juice boxes, and making calls on cell phones to see if they should wait for groups who had not yet arrived.[2] The plaza was packed with approximately 300 children who were ready to go. Adults announced instructions indicating in which order the groups should organize themselves to form a defined line. The youngest children—between the ages of 6 and 8—gathered in the front. Blow horns were passed out to child leaders for each section of the line, and drummers were concentrated in the center. They marched through the streets of Lima, stretching out over whole city blocks, state police escorting them through traffic. As they marched, the young people chanted: "Working, school, and organizing are a good combination! We claim our right to work as a human right! Long live International Workers' Day! Long live all the workers!" (*El trabajo, la escuela, y la organización, son una buena combinación! Por el reconocimiento de nuestro derecho a trabajar como un derecho humano! Viva el 1 de Mayo! Vivan todos los trabajadores!*).

Figure 21: International Workers' Day march, May 2014. Photo taken by author, 2014.

MANTHOC is a prominent member of the coalition of child and adolescent workers that comprise MNNATSOP. It has chapters in multiple regions across Peru and is one of the oldest youth rights organizations in the country. MANTHOC is an example of a unified children's rights group in Peru that is an organized social movement. Unlike the young people of Lomas—who have grown up as neighbors, living near others with similar socioeconomic status, facing similar challenges in terms of lack of state infrastructure, and situated within a similar visual landscape based on place—the members of MANTHOC come from different areas across Peru, not just from Lima, and define their connection through their participation in the movement itself. That is, their connection is ideological and values based, rather than primarily spatial or geographic.

Building on the discussion in the last three chapters of the ways that children in Lomas de Carabayllo express observations of the state through affect and longing, the second part of this book looks to how a movement of working young people—whose legal and political demands complicate understandings of childhood subjectivity—provides important insight into the "spatial frame" of how state violence appears in Peru. While the Lomas young people pointed to the contradictions of public policy narratives that work to cast the Peruvian state as a neutral site for engagement and action, the MANTHOC young people show the limitations of understanding these sites largely at the individual rather than at the collective level.

MANTHOC, as a long-established social movement and organization in Peru, seeks that the state recognize its work, its members argue that as workers they should be seen as political agents and active citizens.[3] The claims of MANTHOC, as well as its demands, happen collectively and as a movement. The members use rights language as a centerpiece for their organizing, strategy, and philosophy. They actively helped draft and shape the comprehensive national law on children and adolescents (Código de los Niños y Adolescentes) in the 1990s. They, for years, have lobbied for fair labor conditions for children, as well as for more structural issues like environmental justice. This chapter introduces key tenets of the movement along with the broader ideological development MANTHOC. The next chapter shows the multiple ways MANTHOC enacts its mission today, highlighting the importance of understanding MANTHOC's approach to advocating for children's rights, legal recognition, and messages of equality. As discussed in the book's introduction, listening to MANTHOC as a collective youth rights movement in Peru provides a particularly valuable lens into some of the key issues discussed in prior chapters about Lomas, helping clarify the question of what it could mean to "listen" to children not solely as individuals but as a collective. MANTHOC expands the discussion about child subjectivity and raises questions about incorporating children's voices in law—key issues that help shed light on broader discussions of child citizenship in any national context but particularly in Peru, which has elevated its public discourse on the importance of the child.

Founded in 1976, MANTHOC was one of the first child workers' group in Peru, and it has grown and developed in significant ways over the years, with a fluctuating membership. In 2013, MANTHOC counted some 5,000 children and adolescent members representing 27 towns across Peru. In 2017, there were about 2,000 young people as members. Unlike the children in Lomas, who are not organized and do not see themselves as a collective or a united group, MANTHOC is organized into what they describe and envisage as a union, and the leaders organize and mobilize around a clearly defined children's rights manifesto. Part of this manifesto calls for a clear rallying around identity in politics, and these children make their claim as workers when they pressure the Peruvian state for fair labor conditions and increased public child participation.

The members of MANTHOC whose voices are documented in this book live in various neighborhoods across Lima. Many of them work as street vendors selling candy, bread, and other items. Others work in their homes—cooking, cleaning, and doing childcare.[4] They and their adult allies routinely use the language of rights to describe and publicly advocate for what they call the "integral protagonism of children and adolescent workers," the fundamental belief that children can organize and have overt political agendas and concerns (MANTHOC 2016).

Relatively little has been written in English about working children's protagonism (see Cussiánovich and Méndez Quintana 2008; Taft 2019). However, Alejandro Cussiánovich—who is one of the most prolific writers, educators, and theorists behind the larger working children's and children's rights movements in Latin America—has written extensively about the concept in Spanish. His numerous books on the topic and his ideas

Children, Protagonism, and Organized Labor   111

have been core to the theoretical development of the MANTHOC movement. The ideas presented in this chapter are based on multiple interviews with Cussiánovich, engagement with his scholarly work, and the ways MANTHOC members use and understand these ideas in everyday practice.

MANTHOC's social and political mobilizing, as well as their use of rights language, challenge dominant narratives of childhood, such as those discussed in the first half of this book in the context of Lomas, of children as national symbols "of nature and the object of protection and enculturation" (Stephens 1995:10). Through their movement practices, MANTHOC members disrupt core binaries on which many children's rights narratives rest, particularly in terms of natural differences between adult/child, individual/collective, and subject/object. The MANTHOC movement is unique not just because they are children, but also because the rights they seek are not just as protected (objects) but rather as what they term protagonist (subjects). To understand the way MANTHOC members represent themselves, and the tensions and complexities their movement struggles with, this chapter traces the history of how these young people framed their movement in relation to national state discourse, as well as political and historical factors: namely, Peru's history of internal armed conflict and the general rise of rights-based language in the country.

Despite MANTHOC's focus on celebrating children's voices and protagonism, similar to the young people of Lomas who are navigating legacies of violence and constant environmental health risks, children's "voices" cannot be fully understood without social, political, and historical context.[5] As legal scholar Sandra Levitsky notes, it is often hard to discern the exact conditions or particular circumstances that "unleash the emancipatory potential of law" (2018: 258). But as the young people discussed in this book show, listening to their voices, especially those who have experienced violence and/or been made marginal by the state, helps to exemplify where rights and law discourse come from and what influences those voices. If understood in a relational way, as discussed in this book's introduction, listening to children's "voice" becomes not only about the sole individual child, but also, and equally important, about the contextual backdrop and specific conditions against which they speak.

For MANTHOC, part of the historical context for the emergence of their movement traces back to the social and political moment of 1976. At this time, under the military rule of General Velazco Alvarado, Peru had high unemployment rates with working-class and poor people most affected. It was a tense time, especially for many social activists, and many union members and labor leaders were being fired from their jobs because of their beliefs and union affiliations; it was a time of general repression of social movements. Youth labor leaders in the Peruvian Young Christian Workers group (Joventud Obrera Cristiana, JOC) were among those who feared they would lose their jobs. Because of this economic insecurity and sense of fear, the members called for a general strike on July 19, 1977. In order to plan for the strike, there was a national gathering of eighty members of JOC (Taft 2019: 6). The meeting took place in October 1976, led by a group of young people, to explore and articulate the consequences of the current economic, social, and political climate. The meeting underscored how the young child workers, union members, agreed about the importance of them being recognized as social and political actors. This national meeting of JOC spurred the founding of MANTHOC. The members came up with the name of their movement on March 15, 1979. The young people chose the "Movement of Working Children and Adolescents from Working-Class Christian Families" as a way to identify themselves and the multiple pieces of their identities.[6]

Today, MANTHOC describes and conceptualizes state engagement broadly. The members dream of a world in which their labor and voices are recognized, and they believe that this new kind of world is possible. By tracing some of the broader complexities and contradictions they have faced as a movement through their use of rights discourse, this chapter highlights the ways their organizing strategies reflect insights about the workings of Peruvian state power not just in terms of individuals, institutions, and bureaucracy. They help clarify what it could mean to listen to young people's subjectivities through collective movements, and, in doing so, MANTHOC offers new ways to understand the state as more than just a bureaucratic site.

MANTHOC *as a Movement*

MANTHOC initially developed out of discussions among its founding members about what it could mean to be working-class children and organize as a collective movement. Many of the early members of MANTHOC had been youth labor leaders in JOC, and when they lost their jobs in the late 1970s, they were motivated to see what could happen with collective youth organizing. As Latin American scholar Jessica Taft details, MANTHOC members "had been organizing in the factories, but now felt that the future young people's work was not going to be in the factories, and if there were no youth in the factories, they needed to organize outside workplaces, in the neighborhoods" (Taft 2019: 21). As such, one of the first principles that the members of the MANTHOC movement developed was the need for autonomy. The young members did not want to be an appendage of a large-scale or international organization, despite the potential benefits of such an association. The local Lima branch of UNICEF, for example, receives significant benefits from their association to the larger international organization. But they also must adhere to particular global standards, follow certain global mandates, and base their initiatives on those issued from headquarters. Instead, MANTHOC's members wanted to be recognized as a movement and chose to frame themselves as a "movement" (versus an organization). This decision was a political choice that helped express their desire to remain autonomous from any international organization.[7]

Another principle the group decided upon was that they, as MANTHOC, wanted to be represented in their own right. They did not want adults to speak for them or to serve as interlocutors for their views. They wanted to represent themselves. According to Cussiánovich, "adult sympathizers and educators could accompany, support and collaborate but must not direct the organization: working children were its heart and soul" (Cussiánovich 2001: 158). This is an important distinction because at different moments in recent Peruvian politics, there have been a number of child-centered public policy efforts, particularly within the center-left political party American Popular Revolutionary Alliance (APRA) to represent children's interests. Members of MANTHOC wanted their own voices to be part of the political process and what they refer to as public space.

114   Young People Together

Institutionally and organizationally, the idea of children's "own" voices means that young people are the members in the organization who vote, who take interviews, who debate and discuss the political agenda, and who speak publicly. They are organized into small base groups and also have community, regional, and national coordination committees. Children hold leadership positions in all the chapters across the country, and they hold regular (virtual) meetings across all coordinating committees.

For many of the early formative years of the MANTHOC movement, members were vocal about the importance of child autonomy as a key principle to their values and success. After much internal debate and reflection, however, in 2013 the movement decided to make a fundamental change, and they publicly acknowledged and rewrote their constitution to accept adults as key allies (*colaboradores*), presenting the movement instead as a collective. This was partly for organizational reasons: The effort to coordinate action by large numbers of people necessarily involves adults in critical organizational ways. But the shift to include adults in the organizational structure also became a political strategy: They wanted to create a movement that keeps children at its center and recognizes them as subjects deserving of agency, but that also could have an egalitarian and collaborative relationship with adults. Furthermore, many of the adult allies were former MANTHOC members themselves, making its intergenerational aspect important to the movement's identity. Even so, having the movement remain primarily child-centered, and yet also recognizing the dependence on adults, is difficult to negotiate in everyday practice.

A third important principle of the original MANTHOC mandate was that the movement aim to help all working children in Peru and not just the members of MANTHOC. This element is perhaps one of the most distinctive as it is based on the possibility of bringing the goals of the movement to the larger population, especially those the state marginalizes. Their choice of reaching not only those who are "members" of the movement, but all working children, is politically significant in that it imagines collectives larger than just individuals. This emphasis draws on the liberatory movement history in Latin America and shifts the mission to take on a particular class orientation. The young people of MANTHOC have always been explicitly interested in helping other poor children in Peru, particularly those who work. In Lima, for example, MANTHOC has chapters in all four "cones" of the city, as well as the center. Each chapter is self-organized, based on the specific needs of the children who live there, but also coordinated across chapters.[8] The self-identification on the part of MANTHOC members towards poor, working children is fundamental to their ideological agenda and grew, in part, out of their orientation towards what Alejandro Cussiánovich calls a "pedagogy of tenderness" (see Cussiánovich 2007).

These primary principles that drive MANTHOC as a social movement highlight notable responses by working-class young people in Peru during the 1980s and 1990s—youth educated in the language of rights—to the legacies of violence and the deep poverty and injustice that many young people faced during the latter decades of the twentieth century. This era was the same time period when, as discussed earlier, many of the parents of the young people of Lomas were leaving the rural regions of the country due to the armed conflict and moving in search of work and schooling. Although the daily lives and consciousness around rights language of the youth members of MANTHOC and the youth workers of Lomas are expressed differently, they share the larger historical and national contexts that provide the legal and political backdrop for the ways they frame and respond to the state in their lives.

As discussed in the last three chapters, the young people living in Lomas, who are not engaged in collective political activism, reveal specific ways through which they understand, and by extension, shed light on key aspects of state power in their lives, particularly through affect and an embodied discourse. The young people who are members of MANTHOC provide a different but strongly related contribution for questions one may consider when listening to children's movements and children's voices in law. Because of MANTHOC's explicit engagement of human rights language, and children's rights in particular, the ideological development of the movement highlights key (contradictory) tensions that have arisen under neoliberalism. The Peruvian state has pushed particular groups of young people further away from political subjecthood, even alongside and congruent with more policies of children's rights and participation of children's voices in the public sphere.

116   Young People Together

The young people of Lomas demonstrate how they see such contradictions play out in the everyday lives of their peers and families, and what it means to be made marginal by the state and living within the effects of Peru's legacy of conflict and disenfranchisement. The movement of MANTHOC shows another aspect of state contradiction under neoliberalism, and these members experience the tensions differently as a result of their shared pedagogy, their discussions of children's rights language, and their cultivation of a political consciousness. In their articulations of childhood subjectivity as collective, they simultaneously expand the very spatial understanding of the state beyond just individual actors and governmental subjects. Through their movement approach, MANTHOC members offer an interpretation of the state as located beyond bureaucratic sites. But to hear that insight, one must understand that their movement holds space for complexity and iterative approaches and is grounded in a pedagogy of collectivity.

Un-Crisis and the Pedagogy of Tenderness

The MANTHOC movement was influenced by, and helped influence, Peruvian activist-scholar Alejandro Cussiánovich. His theoretical concept for and with child workers has been central to MANTHOC's goals and to their current mission statement today. For the communities in Lomas, the young people's political theorizing is largely inductive; for MANTHOC, the political theorizing is primarily didactic and significantly influenced by Cussiánovich among others. For MANTHOC, a "pedagogy of tenderness" is both a theory and a practice that understands reflexivity and reflection as fundamental to social activism.

Cussiánovich's approach is one based on self-reflection, love, and kindness (2010). It is a relational theory—not just between adults and children, but also between children and children—and links to the cultivation of learning and reflexivity. The theory has emancipatory goals: It aims to serve as a tool for relational understanding and being.[9] He writes: "The Pedagogy of Tenderness is part of the antipode of any attempt to instrumentalize the affective world, relationships, and bond based on trust and transparency, [the lack of which has been] an effective strategy of colonization" (Cussiánovich 2015: 33). The relational element of this pedagogy, in other words, depends on a spatial and conceptual logic that disrupts a hierarchal order and that holds room for multiple knowledges and forms of knowing.

In his book, *To Learn of the Human Condition: Lessons About the Pedagogy of Tenderness*, Cussiánovich outlines the significance of the theory and what it has meant for the larger coalition and movement of working girls, boys, and adolescents, NATs (Niños y Adolescentes Trabajadores).[10] Cussiánovich's thinking influenced MANTHOC's theorizing during a historical moment in Peru when other social movements were either stunted, shut down, or turning to violence in the face of the internal armed conflict. MANTHOC used rights language nearly twenty years before the International Convention on the Rights of the Child. Consequently, much of the movement's theoretical stance has since been influenced by Cussiánovich, as a trusted adult ally and theorist who has bolstered rights language to offer global legitimacy for youth as political subjects in the face of economic injustice and deserving of dignified conditions.[11]

Early in his career, Cussiánovich worked as an educator for young people, both formally (as an elementary school teacher) and informally through his work as a priest and activist. He worked with migrant women workers, and then child workers, and began prolifically writing about agency and subjectivity. He began theorizing about liberation theory in the 1970s, in the context of the "popular education" movement that spread across Latin America, under the influence of Paulo Freire. Popular education theories used pedagogies of peace and nonviolence to enter into discussions about social justice. In Peru, the emergence of this popular education trend across Latin America also aligned with Lima priest Gustavo Gutiérrez's seminal book *A Theology of Liberation*, looking at the relationship between Christianity and class and political consciousness. Gutiérrez argued for a type of Christianity that recognized systems of domination, alienation, and exploitation; in the face of such systems, he called for a path to political action and political liberation (1973).

The class consciousness of liberation theology resonated with Cussiánovich. As a former priest himself, his training in theology and philosophy shaped and influenced his basic principles and teachings. In the early 1970s, Gutiérrez created a group of theologians in Peru called the Movimiento

118   Young People Together

Sacerdotal Onis. Cussiánovich was central to the success of that movement and the articulation of liberation theology in Peru and was a founding member of the Institute of Popular Education, the Peruvian Institute of Education in Human Rights and Peace, and the Organization Educational Forum. In 2000, he joined the faculty of the Master of Social Policy at San Marcos University, focusing primarily on children and childhood. He was a founder of IFEJANT (Training Institute for Educators of Child, Adolescent and Youth Workers, Instituto de Formación para Educadores de Jóvenes y Niños Trabajadores de America Latina y el Caribe), which functions as a training school and institute for adults who want to work with child workers as allies.[12]

The liberatory solutions the MANTHOC members created, and named, were necessarily related to the context of country conflict and the overarching political and historical landscape.[13] Beginning in the mid-1980s, rural areas such as Ayacucho were particularly affected by political violence and armed conflict, and the young people in the local chapters of MANTHOC could not ignore the violence that surrounded them.

According to Cussiánovich, in MANTHOC "the reference and reflection of tenderness was always present because of the context of violence, both at the state and regional level, and also the problems the girls and boys were suffering" (Cussiánovich 2010: 49). The families and young people who joined MANTHOC developed a language and set of strategies to resist and respond to the intensified context of violence. In this way, the emergence of MANTHOC's values, and the theorizing by Cussiánovich, were largely shaped by a backdrop and context of multiple scales of violence (see Bueno-Hansen 2015). Cussiánovich writes:

> The pedagogy of tenderness is a necessary factor, even if insufficient, to the satisfaction of learning about the human condition in Peruvian society in the framework that has been written about in the Truth and Reconciliation report and the havoc of the condition of poverty and fragmentation within the country. It is insufficient because in order to live and restore these conditions, it becomes not only a pedagogical question, but fundamentally a question of politics, ethics, and culture. (2010: 215)

Children, Protagonism, and Organized Labor   119

In the 1980s, during the initial years of MANTHOC's organizing, the movement's members felt the formal education from state-run schools did not fully recognize or value the labor of young workers like those of MANTHOC. Consequently, MANTHOC members decided to articulate what an alternative theoretical and affirmative stance for their identities could and should look like, creating different schooling curriculums as part of their vision and mission. Refusing the dominant frame of child work as solely, or automatically, oppressive, members of MANTHOC sought to mobilize around the ways that their daily labor, through critical self-reflection and dialogue, could be a tool for learning and empowerment. Fundamental to their organizing and the orientation of the movement was the influence of Cussiánovich and his teachings about nonviolence, caring, and affect.

MANTHOC developed its approach towards tenderness and collectivity in the midst of Peru's internal armed conflict and at a time when law and order dominated the government's public discourse. MANTHOC's focus on nonviolence and tenderness was in direct contrast to the government's discourse of fear, violence, and discipline that underpinned important areas of policy at the time, including the Fujimori government's anti-terrorism legislation enacted in response to the emergence of Sendero Luminoso. Some of these state laws began to be used as a tool of punishment and a scare tactic in the face of "terrorism." As discussed earlier in this book, governmental responses to the conflict were often extremely violent themselves and led to legacies of collective memory of different forms of violence and the suppression of fundamental human rights protections.[14] Thousands of innocent people were sentenced to jail, mass media was censored, and the judiciary was taken over.

During this period, social and political organizing was under siege, and freedom of expression and activism faced threats of violent crackdown. In this way, the government's language and focus on law and order gave rise to more violence.

This period in Peru's history, and the government's embrace of a discourse around law and order, is symbolic of a broader discursive tendency of states who employ authoritarian tactics. Historically, in countries around the world, during moments of formative and public crisis, states often frame a law and order discourse as a guiding light, so that it be-

120   Young People Together

comes a narrative of order amongst disorder.[15] These moments of crisis are frequently accompanied by increased rhetoric about global order (Otto 2015).

Cussiánovich's pedagogy of tenderness, in conjunction with conversation with MANTHOC members (and a key part of MANTHOC's origin story), emerged directly in the face of the history and moment of this kind of crisis governance in Peru. Contending with multiple scales of violence and a national framing of "crisis," MANTHOC employed what Dianne Otto terms "un-crisis" thinking—the "flip side of crisis thinking"—with the hopes of turning moments of crisis towards more progressive ends (Otto 2015: 135). For the young people of MANTHOC, this meant focusing on relationality, collectivity, and movement building. They developed an orientation that went beyond just employing the rhetorical language of agency and rights. Instead, they paired this rhetoric of an expanded set of legal recognition claims as children with a stance of tenderness and didactic nonviolence— specifically against a backdrop of state violence and a national discourse of law and order.

In this way, MANTHOC's history and orientation towards collective care as a key organizing principle adds an important dimension to the discussion in Chapter 1 about relational listening practices, in so far as it suggests that those practices grow out of particular historical contexts and site-specific legacies. MANTHOC illuminates how a relational listening practice also demands a pedagogy that is oriented toward being able to listen to multitudes.[16] It is a practice that leaves room to hear movements in conversation with one another, to attend to their content, and, importantly, to hold possibilities for tensions and contradictions within and among movements themselves.[17]

"Jesus Was a Child Worker"

One afternoon in July of 2014, I went to the center of Lima to one of the base offices of MANTHOC to speak with Geny, a 15-year-old member of the movement. MANTHOC has several locations throughout the city, one connected to a parish and several connected to neighborhood community centers. Children gather in small groups at these various locations and meet either weekly or monthly depending on the chapter. At this particular office the building is part of a larger housing cooperative. I was shown into a room with large windows overlooking a small courtyard. I had gone there that day because I had some specific questions that I was hoping to have answered by someone from MANTHOC, questions particularly about the influences of Christian teachings on the movement. From the very start, Christian teaching had been an important part of the movement's approach. As a movement of youth workers, MANTHOC's interpretations of state power, and its perception of having agency within a broader legitimate political sphere, were informed by its stance on religion. As many scholars have noted, religion has long been an important place to recognize how legal practices are shaped and understood. In particular, Western law has often been shaped and formed in relation to Judeo-Christian traditions. But, "Euro-American law—in ways analogous to Islamic or Native American legal systems—is not devoid of religious impulse either in its myths of legitimacy or in the formulation of its foundational concepts" (Darian-Smith 2013: 324). MANTHOC exemplifies this insight. Walking into one of the main offices in the Lima MANTHOC office, one sees a large poster that reads in big letters "Jesus was a NAT!" (a child worker). An image of a white Jesus accompanies the lettering. The sentiment is that Jesus's age is often overlooked. Jesus, MANTHOC members remind one another, was a child worker.

The use of Jesus as a model child worker for MANTHOC is not by chance. The Christian stance has a contextual legacy given that many of the early gathering spaces for MANTHOC were churches—physical spaces where children and adults could come together in conversation. One of the features of the MANTHOC movement, and a core element of its interpretation of collective action, is its orientation towards Christian religious beliefs that place nonviolence and reflection at its center, as well as social justice and caring. A core element of MANTHOC from the beginning was an articulated Christian belief that there is God in all people—children and adults. One doesn't need to be Catholic to be in MANTHOC, and the young people make it clear that all religions are welcome, but it is a Christian organization.

Geny was 15 years old when the other children in Lima chose her to

122   Young People Together

be a MANTHOC representative. By 2014, Geny had been involved in the movement for seven years. She explained the role religion plays in the organization in this way:

> In MANTHOC we spoke about modifying [the name] within the movement. At the national assembly we spoke about if the word "Christian" should be in the name or not. And we think it should, not because many of us see ourselves as Christians because we go to Catholic church, but rather we see the word "Christian" because in every action that we do we always feel the presence of the child, Jesus Christ. We see him as a model because he was a worker, ever since he was small he was a worker. So for us that is a model of life. When we reflected, we said that we can't get rid of the word "Christian" [in the title of MANTHOC] if Christianity is what we see in everyone. In every action we do, we feel the presence of Christ, in every march that we fight, we feel him as giving us strength to do our work, and to be heard.[18]

This orientation towards Jesus as a model is significant to the organization. Daily practices they embody regarding tenderness towards one another mimic what could be read as a religious orientation, in both the sense of a moral code and in everyday behavior.

Unlike the young people of Lomas, whose perspectives and ideas are established through their locality and sense of neighborhood and place, one of the features of the MANTHOC young people is the grounding in an organized, ideological movement. Their practices of collective reflection, like religion, are important elements that echo core values of the movement and are integrated explicitly into MANTHOC's organizing activities. For example, in the week after the 2014 march mentioned in the opening of this chapter, the MANTHOC representatives met in Lima to reflect on the experience. What went well and didn't go well? How was the MANTHOC representative's speech? What did she say and how did people respond? Although caring, this session after the march was honest and self-critical. Some of the adult and older allies outlined the reasons for what they saw as missed opportunities in the march (for example, the fact that education and work go hand in hand was not highlighted in the way it could have been). The young people made follow-up action plans and articulated lessons learned.[19]

This method of reflection and engagement with one another is embedded in the MANTHOC vision and is core to its pedagogical stance. It is framed by a learned reflective approach that is focused on children responding to other children. The approach also draws on another important idea within MANTHOC's understanding of children and children's humanity—something they term "child protagonism," which understands children's subjectivity as beyond just the individual child.

Child Protagonism

MANTHOC, as a children's rights movement, has long sought to advance legal agency for young people in Peru. MANTHOC's concept of children's protagonism maintains that children can be both social actors and political subjects. It is grounded in the affirmation of childhood and in an orientation of children as people worthy of dignity. While the concept of participation within children's rights discourse is often limited to discussions of inclusion of "children's voice" in civil society, protagonism argues for the need to define and imagine new forms of adult/child social relations, as well as constructing new understandings of child work (Liebel 2020).[20] Fundamental to MANTHOC is their wish for their work to be recognized by and legible to the state. As workers they demand to be seen as political agents and active citizens. In outlining this vision of protagonism, Cussiánovich writes:

> The ideological and emotional background for this approach is love for childhood, as the foundation of all ethical, social and political discourse of solidarity with children. Furthermore, this paradigm calls upon us to break away and constantly overcome the adult centered culture which wields age as a factor for discrimination and hierarchy. And it calls upon us to relinquish the culture of the trustee or tutor as the prerequisite for the consistent upholding of the discourse of citizenship and democracy. (Cussiánovich 2001: 159)

MANTHOC's vision of *el protagonismo*, as Cussiánovich notes, relies on a fundamentally ambitious principle of breaking free of core assumptions

124   Young People Together

about the (hierarchal) order of children as less than, or even as primarily future adults. The idea of protagonism goes hand and hand with an understanding of inherent dignity. The young people of MANTHOC hold ideas and employ practices that push against normative binaries within dominant assumptions about childhood such as formal/informal work practices, individual/collective voice, and even child as object/agent (see Taft 2019).

What child protagonism (*el protagonismo)* means in a tangible way for MANTHOC members is that the young people of the movement who agreed to take part in this book did so on the condition that they be seen as representatives and members of an organized movement. MANTHOC members want readers to know the principles and ideas of the movement, and not necessarily read their story as an individual narrative about one particular child. One of my methodological commitments was to know and understand both groups of young people on the terms and in the ways they wanted. For MANTHOC, this meant they wanted me to learn to understand their movement by going to rallies, attending lunches and meals, doing participant observation at their board meetings, and conducting focus groups with the young people—and they wanted to speak to me as *representatives* of the collective movement. For the young people of MANTHOC, in other words, a core element of self-representation and protagonism was to be taken seriously for their ideas as an organized social movement of workers.

Having children be able to represent themselves in terms with which they identify and feel comfortable is argued by many as critical to doing ethical, sensitive, child-centered research.[21] Taking this claim seriously is one of the reasons why it is valuable to look at children who are in relationship with one another in a range of ways (spatially, politically, etc.) beyond only age. And this same approach also speaks to the complexity of the research with regard to the question of "listening." What should be the balance between honoring their wishes and representing them on the terms they wanted, while also recognizing their vulnerabilities as children, as social and developing subjects? What, in this case, does an ethical stewardship of MANTHOC's core idea look and sound like? These questions are closely related to a fundamental tension with which the MANTHOC members themselves continually grapple: articulating their needs in terms of their identities as representatives of a worker's movement, and not just as individuals of a particular (vulnerable) age—while also trying to not lose or deny the social power and authenticity that comes from being children and arguing for a reimagining of child/adult relations. Indeed, the concept of children's "own" voices is complex. One of the dangers of the concept of a unified children's voice is that it obscures not only the diversity of children's experience but also their deeply relational (and dependent) positions.[22] Complete autonomy is impossible, for all people, but perhaps particularly so for children.

The complexities of how to talk about the concept of protagonism, and to capture its intricacy, became vivid to me in 2016, when I presented sections of this book at a Law and Society Conference in Minneapolis. Far from Lima and speaking to a nearly all North American audience, I found myself challenged to adequately express the complexities of what I was hearing from the MANTHOC young people about the need to reconceptualize children fundamentally as "protagonists." In presenting their arguments, I struggled to speak about MANTHOC in ways that didn't feel too binary. That is, in my fidelity to their exact words and arguments, I feared my descriptions came across either as though members of MANTHOC were autonomous "little adults" or, alternatively, as if there was some devious manipulation happening on behalf of the adults in the movement that I wasn't sharing and that the children were being used as political pawns. Neither I felt was true. One audience member grew visibly frustrated with the nuance, and tensions, I was reporting. She raised her hand and exasperatedly said "this isn't *Lord of the Flies*. Children can't possibly be *that* political, and articulate, in the ways you are presenting. Children are, and must be, dependent on adults."

The exchange clarified how few models exist to listen for the complexities of "children's voice," but perhaps especially with regard to young people who have direct experiences of state and structural violence, and so whose lives *are* "that" political. For this audience member, my descriptions conjured up for her the need to call upon clear distinctions between adult/child, political/dependent, and even, by way of calling forth the image of *Lord of the Flies*, savage/controlled. The exchange crystalized why the proposition that MANTHOC puts forward is, in part, so radical: It is the rejection of a singular protagonist. Instead, in their notion of protagonism, MANTHOC relies on a relational orientation—one that rejects inherent hierarchal orders, particularly between children and adults.

126   Young People Together

In original ethnographic work with MANTHOC, Jessica Taft notes how, in reaction to a common critique of the movement that they are "just pawns in adults' political maneuvers" the young people sometimes "bend over backwards to argue that these spaces are entirely child-led and express children's autonomous and authentic perspectives" (Taft 2019: 153). I observed the defensive stance MANTHOC members often felt they had to take in the face of the argument of adult manipulation. Yet in the movement's self-consciousness and grappling with these questions, MANTHOC offers a core contribution to both method and content, insofar as the kind of listening and protagonism they are visioning moves beyond just individual children.[23] They are arguing for a world in which their political participation as a movement is possible.

In an organizational meeting of a local chapter of MANTHOC in 2014, one of the young adult coordinators tried to explain the idea of "child protagonist" to three members (all of whom were 10 years old) who were struggling to understand what it meant. She asked if the pencil case that was sitting on the table was human, "Does it have rights? Can it express its opinion? Can it express emotions? No! Children are not objects. You are subjects! You are protagonists! You have the right to express yourselves."[24]

This notion of child protagonist—as fundamentally about the right to expression and who the audience is for this expression—links directly to the importance of children's voices in "public spaces." Sonia, an 11-year-old representative of MANTHOC, reflected:

> In this last evaluation we did of the past four years, the most difficult thing has been to intervene in public spaces. For example, in Congress, where we cannot intervene, which is where the people of Congress make decisions, but also in some other spaces, for example at the provincial "poverty networks." This also happens with public budgets, where there are only businesspeople, and children cannot intervene there by giving their proposals. This has been changing slowly but there still has been an inability to insert our agenda in public spaces.[25]

Sonia cites the desire to enter into public spaces in Peruvian politics in order to be heard. She presents an understanding of public space as a site of politics where only certain (adult) people can participate. Public spaces, for MANTHOC, are similar to what the young people of Lomas in Chapter 2 described as politics—a site for government intervention. Part of the core notion of the development of protagonism for the MANTHOC young people, therefore, is about having the opportunity to use and engage their voices in the public sphere, and to become political subjects, rather than solely objects of the polity.

Protagonism and Public Space

The young people of MANTHOC strategically depend on the language of law and rights. They look to international conventions, and to the state, as spaces that are able to provide (legal) recognition and protection of their identities as child workers.[26] In this way, rights language, for the young people of MANTHOC, serves as aspirational language rather than what they see as happening on the ground. But MANTHOC members want the Peruvian government to actualize their rights as agents and also as workers—specifically, they want formal changes to codes, laws, and public platforms for engagement. Part of the enactment of protagonism, as members of MANTHOC have described, is the entry of child voice in what they term "public space." MANTHOC members use the concept of public space in relation to protagonism to mean more than just a geographic location.

> We are not considering "spaces" for participation in geographical terms. A more appropriate term may be *milieu*, which synthesizes a human, cultural, social, economic and political reality, and refers to context, social relations, projects and life styles. In this sense, "space" implies dynamism, temporality, subjectivity, change, specificity, and process. Or, put in another way, a permanent construction or deconstruction of the lives, daily tasks and protagonist participation of the diverse actors who share a determined *milieu*, which could be described as a way of living. The spaces, then, mark and even condition the social relations found within them. (Cussiánovich and Márquez 2002: 23)

Conceiving of public space beyond geographic site, members of MANTHOC look to law and rights as a public space where they wish to see political

128 Young People Together

and social change. They seek to change and intervene in public politics and change work-related laws and international conventions. They look to the state and state actors as able to validate and provide recognition and protection of their identities as child workers.[27] As MANTHOC members make choices as a collective, particularly in their organizing in relation to law and legality, they reveal crucial insights about the Peruvian state as operating through everyday interactions, exchanges, and interpretations (see Ewick and Silbey 2014).

MANTHOC representatives speak of their wish to have more political influence (*mas incidencia política*). Indeed, their notion of space or increased political influence was one of the central and prioritized issues for MANTHOC's child delegates who spoke at the International Workers' Day march in 2014. One of the children's core demands was that "the central, regional, and local government, invest and implement politics that are favorable for children and adolescent workers and for children more generally, and that they recognize children's capacities and abilities."[28]

In many ways, MANTHOC has arguably achieved their long-time goal of increased political influence in terms of public and state representation. Over the last couple of decades, the Peruvian state began to recognize children as subjects who should be included in public political process, but the changes have been slow. Peru's Code for Children and Adolescents sets the legal norms and mandates for issues such as children and the penal system, child labor, and children's right to public participation. First established in 1990, it has had several revisions since then, and there is a congressional revision committee for this code on which a number of public representatives serve. Children, however, are not part of the revision committee.

On January 28, 2008, a 15-year-old representative of MANTHOC named Layla Villavicencio Garcia addressed this committee in Congress to address the issue of excluding the voices of MANTHOC from public space. In her speech, Garcia shed light on the tension with child as (modern) object/agent.

My name is Layla Villavicencio Garcia, I am 15 years old, I am from Piura, and I am a delegate of the national movement of organized child workers of Peru. I have been a child worker since I was 8 years old in the city of Piura. . . .

First, we question the initiative of the revision of the code of children and adolescents. As an organization of children, we are surprised that the emergence of a commission brought forward to revise the code does not incorporate an organization of children. For example, our group, who are subjects of social rights, should be involved in this revision.

However, there is not one child's organization that is present for this session, and we argue that there really should be. Otherwise are children or adolescents really being considered or taken into account? Especially since this is an issue primarily for children and adolescents in general, and they are not here, then is this committee really able to represent the concerns of children and adolescents? Especially since this revision is based on the principles of the Convention, the best interests of the child, child participation, but that is not reflected here even with so many entities of the state.

Garcia articulates a critical point about children's subjectivity in this speech: that the legal codes at the congressional level are often revised and considered by adults, and children's voices—organized or not—are not part of that revision. Garcia, in this respect, is arguing for the insertion of children's voices and representation within the public space of both Congress, as well as the law as enacted by the children's code. According to Garcia, listening to young people was not just about individuals but collectives, and crucially, the inclusion of young people into an idea of the Peruvian state through everyday law.

In 2010, in response to the Hague Global Child Labour Conference (on the worst forms of child labor), the Latin American and Caribbean Working Children and Adolescent Movement (MOLACNATs), of which MANTHOC is a part, expressed similar sentiments in the following letter:

We raise our voices as the Latin American and Caribbean Working Children and Adolescents Movement (MOLACNATs) to protest the disrespect shown to us by the organizers of the Hague Conference by neglecting to invite us to participate, or indeed, even informing of us that it would take place.

For more than 30 years, our movement has defended its firm position to fight and denounce labor exploitation of millions of chil-

130   Young People Together

dren throughout the world, while at the same time fully rejecting ILO Convention 138, on minimum working age, and remaining critical of Convention 182 on the worst forms of child labor and its IPEC program. As regards to Convention 138, we consider the minimum working age to be discriminatory, excluding minors younger than 14. This convention condemns thousands of girls and boys to the illegal and informal sectors, thus greatly exposing them to exploitation. As regards to Convention 182, which considers the use, procuring, or offering of a child for prostitution, the production of pornography or for pornographic performances, or the use of child for illicit activities, in particular for the production or trafficking of drugs as the worst forms of child labor, we believe that these are criminal offences and flagrant violations of a child's human rights. We are clearly against all of these phenomena but calling them "labor" creates dangerous confusion and leads to purely repressive practices as opposed to truly liberating alternatives.

The letter went on to make specific calls of action for the conference to consider. As in Garcia's speech two years before, one of the fundamental disputes and demands of the MANTHOC movement is about the ways adults make laws *about* children, but not *with* children. Further, in the case of the letter from MOLACNAT, they were challenging fundamental definitions and conceptualizations of labor. And like MANTHOC, they highlight the importance of children's voices, the revaluation of the basic category and definition of "work," and the denunciation of adult-only representation for issues that directly affect children. They expand what it might look like to listen to children as part of movements and point to the dilemmas of "children" as a static and coherent category.

Listening to Movements: Methodological Complexities

If Lomas young people highlight the importance of listening to working children for affect, history, and context in order to better understand everyday workings of state power, the working young people of MANTHOC bring to light some of the tensions, and stakes, in doing so. As discussed in Chapter 1, in relating to both the young people of Lomas and MANTHOC,

Children, Protagonism, and Organized Labor   131

my own methods relied heavily on feminist, critical, and post-colonial principles about ethnographic research and the need to attend to questions of power and standpoint.[29] I found myself hyper- aware and questioning my "reading" of MANTHOC—and in continuous "moments of puzzlement and sudden realization, of making and unmaking" (Cerwonka and Malkki 2007: 175). These moments of making and unmaking came most vividly through my own changing consciousness of how I was defining the identities of the MANTHOC members primarily as young people and understanding their extraordinary actions because of their age. That is, for many of the first years of meeting and following MANTHOC, I found that I wanted to listen to them first and foremost as children. And the young people of MANTHOC were continually asking me to listen and represent them in more robust and intersectional ways—not just as children but as activists and as workers, as both subjects and agents. While intersectionality in recent years has often been used and lauded by many within the academy, the actual development of practices and ethical imperatives that can be used for what Patricia Hill Collins names a "lens for examining how critical analysis and social action might inform one another" (2019: 3) is quite complex in practice.[30]

The need to attend to this complexity in my fieldwork was present from day one. When I went for one of my very first interviews with MANTHOC in 2008, a 12-year-old representative met me outside and said she would be the interviewee. I had spoken to an adult on the phone, so I was surprised. The adult also met us and came with us to the interview room. As we began, the issue of ethics stumped me as I internally debated which consent form I should have them sign. Because I had spoken to an adult on the phone, I had brought only the "adult" consent forms. I had separate consent forms for the children of Lomas—ones that I wrote in ways that seemed more accessible (age-targeted language, formatting, etc.). The simplistic language on the children's consent form suddenly seemed almost insulting, however, given that MANTHOC is a movement striving for recognition as protagonist workers, not just as children.

Even though the interview was technically with the 12-year-old, the adult MANTHOC ally sat next to her to address any confusion, questions, or issues the representative felt unprepared to discuss. Indeed, the adult interrupted the representative at times to clarify her statements. In subsequent interviews even if an adult was not present, an adult collaborator always served as a gatekeeper. Partly, the reason for this seems obvious: The need for structural support from adults—in terms of both organizational logistics as well as conceptual understandings—reflects the fact that the majority of the MANTHOC leaders are 11, 12, and 13 years old. But MANTHOC's original framing of the movement and promotion of a child- centered approach in its main objectives can obscure such dependence.[31]

This paradox reflects a larger dilemma in the general area of children's rights and child participation. The literature on research with children focuses largely on the ethical specificity of working with children because of their status as vulnerable children (i.e., because of their age). The promotion of children's "voice" is central within many international development organizations.[32] Yet, power is often not explored adequately, particularly with terms assumed to be internationally celebrated, such as "empowerment," "voice," and "participation." In this way, MANTHOC's call for child protagonism is not just a theoretical idea but rather a demand to attend to questions of power, power relations, and intersectional identities.[33]

MANTHOC is unique in that its claims for child protagonism go further than primarily welfare claims. The movement also makes sociocultural and economic claims related to the recognition of children as workers. In considering the priorities of these claims, and the ways these priorities have changed and evolved over time, the MANTHOC movement shows both the possibilities and challenges to the existence of an individual or "authentic" voice.[34] In their collective demands, MANTHOC members strive to make particular claims about the labor market (both formal and informal), and they want recognition for how much the market depends on young people for labor in Peru. However, recognition itself does not automatically challenge existing forms of power.

The representatives of MANTHOC seek recognition from the state for their status as child workers, not just as children. The institutional and political claims they make in regard to children's rights are not solely individual (child to child) but are also ideological and representative of their points of view as members of a movement. My categorical separation of consent forms based on age had not accounted for the multiple standpoints and identity claims by the young people. Working with MANTHOC, therefore, continually required an approach that would allow for the intersectional

Children, Protagonism, and Organized Labor   133

aspects of the MANTHOC member's identities, as well as an attention to power relations.[35]

Other meetings I had with MANTHOC representatives over the years continued to reinforce this need to develop an expanded understanding of MANTHOC's claims and what it meant for seeing the members as political protagonists. The meeting with Geny from 2014, for example, who told me about the role of Christianity in the organization, also underscored this. When I arrived for that interview, the youth representatives told me at the outset that 15-year-old Geny would be their key "representative" for the interview to state the main points they wanted to get across for the group. Yet, they didn't just have me meet individually with Geny. Rather, these representatives came as a group and listened to her answers to my questions. They had pads of paper and pencils, and as we sat around a table, they took notes. Geny presented this as a teaching opportunity to instruct them, as well as me, about key principles of the movement. The young people were focused on expressing a shared and coherent voice, and that has meant creating practices of care and collectivity.

If I had just focused on age or listening to the children's individual voices, I might have (mis)read this experience as solely a didactic or ideological exchange. But MANTHOC wants to be understood as a movement. The movement's fundamental argument about the limited tools at hand to see children as protagonists challenges the dominant idea of age as the key part of child identity. Rather than reading them primarily through the lens of individual "children," MANTHOC members demand an expansion of traditional categorization for understanding their primary identity in terms of only age or singular identity status. Instead, they want to be read for multiple identities at once: workers, Christians, young people, organizers, protagonists.

In the fall of 2015, I returned to Lima to present my research findings to the MANTHOC young people and to share what I had found, heard, and understood from my years of research and interviews with the movement. I arrived at the field site with my 6-month-old baby strapped on my back, blurry-eyed from a night of little sleep, and anxious about what it would mean if the MANTHOC members didn't "like" my findings. I came with a PowerPoint presentation, handouts, and happiness to see them.

With Enrique, the research collaborator who accompanied me to all in-

134   Young People Together

terviews in both Lomas and with MANTHOC, I told the MANTHOC members why we had returned—that it was important, as part of the ethics of taking them seriously as research participants who had given me so much faith and time, to present what I heard and observed over the years. And I also wanted to give them the chance to clarify what I thought I heard or ask me questions. I wanted them to have the opportunity to be actual subjects, not just objects of research. Although Enrique and I had said all of this in Spanish, one of the adult MANTHOC collaborators in the room stood up and tried to repeat and summarize what we had just said. She told the kids that we were there to "honor their rights." This translation and interpretation of my explanation reverberated for me. Rights discourse was the means through which these young people have been taught to translate and understand "the political."[36] Indeed, legality and rights language have become crucial discourses through which to see and understand themselves in relation to each other and their work (Liebel 2020).

A fundamental methodological complexity of this aspect of the research has been how best to respect and understand the multiple identities of MANTHOC as a social and political movement (rather than just as a collection of individual children), as well as what this shift would demand in terms of relational listening practices. How does one stay attuned to large-scale, global patterns of entrenched inequality, particularly as it relates to young people, while also focusing on the local, the particular, the actual, the everyday? The representatives of MANTHOC seek recognition for their status as child workers, not just as children. While much of the scholarship about young people focuses narrowly on age (i.e., how to listen and do research with young people because of their age and status as children), MANTHOC members reveal a critical assumption with this approach: Namely, the institutional and political claims MANTHOC members make, as well as the core principles of their movement with regard to children's rights, fundamentally disrupt patterns of viewing childhood primarily through single identity categories of age. Instead, MANTHOC members use human rights language to make ideological claims as representatives of their collective points of view and as members of a social, political, and class-based movement, and not as individual children.[37] Rights language, in other words, works to help them gain legitimacy for their (global) identity claims—it is a recognizable, international frame. But one question, addressed in the next

Children, Protagonism, and Organized Labor   135

Figure 22: "Long live the workers!" Poster drawn by MANTHOC members for International Workers' Day march in May 2014. Photo taken by author, 2014.

chapter, is if, and how, the elevation of rights potentially also flattens other claims—particularly in terms of their conceptualization of citizenship. Methodologically, MANTHOC offers an important lesson about how there is still much more to be studied and attended to with regard to listening to children's movements, as well as the tensions and opportunities that doing so creates (Taft 2019).

MANTHOC members want to be seen by the state as political beings and do so by emphasizing their status as workers as well as agentic children. They seek recognition for their work and organize their movement around claims of inclusion of children's voices in the social polity—a site they associate with the public sphere. To make these claims, they use a language of rights, representation, and protagonism. MANTHOC members disrupt the myth that children can't be organized actors in public spaces (either as protagonists and/or economic agents), and as an organizing strategy they code their activism through rights language as a way of taking up and understanding politics. Rights language for MANTHOC members is a recognizable discourse for global exchange, and that fits within a much broader view of what it means to be a worker and what it means to be a citizen.[38]

In many ways, the idea of a child citizen, like the kind that MANTHOC advocates, pushes for a reconceptualization of adult/child power relations and opens up new understandings of child subjectivity. More specifically, this conceptualization pushes for ways of relational and intersectional listening practices beyond just tokenism. The MANTHOC young people offer an explicit model of how they wished to be listened to and how it includes an attention to the complexities of movements and collective identities. But they also reveal the challenges of doing so in ways that are able to attend to intersectional elements of identities (in this case, beyond that just of age).

In making these arguments, the children of MANTHOC rely on an interpretation of rights that is associated with public space and where they can best engage politics, the market, and the state together. Indeed, for MANTHOC, whose members consider their identities as workers to be crucial, the market becomes a fundamental platform for their politics. As such, they are clear that they do not seek to end child labor. Instead, they are fighting for the recognition of child workers within a vastly unequal global market, and for the radical shift towards more dignified and just conditions. To listen to MANTHOC members, therefore, requires a reckoning of methods—for example, what it means, or could mean, to listen to children beyond just the individuals; what it means, or could mean, to listen to children in intersectional ways and ways that hold multiple parts of their identity. And these questions also demand asking what such listening reveals about current understandings of state power in Peru.

5

Child Workers and Child Citizens

Rights, Recognition, and the Language of Equality

AT THE WORKERS' DAY MARCH in Lima on May 1, 2014, Daniela, a 13-year-old MANTHOC representative, stood confidently with a microphone in her hands in front of a crowd of hundreds of people. There were adults standing on the platform around her—the union representatives from various workers' movements. In the crowd at the street level below, about twenty MANTHOC members stood with homemade signs, and they jumped and cheered for Daniela as she was getting ready to speak. I stood with them and watched as Daniela delivered these words:

> Good morning, everyone. My name is Daniela and I am 13 years old and am in my second year of secondary school. I work in a store in my house. Today is the 1st of May and it's the day for all of us workers who fight for our rights. Happy day of the worker!
>
> We are here today because we want the work of boys, girls, and adolescents to be recognized. We want to be respected and not discriminated against because you see us working in the street and that

137

you protect us. We are a reality of Peru and we [child workers] help and sustain the economy. We work to sustain our families and to have a good education.

We ask that you see us as useful because that is how we identify. We want to be recognized as useful in our families and also [that you recognize] that we study. The truth is, working doesn't imply that we don't study. Child workers study and, in fact, we are at the top of our classes.

We ask that you see us this way, that you recognize that we are equal to you and that we are able to achieve our rights and that you respect us as we are. We are also people and we have opinion. We are workers just like you.

Happy Workers' Day. Long live the workers! Long live all the boy, girl, and adolescent workers!!

The labor union's invitation for a MANTHOC representative to speak at the march was a significant milestone for MANTHOC; it was one of the first times since its founding in 1976 that the organization was given the platform by the union to publicly outline their agenda and wishes. Moreover, the decision by both MANTHOC and the adult union leaders to choose Daniela to speak was notable because she was one of the first children to speak at a union-organized event. Daniela stood with a microphone, sharing the stage alongside seven adult men and three adult women from various labor organizations. Daniela spoke with authority to the crowd as the national coordinator for MANTHOC, and she delivered a message about the politics of justice, rights, and equality.[1]

Daniela's rallying May Day speech highlights several important questions: Is genuine child voice or authentic child participation possible in the realization of "equality"? Should only adults be taken seriously in the public sphere and at workers' rallies? In contexts of inequality, can children play a role as social and political actors? By demanding recognition of children as subjects worthy of essential rights, and by promoting a notion of child work that is not at odds with a child's education, Daniela unsettles and expands certain assumptions about childhood and voice.[2] In her speech, she articulates justice claims for workers' rights but also makes a call for a certain kind of recognition from the state that includes children's voice.

Through MANTHOC's discourse, as deserving subjects of rights and what they term "dignified work," MANTHOC young people issue a challenge to move beyond dominant binaries of adult/child, formal/informal labor, equality/difference, and public/private spheres. When MANTHOC members use the terminology of equality and justice, their tacit point of reference is often the state. They infer the state in a variety of ways: to grant them equality as workers, to grant them recognition as subjects deserving of rights, to make them visible as subjects deserving of dignified work. As such, it is not just that MANTHOC members seek for their subjecthood to expand (i.e., viewing children not just as solo subjects and agents of the law, but also as collective subjects), but also that they are positioning these claims with public policy in mind, and, in turn, with imagined ideas of, and knowledge about, the Peruvian state. In this way MANTHOC members frame their subjecthood not merely in the sense of being acted upon *by* the law but also recognize that their subjecthood is enlarged by acting *with* and *through* the law. At the same time, since they are not political agents or subjects in the eyes of the state—and since they are without the means to demand things of law itself (voting access, political representation, etc.)—their power to shape the contents of law is often limited.[3]

In Daniela's speech, and in many of their general advocacy campaigns, MANTHOC pairs the concepts of "child worker" with "child citizen," disrupting certain recognition claims both in terms of their agency as children and their identities as workers. As discussed in the last chapter, MANTHOC's notion of child subjectivity pushes for a reconceptualization of child participation beyond being a solo or unified voice.[4] At the same time, as this chapter shows, the particular concepts that MANTHOC has used in the last ten years have linked subjectivity with citizenship and legality. In Peru, like elsewhere, the claims and discourse of citizenship are shaped by both context and history and are imbued with gendered, racialized, classed, and geopolitical implications—as well as a long lineage of serving exclusionary and colonial purposes.[5] Over the last forty some years, MANTHOC has adapted its campaign language to reflect the times: from needs, to rights, to citizenship (MANTHOC 2016). Core to MANTHOC's strategic organizing has been a nimbleness in its terminology and a pragmatism in its shifting language and advocacy frames. MANTHOC's organizing makes visible how the very categories one uses to make claims for political subjecthood matter, and in

140   Child Workers and Child Citizens

what ways. The iterative approach the MANTHOC movement has taken towards claim making over the years reflects not only its political nature but also important insights about the state as fluid, changing, and expansive.[6] MANTHOC, through its collective and evolving demands for working children's rights, reveals how state power in Peru is not static nor a technical site, but rather a daily site of negotiation and struggle.

Listening to the demands of MANTHOC and following the strategic, careful decisions as to why, and for what purposes, it has transformed its language over more than four decades, reveal a hierarchal order in which the Peruvian state has treated political subjecthood. The changing discourse of MANTHOC reveals how legal categories have been handed to them by the state: from objects of the law, to subjects of the law, to citizen subjects of the law. These logics underpinning this positioning vis-à-vis the state are grounded in a longstanding colonial and imperial order, particularly in terms of the effects in Peru of Spanish conquest, and an enduring orientation towards law and legal subjecthood. MANTHOC, conscious of this history or not, has picked up on present-day discursive shifts from the state, and in its quest to be legible to the state has made its own discursive shifts in advocacy campaigns (from needs, to rights, to citizenship).

Given the ways MANTHOC members wish to change policy through mass mobilization, looking at what they understand to be the language of state "legibility" (Scott 1999) reveals as much about them as a collective movement as it does about the state itself. MANTHOC's iterative and malleable approach over the years makes visible how it has come to understand certain concepts (such as equality or citizenship) as required frames for state recognition. As one of the oldest child workers' movements in Peru, tracing what discursive strategies and negotiations MANTHOC's members have wrestled with to achieve state and policy recognition provides critical insight into what constitutes state legibility in Peru. It also reveals that their adaptive, creative approaches and sites of internal contestation within the movement provide them with direct knowledge, and ways of knowing, state power.

MANTHOC's definition of work and its elevation of the concept of citizenship highlights how the movement envisions the state, but also, importantly, how the state envisions political subjecthood. At the same time as MANTHOC's discourse unsettles certain binaries about recognition such as child/adult subjectivity and formal/informal work, the movement's leaders are reading and interpreting the state in order to make such recognition claims. In this way, MANTHOC's reading of the state and state logics—what is deemed important for eligibility to be able to make collective claims—exposes how the state depends on a spatial scheme and colonial logic: an ordering and hierarchy of knowledge, a privileging of the market, a prizing of the citizen-individual.

This can be seen in several ways. In its evolving campaign and organizing choices to use a discourse of citizenship and equality, MANTHOC reflects not just the framing of local Peruvian politics and the growing inequality in Peru specifically, but also global austerity more broadly. This discursive shift from using rights language in the 1990s to rights-citizenship language in the 2000s is not just happenstance, but rather maps onto the larger political economy and reflects pragmatic choices, tensions, and negotiations that the organization has made over the years about how best to be legible to state actors and others. Looking at MANTHOC in this way helps brings into view how the movement sees the myriad of negotiations, compromise, and nuance in understanding recognition claims as part of a very broad reading of the state. At the same time, while MANTHOC's discourse and framing of state legibility over the years has been fluid and evolving, the state's hierarchal order—and its use of a spatial scheme to enforce that order and to keep the state as a largely depoliticized site—has remained intact.

Defining Work

One of the core areas in which MANTHOC members seek recognition from the state is through their identities as workers. The MANTHOC mission statement from 2009 reads: "to contribute to the promotion of protagonist organizing of children and adolescent workers (Niños, Niñas y Adolescentes Trabajadores, NNATs) and the development of capacities, as a way to better our conditions of work, health, education and quality of life."[7] The movement's need to defend work as "morally and legally legitimate" (Taft 2019) was not as relevant for the first fifteen years of its collective organizing, but became more so during the 1990s in the face of growing pressure by the United States and other nations for Peru to ratify ILO Convention 138 on the minimum age.[8]

MANTHOC members seek to reclaim the very categorization of child labor and move away from it being automatically categorized as inherently (a) monetary and (b) harmful. They oppose dominant understandings of child work as something inevitably dangerous to children without an examination of the larger context and content of that work. MANTHOC focuses on child work as a human right, arguing that children can be recognized as both workers and children. MANTHOC, as a movement, believes that mainstream discussions of child labor do not adequately distinguish exploitive work (such as child prostitution or child slavery) from other types of, and possibilities for, "dignified" work and that the lack of discernment is extremely problematic.[9] For the members of MANTHOC, child work should include not just activities that are part of the formal labor market (i.e., activities for which children earn money), but also activities that make up parts of everyday life (including cooking, cleaning, and childcare) (see Liebel 2012; Liebel 2020; Taft 2019).

In 2009, MANTHOC, along with other children and youth workers' groups, co-wrote and sent out a national press release detailing the following four main demands:

- That work be recognized and valued as a human right, as noted by the Universal Declaration of Human Rights in article 23. Work is an indispensable condition for all humans without exception.

- That the Peruvian government increase the education budget from 2.8% to 6% of the GDP, as has been done in many countries in the region. Improving the quality of education is vital for human development and the exercise of citizenship.

- That the Peruvian government devise a budget for the programs and plans that have been created for the development of children and adolescent rights, as recommended by the UN Committee on the Rights of the Child.

- That the participation and organizing work by children, adolescents, and young people be critical in the building of a truly democratic society.[10]

MANTHOC's objectives and principles, as shown in these demands, consider work to be a human right, not as something automatically problematic (as is often the case with international discourses of child labor). Indeed, the assertion that "work is an indispensable condition for all humans without exception" is not always adopted or discussed, even within the human rights framework. While there is a notable body of scholarship about *protecting* children from child labor as part of the international human rights literature, the ways that organized children are defined within the labor movement literature are less clear and often left out of the scope of debate completely.

In their definitions of work, representatives of MANTHOC are careful to distinguish "dignified" work from harmful work. They are clear that their conception of child work doesn't include work the ILO names as the "worst forms of child labor" (article 3 of ILO Convention 182) that jeopardizes children's physical and/or mental well-being. For example, much of the work done by the young people in Lomas—recycling glass bottles in the nearby landfill—would not meet MANTHOC's definition of dignified work because of the physical and environmentally harmful conditions. In their memo for National Workers' Day in 2009, MANTHOC defined dignity in the workplace in the following way:

- Dignity to say "stop" to all injustices committed against us.

- Dignity to say that we want to work in decent conditions and to be recognized as youth, teens, children, and employees.

- Dignity to assess the organizations [for which we work] and require our protagonist participation in all that concerns us.

- Dignity to denounce the exploitation that many of us suffer.

- Dignity to say: our opinion counts.

MANTHOC's definition of, and specificity about, dignified work (as opposed to harmful work) is a fundamental distinction in that it serves as a bedrock to what its members see as enabling them to create a collective movement. By grounding the movement in calls for dignified work and dignified conditions, new possibilities emerge for shared identities and shared purpose that wouldn't be possible if the specific type of work MANTHOC's members are speaking about were based on current (exploitative) models. Two allies of the movement note, "without disregarding the condemnation of the violent, unjust and inhuman aspects of children's work, we set our hopes on the recognition and appreciation of working children's capacity for organizing themselves, putting forward proposals and taking up antagonistic positions" (Schibotto and Cussiánovich 1994: 92). In transforming their social group into a "collective subject" that is fundamentally tied to work and labor, MANTHOC's young people embrace a position distinct from many other international uses of children's rights in that the subjecthood that is imagined is not the individual, liberal rights holder, but rather an imagined collective of workers. Further, their subjecthood is grounded in, and draws on, their interdependence: as children, as workers, as members of a collective.

The members of MANTHOC focus on the capabilities of children's work and their right to be recognized by the state for their status as workers. And, they argue, it is through their work that they gain knowledge and skills—and the capacity to organize as a collective. Julio, a 12-year-old representative of the Lima chapter of MANTHOC, in an interview with me in 2008, reflected on how dominantly the state frames child work in terms of a simple binary of legality versus illegality, and in doing so skirts over some core ideas put forward by MANTHOC, both about the need for dignified work and for the possibilities for a collective, interdependent subject. Julio, who was working at the time as a street vendor selling candy, noted:

> We see that the state and the government can take work away from us, but they can't make us [our identities as workers] illegal because that would be like infringing on our integrity, against something that has come from our culture.[11]

In this way, Julio argues that the state's very definition of work needs to be reimagined. "We see work as a right, because we have rights like health and education. Because it is something that comes . . . from the culture. Your parents teach you to help in the house or to go and sell something." Hector, another representative of MANTHOC, age 11, also argued that the state's conception of work is limited because the state doesn't include its potentially generative and "formative" nature:

At present they are changing some norms, laws of the [children's and adolescent's] code because for us the main concern is work and that [the government] really understand that it is a right. Because we see work as something educational and something formative. Because of this, the norms have to be respectful, but the work should be in dignified conditions.[12]

Hector's statement that MANTHOC views work as something "educational and formative" aligns with the movement's current objective to promote organizing by child workers as vital to the development of children's capacities. The specific kind of work they are advocating for, therefore, is a means to improve daily conditions and is not automatically harmful or at odds with education. Rather, work serves as a generative and life-giving force, both to their individual capacities and to their shared sense of collective. This understanding of work by MANTHOC transcends questions solely of the economy and instead overtly links family, culture, and work.

In May 2009, MNNATSOP hosted a forum on the subject of working children and the global financial crisis.[13] The members of MNNATSOP expanded on the *kinds* of work they want to be recognized as a right, and more specifically:

[W]ork has enabled us with more than an economic income. We have developed capabilities and skills, such as responsibility, solidarity, autonomy, protagonist participation, etc., which would be difficult to be able to develop outside of work. *Our work has enabled us to become humans.* (emphasis added)

"Work" in this statement is grounded in a sense of dignity and imagined possibility, a belief that labor could promote capabilities and skills, rather than be an inherently negative obligation. This contrasts with dominant portrayals of child labor as unavoidably dangerous, problematic, and harmful to children's education and development. Instead, MANTHOC and MNNATSOP argue for children and adolescents to be seen as workers, social actors, and "protagonists," who are able to demand rights (from the state) for dignified work. They seek a world where the public imagination understands

146   Child Workers and Child Citizens

work as a basic feature that allows them to "become human." Becoming human, for members of MANTHOC, is based on claims for specific kinds of work, a feature of which enables children to gain skills and capacities. But to be able to make such claims, MANTHOC members recognize that they must have their collective subjecthood recognized by the state. That is, they are making a call not just for the expansion of workers' rights, but rather for both the transformation of work (that it be dignified) and rights (that their labor rights be seen as linked to their collective cultural rights).

MANTHOC's claims for child participation are both sociocultural and economic in terms of recognition of a new kind of subjectivity of children as workers. The young people's argument about the labor market (both formal and informal) makes visible the dependence on, and agency of, how they constitute the market. But in the case of MANTHOC, to only look at the claims of recognition as workers without also looking at the political order within which the workers want to be recognized would be incomplete. For MANTHOC's members, they identify a political state order that (mis)recognizes cultural and historical logics and focuses largely on the individual. Further, it is a spatial scheme that, as they note, seems to value economics and the market over dignity.

Claiming Rights, Contesting Subjecthood

During the ten-year period that I followed MANTHOC as a movement, although it grew and changed, it remained united as a collective. Unlike many children, members of MANTHOC rely on a collective idiom and set of ideas, particularly around the language of rights and child protagonism. While the movement's advocacy claims (directed to the state) have changed over its history (largely as categorized from needs, to rights, to citizenship), a central component of its organizing is grounded in education and the transference of core ideas to others across the movement. The young people teach one another, and have been taught by older allies in MANTHOC, sharing between them specific language to strategically express their claims and wishes as citizens, protagonists, and child workers. Their collective demands and their claim making is located firmly within the boundaries of certain imaginaries—namely, deeply rooted histories of inequality in Peru.

As described in the last chapter, the history of the MANTHOC movement emerged during a national moment of internal armed conflict. As a movement, the strategic choices its members made about the most effective approach for their claims were influenced by a range of progressive theorists, and they found that the language of rights and citizenship resonated. Rights language allowed the young people of MANTHOC a way to interface with state actors in the context of ongoing state injustice, and it has allowed recognition of their protagonism under current policies of neoliberalism.[14]

The young members of MANTHOC have grappled with what discourse most resonates at the national level to make their claims heard. The ways working children are often excluded as meaningful subjects of law and citizens in Peru and beyond has made their struggle for recognition arguably even more complex. Given the multiple and intersecting aspects of many of the MANTHOC children's identities, and that they are not seeking to be identified by the state solely as children, the language of rights and more recently the language of citizenship are a recognizable framing for the Peruvian state. The discourse of child citizenship makes them legible to the state in ways that other young people, like those of Lomas, don't have. To listen to the young people of MANTHOC, therefore, renders visible the very idioms demanded by the state for children, as well as all the contradictions, compromises, and negotiations at stake.[15]

MANTHOC members show the complexities of children using rights-based language in the age of individualism and neoliberalism in Peru, and how the movement's rights-based language can challenge some forms of state power and power relations while simultaneously reinscribing others. The MANTHOC movement uses a discourse of rights (children's rights, worker's rights) as a mechanism to critique and reconceptualize claims about rights, law, and the state. At the same time, given the historical and ongoing backdrop of state violence and dispossession within Peru, the desire by MANTHOC members to expand the very categories of recognition, through a language inherited by the state, entails complexity.

Carlos's experience with MANTHOC exemplifies how the movement has struggled to discern the language of the state to gain legibility. Carlos was a little boy when the political violence in Peru began. He lived in a tiny pueblo near Chiclayo, the northern jungle in Peru, and was involved with MANTHOC since early childhood. As a man in his early 30s (and one of the key adult national collaborators for the organization), Carlos reflected

148   Child Workers and Child Citizens

back about his involvement with MANTHOC as a child. He noted that he couldn't recall not being a member of MANTHOC. His mother and sister were among the organization's first leaders in Chiclayo. Carlos remembered the splitting of left-leaning social movements in the early 1980s as people in rural areas were recruited, and committed, to Sendero Luminoso. In this context of fear and distrust, social movements were splintered. The kinds of joint organizing/joint movement work became harder to undertake during this period of heightened distrust and a state of emergency, with a national curfew. Left-leaning movements began to strongly distance themselves from each other, disagreeing about the best path towards liberation. He recounted:

> Some of the movements were turning to violence, they criticized the [other] movements because they said you want peace and power, but you aren't willing to fight for it. That was the criticism that they had of us [MANTHOC members]. It wasn't only the government who was the object of the violence from armed movements, it was also anyone who disagreed with them or who didn't commune with them.[16]

Carlos described how difficult it was at the time for community members and members of MANTHOC to regularly gather for meetings, not only because state regulations enforced a curfew and kept them off the streets, but also because of their own fear.

Carlos also remembered how, when they could, MANTHOC young adults and children would gather at a local church, slowly gaining the language to talk about their work as children and their belief in social justice. As the organization began to grow, however, so did the political violence in the region. Political gatherings, organizing, and collectivist movements were viewed by state actors as threatening and dangerous, because of how collective mobilization could be seen as linked to group violence and the Sendero Luminoso ideology. Carlos described the climate of fear and danger for anyone associated with social movements:

> We couldn't have any literature in our home or any place that was at all progressive or left or that appeared to be like that. At that time,

Rights, Recognition, and the Language of Equality   149

my mom told me that all of the books that stated something like that—we had to bury or burn.[17]

Similar to the multiple scales of violence discussed in Chapter 1 with the Lomas young people, Carlos's story illustrates what it means to understand and conceptualize violence not just as immediate and individual, but also structural and collective. In his description of that time, Carlos reflected on the violence in ways that were analogous to the way Lomas parents did—that it was perpetrated not only from members of Sendero Luminoso but rather from multiple sources. He recalled the sense of overwhelming anxiety and fear in that time that many of the Lomas families spoke of. For MANTHOC members, the context of fear was partly a result of the anti-terrorism laws and governance enacted by Fujimori. The fears of being associated as a terrorist group impacted the organizing of MANTHOC, as well as many other left-leaning social justice and activist groups. The constant backdrop of fear—especially for a social justice movement like MANTHOC—affected the members directly. Carlos recounted being a teenager and watching the movement grapple with the tensions of the multiple scales of state and civilian violence:

> When Fujimori was in charge, that was the other extreme—he confronted violence with more violence and I think in that time it affected MANTHOC because MANTHOC was always against violence. . . . We felt that it also was part of our duty, our political duty, the manifestation of our citizenship, to show that we were not in agreement, and that we had to demonstrate what we feel about that [context of violence].[18]

The cultivation of a particular stance of not only being "against violence" but also grounded in what went on to be their pedagogy of tenderness became a fundamental element of the mission and workings of MANTHOC. And it was articulated very precisely in the face of multiple scales of violence by the Peruvian state.

As discussed in Chapter 1, the parents of the children in Lomas who were affected firsthand by the political violence of the 1980s often talk about

150   Child Workers and Child Citizens

the immense social isolation of that time. For many of the families and young people of MANTHOC, the violence and social isolation in the 1980s and 1990s also affected them and, at the same time, offered a backdrop to strengthen and articulate a collective and theoretical stance of a pedagogy of tenderness. That is, at the time when members were forming the core values of the MANTHOC movement, they were simultaneously doing it in the face of daily fear about what it meant to be activists. As such, the fact that respect and community are fundamental to the mission of MANTHOC is not a fluke, but rather are grounded in the historical and political context of multiple scales of violence in Peru.

Both of these responses—by the parents of the young people of Lomas and the founding child members of MANTHOC—have shared memories and experiences of the history of violence in relation to the state and law in Peru. The examples of slow violence discussed by the young people of Lomas in terms of the environment, and the examples of violence (or anti-violence) that were expressed by MANTHOC position the concept of rights and legality in ways that extend beyond one singular domain (i.e., the nation-state). Violence shapes the very ways the young people see themselves and understand inequality.

MANTHOC members offer an important contribution to both the concepts of violence and the workings of state power in Peru. For them, their collective choices to change with the times and to use discursive framings recognizable to the state cannot be divorced from how their movement began: in the face of state violence. As a movement that has always imagined itself in conversation with the state—a state not separate from, or able to be separate from, the workings of everyday life—MANTHOC's articulation of its movement in relation to rights, and more recently in relation to citizenship, is firmly tied up with current violence. MANTHOC members read the Peruvian state as needing to widen its recognition categories—who constitute deserving subjects of law (i.e., as children, as workers, as political actors). In making that interpretation, and even in making those claims, they expose a particular working of state power in Peru: a power that relies on a framework of neutrality and equality, while sustaining disparity and organized abandonment.[19]

Child Citizen and the State

MANTHOC members shifted towards the language of citizenship and rights in the early 2000s, at the same time as the Peruvian state was doing the same in its public policies. For example, MANTHOC's members decided to use the term "productive citizens" when they made their claims for dignified work conditions—as Daniela, the 13-year-old spokesperson did in the quoted text at the beginning of this chapter—partly because that is the current dominant discourse from the state. And as the language of the state, it is also a currency embedded with gendered, racialized, classed, and geopolitical histories and grounded in the historical and geographical context of place.[20] Like many places with legacies of colonialism, Peruvian citizenship claims have been historically structured by inequality and have emerged largely alongside practices of discrimination and exclusion. As Peruvian scholar Pascha Bueno-Hansen writes, historically,

> Peruvians' distance from or proximity to the modern ideal determines their access to citizenship . . . those who more closely resemble the lighter-skinned, heteronormative, Spanish-speaking, able-bodied, and literate male have more access to citizenship. (2015: 8)

The colonial and gendered history of the construction of citizenship in Peru has long been "conditioned upon certain assets, such as being male, having formal education, registered property and proven commitment to the sovereign political body to which the citizen belonged" (Stepputat 2005: 63).[21] Indeed, the language of rights and citizenship in Peru is necessarily shaped by, and imbued with, current and past experiences of state violence.

Given this context, MANTHOC's pairing of the two concepts of "child worker" and "citizen" disrupts certain recognition claims (as discussed in Chapter 4), both in terms of their agency as children and their identities as workers, which pushes for a reconceptualization of adult/child power relations and opens up new possibilities for understandings of children's collective subjectivity. At the same time, because of the specific ways state development in Peru has been historically, and problematically, linked to citizenship, the currency of rights and citizenship often also sustains and maintains certain hierarchies. Like many of the political slogans and murals in Lomas, the language of rights in Peru depends on ideological assumptions about the state as the imagined grantor of rights.[22]

Through the ways MANTHOC members understand protagonism and employ a discourse of children's citizenship, they seek to expand young people's legal subjectivity and agency. In their discussions about recognition from the state in terms of citizenship and rights, the citizenship model they employ views participation largely in terms of the public or formal sphere.[23] Their object of desire and focus remains the (neutral) nation-state—and relies on an idea of separate public and private spheres.[24] Environmental scholar Elena Shever makes visible some of the stakes involved in the logic of public/private spheres when writing about oil and neoliberalism in Argentina. Shever notes the process of oil extraction, under neoliberalism, changes the very dynamic of what are considered private and public domains. "Oil extracted from public lands becomes private property and available for ownership by corporations and individuals, including both Argentine citizens and foreigners" (Shever 2012: 78). Shever argues, this process of "redomaining" from public to private or from private to public is happening across Latin America because of neoliberalism, and that state and corporate actors become enabled to make claims on properties previously deemed private. Further, she notes the myriad ways this has direct effects and implications for the types of citizenship claims that can be made, as well as the everyday implications for daily life. Private lives, under neoliberalism, are not easily discerned from public lives, because of the economic, national, and colonial interest at stake.

The ways MANTHOC has strategized and navigated discussions of citizenship and even equality, as a means to make their demands and claims towards the state, reflect some of these same neoliberal state logics. MANTHOC members elevate a discourse of equality and a pedagogy of tenderness and live these commitments through ensuring everyday practices of care, elevating respect and kindness, and continually shining a light on the political order of hierarchy (particularly in terms of age). Given the depth of traditional hierarchal relationships in Peru (for example, between adults and children, between boys and girls), in many ways these interpretations are grounded in a view of liberation. Yet, in her public speech, Daniela anchors this vision in the language of equality, and she notes how enactment

Rights, Recognition, and the Language of Equality 153

of children's citizenship is linked to productivity and to a formal economy. "We are workers just like you." For Daniela, and MANTHOC, eligibility for citizenship is understood as linked to the market.

To be legible to the state and for policy campaign purposes, MANTHOC calls forth a "neutral" citizen worker in its speeches, invoking an adult, male, racialized model of citizenship. When appealing to the Peruvian workers union, and also to the state, the categories of relevance MANTHOC depends on are those associated with an imagined ideal type of political subject, a public worker. MANTHOC members face a dilemma in that, in order for their claims about child work to be recognized, what is most legible to the state is an argument about sameness and equality. When the children speak of being workers "just like you," they are making an argument about the human subjectivity of rights and work. Difference, in this reading, is presented as the obverse of equal.[25] In doing so, they seem to be asking for an erasure of their age differences, and, instead, for a focus on their collective identity as workers to be the primary shared feature. In their desire to be recognized as workers and children, MANTHOC members rely on a framing with primarily two potential options: (1) for children to conform to the adult/citizenship/worker model that is largely grounded in hierarchal understandings of the state and market as (neutral) sites for negotiation, or (2) to risk an illegibility as subjects of the law and to have their work (as children) not be valued or recognized by the state. The current Peruvian dominant notion of "citizen" they imagine, in other words, is shaped in relation to how citizenship as a concept has historically, and presently, been formulated in Peru in largely singular, binary, colonial, and historically exclusionary ways.[26]

The Declaration of the Fifth Meeting of Working Children of Latin America and the Caribbean to the International Community, written in August 1997 by the children and adolescent workers (Niños y Adolescentes Trabajadores, NATs, including MANTHOC), articulated the ways the UN's Convention on the Rights of the Child didn't go far enough. They wrote a manifesto about the ways specific children's articles, namely the rights to be heard (article 12), to organize (article 15), and to be protected (article 31) fail because they are not meaningfully practiced. They note:

> We are listened to, but our views are not heeded. We are given the right to organize ourselves, but our organizations of working chil-

dren and adolescents are not recognized. We are protected, but we are not allowed to participate in the development of such protection programmes. (Liebel 2001:172)

The young people contrasted what they see as hypocrisy of the instrumentalization of working young people versus how they themselves are able to experience and see the (productive) role of work to find solidarity and shared identity. They proclaim:

> In order for our views to be taken seriously, our organizations must be fully legally recognized both on a national and an international level. Our democratically elected representatives must have a say and be able to vote in all local, national, and international bodies in which decisions are taken concerning policies affecting children and their work, in educational policy, labour policy, and in plans for social security and community development. The presence of the NATs within these bodies, in common with delegates from other social organizations, would be the best guarantee in the struggle against exploitation, poverty and exclusion, and a great step towards the realization of human rights. (Liebel 2001:172)

In this declaration, the children and adolescent workers argue that, for their rights to be fully enacted, they want their work and views to be "taken seriously" by public (state) actors at the national and international levels. They wish for equality and respect and feel that it would be granted if they had a say and "vote" in spaces where decisions are made. One of the implications of this statement is the children's observation that serious decision makers are in the formal, public realm, and that for children's rights to be realized, children need to be recognized or seen as equal to adults. Human rights, in this statement, means a valuing of "neutral" equality and is based on a gendered, classed, and racialized interpretation of citizenship and participation (see Perry 2018).

Such a view is partly related to the current neoliberal moment that demands strategic choices for recognition.[27] But it also traces back to when the MANTHOC movement was born and what it meant to have the movement develop in the context of the internal armed conflict of the country.

The social justice mission of MANTHOC, and its belief that empowerment comes from organizing, illustrates that "politics" is seen as something to be played out in the public sphere. As Carlos noted earlier in the chapter, MANTHOC members saw public marches and visible social organizing as part of their "political duty" and the "manifestation of their citizenship." This splitting of public versus private depends on a particular interpretation of politics, grounded in colonial logics and hierarchy, which serves "Euro-centered capitalism" (Bueno-Hansen 2015: 144) and is tied to the neoliberal context of Peru and the use of rights language.

Part of the complexity of MANTHOC's strategy of using public discourses and campaigns that reflect state notions of politics and citizenship, as related to its discourse of equality, is that it also actively seeks to disrupt gender blindness in everyday, lived experiences. Isabel, one of the very early founding members of MANTHOC and now an adult national coordinator for the program, was 7 years old when she joined the organization in 1981. She noted the changes that MANTHOC has consciously made over the years regarding gender and equality, particularly in rural areas. Isabel remembered when MANTHOC, as an organization and movement, had the self-realization that all elected national representatives were boys—and that all adult collaborators (allies) to the organization doing the day-to-day support work were women. She reflected: "We decided to create the criterion that there always has to be equality of gender. . . . Since 1994 we have now said there can't be only male representatives."[28]

Isabel went on to talk about how this internal policy of gender equality in their representation has, at times, proven difficult in the context of sexism and patriarchy, particularly in rural areas. The task, according to Isabel, was not just to convince girls they "have the equal possibility to overcome and be able to participate" but also to have girls feel as entitled to the process as boys do and "to understand that they [girls] are important." Isabel reflected on daily examples of what such a commitment looks like in practice, and what specific techniques MANTHOC has used over the years to promote gender equity within the movement:

> For example, now we have groups in Ayacucho in a small town. In that place, the girls are 15 and 16 years old when they get their part-ners and at 17 they have children. So that is to say that they have a

156   Child Workers and Child Citizens

> different worldview, and they are mothers at younger ages and then keep having children until they are about 40. . . . So for that reason we say that it's more cultural. The girls are more passive, and the boys aren't. You see girls hiding, they don't want to speak, they won't speak, but who is willing to speak? Boys, boys, boys. So we say, that's not how it is. We have more work to do. . . . Now MANTHOC has funding to work on the equality of gender. We have funding to do more activities focusing on this, but even until today machismo continues. It continues.[29]

Teaching the members of the organization explicitly about these gendered power dynamics—and naming the process as difficult to fight because of patriarchy—reflects the lived political commitments of MANTHOC as a movement. While the language of equality or quotas for sameness may not automatically lend itself to structural change, the daily practice by the leaders of MANTHOC is not "gender blind."

At the same time, in its public campaigns, MANTHOC reflects how dominant discourses of "equality" are often used as a shorthand for the portrayal of neutrality, or, as Wendy Brown called it, "depoliticization" (2006). MANTHOC uses dominant notions of citizenship they see modeled in public policy and strategically use them as a means to be relevant to the dominant discourse about rights and labor in Peru. In Daniela's opening speech for the May Day rally, she spoke of MANTHOC members wanting to be recognized as "useful" and about being recognized in terms of equality. Daniela suggests that through the act of being recognized (by the state, by adults, in this case by the workers' union), their citizenship would become productive. What MANTHOC members have heard, and then employ to forward and creatively adapt for their own advocacy campaigns, are the dominant ways in which the state and state policies understand and view (adult) labor. Through the categories of "useful" or "productive," MANTHOC uses economic terms demanded from the state, for recognition in the public sphere. In doing so, Daniela's speech privileges the public sphere as the site in which citizenship is developed and as the site in which young people (should) understand themselves.[30]

Daniela's speech, and the discursive implicated features of child citizenship, raise several challenging questions about the nature of "children's" voices. As explained in the prior chapter, questions about representation are ones that MANTHOC takes seriously and that members actively theorize. Further, their literature and public discourses present a clear agenda about their redistribution claims (their goals for their citizenship to be recognized in the public sphere and for the possibilities for dignified work). Similarly, in everyday practices, MANTHOC members are taught, and teach each other, respect, tenderness, and gender equality—all of which they treat as political acts.

Beyond these particular questions that MANTHOC raises about children, subjecthood, and citizenship, however, is also a reflection about a (violent) state logic and order that uses a language of equality. MANTHOC young people have pragmatically used state categories for policy advocacy campaigns, and in doing so reveal logics of state power. Through their interpretations of framing education as compatible with work, for example, they rely on an argument about the importance, and value, of the (neoliberal) individual subject. Because the movement is over forty years old, its discursive strategies have shifted over the years, revealing the tensions, ambiguities, and complexities of seeking (state) legibility.[31] In this way, MANTHOC as a movement underlines the importance of not treating the state as just a technical, static site (to "add" children as subjects in and stir), but rather one grounded in historical, political, and as MANTHOC reminds us, economic logic. Rather than seeing the state as outside or divorced from the claims MANTHOC makes, and is able to make, this chapter has suggested that the movement has continually had to negotiate, adapt, and wrestle with how to make its arguments legible to the current moment.

Equality Protectors

On May 1, 2018, I showed up at the park early, as I have in years past, to take part in International Workers' Day with MANTHOC. We are gathered in the same park as in previous years, but there is less of a crowd of young people prepared to collectively march. The accompanying adults of the movement are the same as previously—and, like years past, they are cheerful but intently focused, as they run around the young people handing

158   Child Workers and Child Citizens

out pamphlets and chants. There are also youth leaders who look to be 15 and 16 years old, and they are organizing and making calls to see if more young people are coming.

I ask if someone will be speaking at the national stage this year. Daniela, who has spoken in years past, has been elected by the group to do so. But, in contrast to before, the group tells me it's unlikely she will be given the stage because the adult union organizers who have planned the speaking part of the day's activities don't agree with MANTHOC's position on child work. The adult union members have invited MANTHOC members to come and be part of the march but not to publicly speak on stage.

To be visible in the crowd, this year MANTHOC members are wearing blue vests that read "equality protectors" (*protectores de igualdad*) on the front and have cartoons of children displayed on the back. Others have worn matching t-shirts that say "it's time to talk about it #childlabor." One of the MANTHOC members holds a large handmade sign that reads "We are part of this reality."

The sign sticks with me, and I wonder to myself whose reality they are referring to. The "we" in this statement seems open for interpretation: It could be child workers, it could be MANTHOC members as a collective movement, it could be MANTHOC members as children. Their continued desire for recognition—in this case, not just from the state but now also from other adult union members—is what grants them eligibility to be seen or at least heard on a national stage for International Workers' Day. But maybe, as they note, recognition as a collective of child workers is also what grants them permission to feel like their work is recognized in "this reality"? The contents of their collective demand for dignified work and for children to be able to participate in public life go far beyond a call for the protection of "equality." But, as I have learned from MANTHOC members, the language of equality is what is most legible and what resonates in national terms, for them to make their claims.

My child is now 2 and much heavier on my back than he was in previous years. We march out of the park and into the streets with the young people, the drummers in front. The energy is electric, even if a smaller group this year, and even with the disappointing news that MANTHOC members won't be welcomed on the speaking stage.

MANTHOC has just released its own articulation of the movement's history, its values and mission. It's over 200 pages, laid out with original photographs of early meetings and black-and-white images of children throughout different phases of its history. It's a remarkable accounting and documentation of the history of the movement.

A few days before, I had taken part in a formal presentation by a local NGO of the evolution of child labor laws in Peru. Because of the trade agreements with the United States, the Peruvian child labor laws are much stricter and more explicit than when I began my research ten years earlier. When I asked a colleague at the event about groups like MANTHOC and those fighting for dignified working conditions, the colleague told me that MANTHOC was "less relevant" now because of how much clearer the official governmental stance against child labor had become.

I stay as long as I can at the march until my child becomes too fussy. As we are leaving, I see Daniela at a distance across the crowd. Knowing she is prepared and ready to speak if given the platform, I imagine what she will say. She will continue to fight for all working young people to feel their subjectivity collectively recognized, even if not given the stage.

I see a mural on the outside of one of the MANTHOC base locations in Lima. It reads "MANTHOC. Peace is the way." The image is of two faces speaking to each other with a heart in the middle of their dialogue. It is in contrast to the murals in Lomas, shown in Chapter 3, where the major discourse surrounding the young people was one of empty political pleas, painted by adults employing rights language. Instead, this mural, painted for and by the young people of MANTHOC, is one of dialogue and exchange, with sunshine and peace as the centerpiece. This mural adheres to MANTHOC's main principles including a pedagogy of tenderness in which discourses and practices of love, relationship, dialogue, and Christian values are front and center.

But this mural also captures the complexity with which MANTHOC has had to contend in using equality and individual rights language in the age of neoliberalism. Without an explicitly critical (gendered, racialized, or decolonial) frame of analysis, there is a danger of unwittingly construing, or perhaps as reading, the state as a neutral site. In the MANTHOC mural, the figures are without obvious gender coding and appear to be white.

Figure 23: Mural in Lima drawn by members of MANTHOC. Photo taken by author, 2014.

One figure, in front of mountains, is wearing a cap that is typical in rural areas, making more of an imagined gesture towards the hint of Andean ethnicity, certainly more than in the murals in Lomas. That it is not easy to discern the genders of these figures highlights the imagined "neutral" citizenship model that MANTHOC has problematized, a model that seeks formal and public recognition and that privileges a discourse of rights and equality. While the language of peace and tenderness is often associated with being apolitical, MANTHOC members show it is not a language devoid of politics.[32]

The ways MANTHOC members associate participation primarily in terms of the public sphere, and recognition primarily in terms of the state and citizenship, reflect how they understand the workings of the Peruvian (neoliberal) state. The various framings that MANTHOC members have strategically used over the years in order to be legible to the state arguably relate to what they see, or do not see, as the purview for their political action. But these discourses also, critically, serve to act as windows into part of how state power, and state depoliticization, works in Peru. In their use of state terminology for advocacy, MANTHOC members both challenge and confirm categories of law and state power and have done so in response to the backdrop of wide-scale structural violence and inequality. Like the children of Lomas, the children of MANTHOC are affected daily by the material experience of vast inequity and poverty. Further, they are affected by the legacy of the internal armed conflict in Peru and the ways this history of violence has mapped onto and shaped their political movement. For MANTHOC, this past and present violence means a conscious turn towards tenderness, religion, and reflexivity. It also means a turn towards the language of rights and citizenship.

At the same time, in their pragmatic and evolving discursive choices to be legible subjects to the state, they speak of citizenship and individual rights, and use a language of equality. These are the familiar categories that have been handed to them from the state, as well as the market. Therefore, the structural changes the movement seeks are in terms of public recognition from formal (state) institutions. This alignment and orientation towards "productive citizenship" that Daniela speaks of in the opening of this chapter is imagined primarily in relation to the public sphere, which reflects and underscores the current political and global landscape and the legal conventions that are both privileged, and also ignored, by the state.[33]

But the complexities lie in its history. The founding members of MANTHOC took the legacy of violence and armed conflict in Peru and laid "uncrisis" thinking into their foundational mission. They placed an orientation towards a pedagogy of tenderness, community building, tools for dialogue, and collective organizing as centerpieces for what they do and what they wish to do. They continue to negotiate, struggle, and adopt their messaging in the face of inequalities and idioms of state logic. Their interpretations and usage of law, citizenship, and statehood therefore both maintain and also open up new possibilities for these categories. These are the young people who have used the discursive currency of the state. Listening to them reveals the multiple forms of violence they see and contend with— against the collective, against the worker, against those made most marginal. And in revealing the kind of state they see and understand, one is able to get a clearer picture of the political and spatial order on which the state depends.

PART III

6

Looking for the State

The Politics of Children's Participation in Peru

IN AN ADDRESS TO THE Peruvian Congress on July 28, 1991, Alberto Fujimori noted: "Peru is the first country in the world to devise and approve a National Plan of Action for Children." The plan, he continued, reflected a belief that "every investment oriented to the protection and safeguarding of children is, in reality, the most prized investment that a nation can make in the long-term." Despite his words focused on "helping" children, Fujimori's stated commitment to countrywide reconstruction in the National Plan of Action for Children (Plan Nacional de Acción por la Infancia or PNAI) masked the notable distance between the discursive goals at the time of this speech and political realities in Peru. Between 1996 and 2000, for example, Fujimori's government used coercive tactics to sterilize at least 270,000 women, targeting poor Indigenous women, misinforming victims or offering them food aid if they submitted to sterilization.[1] Fujimori's public call to invest in children as a form of "national reconstruction and peace" contrasted with the state's role in the deadly armed conflict as well. The Peruvian state paid lip service to human rights

165

166   Looking for the State

and children's rights, while implementing policies and practices to undermine and violate such rights.

As the previous chapters have made clear, young people living and working in places like Lomas, and those leading and organizing in political movements like the members of MANTHOC, provide a number of important insights about state power and state violence in Peru. Namely, they help bring into view the impact of Peru's legacies of intersecting violence, armed conflict, economic inequality, racial and gender hierarchy, and the specific vulnerability that grows out of land dispossession and environmental degradation. Their insights emerge in ways that are tied to the particular national context of state policies and state discourse in Peru (like Fujimori's PNAI) that rely on the language of children's rights, equality, and participation. Moreover, they also show how Peruvian state actors have historically used and interpreted those concepts to advance what the young people of Lomas and MANTHOC reveal to be a spatial scheme that depends on a political order of hierarchy, rationality, and a depoliticized state.[2]

Since Alberto Fujimori's presidency, the legislation and public discourse in Peru about children and childhood have made the status of children more visible on the country's political agenda. In many ways, the state's investment in Peruvian children in public policy has served as a symbolic placeholder for nationalism, modernity, and a call for an investment in the future. At the same time, as a relational listening approach to the young people of Lomas and MANTHOC reveal, the historical phenomenon of enlarged public policy discourses about investment into children in Peru has been matched by the rise of material and environmental conditions of inequality, as well as economic interests, that have undermined the stated goals of those discourses.

Largely in the name of participation and equity, the state in Peru has long relied on the category of childhood and child as symbols of nationhood and nation building. It has promoted policies that speak to the participation of children and child's voices, while at the same time, creating and deepening conditions of precarity and austerity. This chapter, expanding on the prior chapters' discussions of young people's framing of the state and the state's role in their marginalization, looks at how Peru's (state) discourse about children's rights in public policy has cast itself as a neutral site for engagement and action, specifically through a lens of child protection, and

The Politics of Children's Participation in Peru   167

in doing so has promoted a depoliticized order, what I term in the introduction an imagined "spatial scheme" between children and the state.

This depoliticized order can be seen in numerous ways in the lives and voices of the young people in Lomas and the members of MANTHOC. It is also evident in the state's efforts to advance children's rights. For example, in 2011, Lima became one of the first cities in Latin America to implement an Advisory Board of Girls, Boys, and Adolescents (Consejo Consultivo de Niñas, Niños, y Adolescentes de Lima Metropolitana, CCONNA) to actively promote an "agenda for the rights of children."[3] This is a formal group with representation from local youth organizations, including at different times representation from MANTHOC, MNNATSOP, and other prominent children's rights groups. The council includes representatives from NGOs and civil society organizations as well as several adults from Lima's municipal government. The group's mission statement proclaims it promotes "responsibility, empathy, social sensitivity, and protagonism." While the Lima's children's advisory board is the most robust in the country, the mandate for its existence and its structure is written into municipal law (law 27972) at the federal level. The municipal pamphlet explains why such an advisory board is important:

> Because it is a political, public space where we can consult with organizations about projects and actions that we are taking for the municipality for and with children. [The advisory board] is where we monitor and promote compliance with the existence of our rights.

The board consists of children between the ages of 9–17, each representing a formally "organized group" of children and adolescents. The municipality considers organized groups to be people brought together through church, sports, or arts; or child workers or Afro-Peruvians; as well as groups for street children or disabled children. The board includes children at a range of socioeconomic levels. The advisory group uses a structure similar to MANTHOC in that it has general members and a coordination team of elected representatives.

Since 2011, Lima's children's advisory board model has evolved and strengthened. In one of Lima's richest districts, Miraflores, the mayor identified the advisory board in the local newspaper as a project to promote Lima

168   Looking for the State

as "the city of children" where participation and voices matter.[4] The group has consulted on a range of local and international children's rights initiatives, including public policy projects at UNICEF and the World Bank.

On paper, this board is an exemplary participatory practice for children, a complement to Peru's strong discourse about the inclusion of children in its public policy imagination. Yet, because of the ways politicians have historically used the imagery of children as symbols of nationalism and purity, this board also points to the ways the language of participation can be used to reify or obscure state power. Through the elevation of a language of equality and rights, the categories of childhood, and children, have been used in Peru to legitimatize state development projects.[5]

Much of this is done, as this chapter will show, through positioning the state as a neutral or depoliticized site for participation. As elucidated by the young people in this book, the particular interpretation of children's rights discourse and the language of equality employed by state actors in Peru is largely one that is grounded in a citizen-individual, and that relies on institutional, technocratic, and static interpretations of the scope and reach of the state. Further, it relies on a particular spatial scheme where young people are imagined as furthest away from politics.

This final chapter takes up this paradox. In a moment when human rights are under significant threat across the globe and certain children are made deeply vulnerable by growing austerity, environmental violence, and increasing inequality, there is an urgent need to find ways to grapple with the kinds of contradictions at play in the elevation of child participation discourse, as well as some of the stakes. In Peru, the symbolic use of children and childhood has long been used by politicians in the name of progress, participation, and rights. Evident through the framing of policy discourse around children's rights—in the practices of participatory budgeting, government children advisory boards, and even in Peru's National System for Children's Rights—this chapter discusses a variety of ways the state relies on children as symbolic actors, while forwarding policies and actions that further disparity and state violence.[6] Such tension, in and of itself, is not new or necessarily even unique to Peru.[7] However, as this chapter discusses, the insights afforded by the young people of Lomas and MANTHOC elucidate the complex ways state power plays out in terms of a privileging of

The Politics of Children's Participation in Peru   169

rationality, the citizen-individual, and the seemingly non-negotiable imagined neutral state.

Public Policy, Participatory Budgeting, and Dilemmas of State Recognition

What we want to do with this law is to make sure their voice is important and is heard, that *they are treated as citizens and not as little children* who are not asked or consulted about anything.[8]
—*President Ollanta Humala, Bagua,
September 6, 2011 (emphasis added)*

In 2011, Peru expanded its participation laws. Then-president Humala promulgated the International Labor Organization Convention 169 (ILO 169) and ratified the Law of the Right to Prior Consultation for Indigenous and Native Peoples (Ley del Derecho a la Consulta Previa a los Pueblos Indigenas u Origiarois *no.* 29785). While prior consultation had been written into the Democratic Constitutional Congress of 1993, under Fujimori, it wasn't until years later, and with much contestation, that Indigenous and native people would see this institutionalized. Peru was one of the first Latin American countries to ratify ILO 169, which is an international treaty acknowledging the rights of Indigenous and tribal people to *consulta previa*, meaning they would now be consulted about policies that affect their culture or heritage. He also provided assurances about the *presupuesto participativo* (participatory budgeting). A number of Peru's neighbors followed, and discussion of the language and laws around these issues is stronger and widespread in Latin America than in other places in the world.[9]

While the treaty provides clear guidelines and strategies describing *consulta previa*, the process for regulation and putting into practice ILO 169 in Peru has been slow. How much power should be granted to the communities during the *consulta previa* has been of the subject of intense debate, and when the regulations of the law passed in 2012, it was granted with the caveat that the state, not the local communities, gets the final say-so (article 23).[10] Peoples of Aymara and Quechua descent have been particularly vocal in calling attention to the tensions of the laws. Their distrust is warranted, particularly given Peru's history of state policies and actions that have not only failed Indigenous peoples but, in many cases, particularly around land and land rights, have caused systemic and direct violence by the continual expansion of extractive practices.[11] While state regulations grant those of Indigenous decent to be consulted, in Peru, like elsewhere in Latin America, the very question of who counts as Indigenous is, in and of itself, political and historically charged. Until recently, Peru's census hadn't included a question about ethnicity (since 1961), and the terminology itself and how it is linked to participation and state rights is historically complex and murky (Sanborn et al. 2016). As has been the case with children's rights, while Peru was a leader in rights discourse in comparison to its neighboring states, working out the details of what those commitments mean in everyday ways is contested.

President Humala's efforts in 2011 and the expansion of laws around "participatory citizenship" shed light on the question of what role children and young people should have, if any, in *consulta previa* and *presupuesto participativo*. As Humala announced when he first introduced the law, he doesn't want people to be treated simply as "little children" who don't have a voice. Young people from the National Movement of Organized Working Children and Adolescents of Peru (Movimiento Naccional de Niños y Adolescentes Trabajadores Organizados del Peru, MNNATOP) took forward this challenge forward: If citizens should be consulted before laws are made about them, should not the state also consult children in relation to policy, especially legislation that addresses children's rights?

The Institute of Formation for Educators of Youth, Adolescents, Boy and Girl Workers of Latin America and the Caribbean (Instituto de Formación para Educadores de Jóvenes, Adolescentes y Niños Trabajadores de América Latina y el Caribe, IFEJANT) addressed children's rights to participatory budgeting in a short manual compiled in 2011. Entitled "The Participation of the Organizations of Boys, Girls, and Adolescent Workers in Participatory Budgeting: A Space to Exercise Our Right to Be Coprotagonists," the document outlines the best process to implement participatory budgeting for child and adolescent workers. Although the opening pages use cartoon images of children and young people, it provides sophisticated information that presumes the reader has a base of knowledge and seriousness.

The prologue notes that the writers intend the manual as a tool to "open your imagination about how to exercise in a better way your personal and collective rights to participate in community life at the local and regional levels." It cites the CRC and Peru's children's rights code, saying that budgetary participation is a "responsibility" and the "concrete median of our citizenship." The manual states: "Participatory budgeting opens a new space for us to provide the opinion of girls and boys, not only in terms of the transparency of the money, but also for children to be considered valid partners in the community."

The IFEJANT manual asserts the need for young people to engage as citizens in democratic culture in order to be recognized as valid partners. Some of the ideas expressed in the document elevate core claims in terms of children's citizenship rights:

> Adults are accustomed to dismissing what children have to say, as if that is something natural and legal. Participatory budgeting is a good opportunity to change this culture that doesn't recognize the right to participate. . . . In the debate about the regional and local government budget, children should confront other opinions, and listen to other budget proposals. That is how we learn to be citizens, to exchange dialogue, to improve our ways to see things, and to learn. In order to be listened to and to be taken seriously, we have to prepare our proposals and understand them. But we also have to learn to co-decide and to discuss and take decisions that are the best for everyone. To not participate guarantees that others become the winners. To be happy we have to achieve what is the best for boys, girls and adolescents, and what is best for our community.

The tone and framing of the manual suggest that having a "voice" at the table secures representation. That is, for the writers of this manual, participatory budgeting for young people is not about tokenism, but rather about putting forward concrete budget proposals and "achieving" the overarching best interests for children. By focusing on individual voice, the rhetoric of participation renders the state—regionally, locally, and even federally—as neutral and technical sites rather than as imbued with power. The discourse of participation and equality focuses on representation rather than redistribution.

One of the major contributions of neoliberalism has been the use of language of participation and empowerment, but also offering depoliticized and largely technical solutions (Cookson 2018). In some ways, the IFEJANT manual about participatory budgeting seems to employ a key strategy of this by focusing on the technical: framing empowerment of young people in Lima in terms of active citizenship in participatory budgeting and treating the state as a benevolent partner. Yet, creating cohesion among children (i.e., the emergence of a collective "children's voice") is not an easy or straightforward process. As the manual notes, it requires learning to value differences as a means to make decisions that are best for everyone. The skills MANTHOC encourages and that underlie Cussiánovich's theoretical stance of the pedagogy of tenderness—self-reflection and the use of dialogue—are fundamental to what they imagine and describe as protagonism. The manual's insistence on pluralism, and that young people deserve to be treated with dignity and respect as a group who can make a difference, all has tremendous value and is no small feat if taken seriously in a hierarchal context like Peru. Research on participatory budgeting documents positive outcomes for participants themselves, who learn new meanings and practices of citizenship through the process.[12]

At the same time, one of the paradoxes that a notion like participation can promote is an illusion of the need to position equality above all else. The imagined child in this purview is inferred to be of a neutral identity: without a named gender, without a discernible ethnicity or race, without mention of class. Instead, participation is linked primarily to the rights accorded by due age (in this case as children). As MANTHOC members themselves show, the myth of single-identity categories does not exist and can often come with the risk of obscuring interlocking systems of oppression.[13] The viewpoint presented in the participation manual demonstrates great faith and confidence in the state to act in the children's best interest, even as it diminishes the role of the state to deepen or create pervasive inequalities.[14] By using the logics of the neutral state and failing to account for the intersectional identities of children, the manual (inadvertently) forwards a binary logic on which the state depends.

The Politics of Children's Participation in Peru   173

Using Bureaucracy to Minimize the Political Subjectivity of Children

As noted in the introduction, Peru's implementation of the 1993 National System for Children's Rights has long promoted an idea of "childhood" in public policy that is about a fundamental consensus among state actors, rather than dissonance. As one prominent children's advocacy NGO director reflected:

> The speeches of the politicians talk a lot about children because it generates consensus. There is not anyone who is going to disagree, theoretically that children are an extremely important sector in the society. But at the same time [children are] only used for speeches. When it comes to putting this into practice it is not always like that.[15]

Developed in 1993, the National System of Integrated Attention for Children and Adolescents (Sistema Nacional de Atención Integral al Niño y al Adolescente, SNAINA) was conceptualized as the coordination of different institutions and public services aimed towards the enactment and coordination of children's rights.[16] Specifically, it says that SNAINA has the responsibility "to orient, integrate, structure, coordinate, supervise, and evaluate the policies, plans, programmes, and actions at the national level designated to the integrated attention of children and adolescents." This language of coordination and integration becomes important because it guides other laws and policies regarding children's rights in Peru. The CCONNA (the Advisory Board of Girls, Boys, and Adolescents of Lima), for example, uses the language of the national system law to guide and confirm its existence.

Despite SNAINA being written into law, the dozens of adult state policymakers who spoke to me about their impressions of SNAINA overwhelmingly said that it exists but does not function. A director of the division of children and adolescents within the Women's Ministry noted that the system has yet to be "articulated."[17] Some respondents, such as a former director of the National Governmental Network to Fight Poverty, were very explicit in asserting that an integrated system simply does not exist. He explained: "SNAINA is only theoretical; it is not happening in practice."[18] Others, such as a former member of the Civil Society Network for Chil-

174   Looking for the State

dren's Rights (GIN), noted that although Peru has the *components* for an integrated system, it has never enacted it.[19] She noted that there is still a lack of institutional integration and coordination at the state level. An officer at one local NGO, Action for Children (Accíon por los Niños), stated:

> Nobody understood this system. If you ask authorities about SNAINA several years ago, some would say that there is a system but it doesn't work. Others will say there is no system, but it works, and others will simply say, there is no system. For us, there is no system, but we have identified that there are conditions in place for the potential of a system, especially at the local level.[20]

The overwhelming response, in other words, was that even as SNAINA exists by law, it does not function in practice. Interviewees expressed a range of opinions as to why SNAINA doesn't work in Peru: absence of leadership, structure of the position, importance (and lack) of hierarchy, and lack of associated funding. Many of the descriptions centered around either individual culpability for failure of implementation or cultural inadequacy. None of them cited larger structural inequality for SNAINA's failure to be implemented. Instead, they attributed the lack of its functioning to technocratic or cultural reasons and flagged the placement of SNAINA as low within the Women's Ministry hierarchy—located within the subdivision of family and community. Housing SNAINA under the family and community division within the Women's Ministry gives it significantly less power than other similar units, as well as serving as a symbolic and discursive imagining that children as a category should be addressed and imagined primarily within the unit of the family.

Such spatial logics are reflected in the placement of children's rights programs. Originally, the governing body (*ente rector*) responsible for overseeing children's rights was located in the Presidential Ministry (Presidencia del Consejo de Ministros), as was SNAINA, to enact these rights. When Alberto Fujimori created the Women's Ministry (Ministerio de Promoción de la Mujer y del Desarrollo Humano, PROMUDEH) in 1996, he shifted the governing body for children's rights to the Women's Ministry. The creation of the Women's Ministry was originally viewed as positive in the sense that it was the first of its kind in Peru and put forward the first cabinet-level portfolio ministry on women in Latin America. Moreover, it seemed to have positive outcomes in terms of "the position of women in legislation and political representation" (Boesten 2003: 116). However, many critics suggest that this same time period also represented state cooptation of women's organizations and women's local organizing. As Peruvian scholar Jelke Boesten has argued, the image of a separate Women's Ministry depended on "a maternalist discourse of development and on the role that women played, are playing, and should play as 'natural' mothers and caretakers of the family and the community" (Boesten 2003: 117). The placement of the *ente rector* for children's rights as enveloped in the new Women's Ministry contributed to a spatial imagining of children as first, and foremost, located within families and with mothers.

The shifting of the *ente rector* from the Presidential Ministry to a subdivision within the family and community unit of the Women's Ministry in 1996 did two things. First, it conceptually shifted the way children's rights have come to be framed (shifting children's rights from their own unit to a subdivision of family and adolescents). Second, since the Women's Ministry had (and continues to have) an especially low level of authority, it automatically affected the level of institutional support and guidance the *ente rector* would be able to offer. Programs using the language of children's rights would no longer be able to rely on their status as an overarching framework working across all ministries. Instead, they were inhibited by being forced by the state to conduct coordination from a low-level, highly centralized ministry.

The placement of SNAINA within the Women's Ministry contrasts with the placement of other state programs that relate to children, namely, Juntos and Crecer both of which are poverty reduction programs. Juntos is the national conditional cash transfer program, which aims to relieve poverty for children and their families in nine of the poorest regions of Peru. Crecer is the national child nutrition program, also targeted to reach the poorest children. Both programs are run out of the Presidential Ministry, which structurally allows for greater autonomy. Moving SNAINA to the under-resourced, then titled, Ministry of Women and Social Development (MIMDES) inevitably makes it difficult for the government to run and supervise such a "national integrated system." The bureaucratic marginalization of SNAINA, which while on the surface may seem to be solely a

176   Looking for the State

technocratic issue, is an example of how state power can be used to dull state effectiveness. In this case, it imposed structural limitations on programs for children's rights, nestling children's rights and even child participation first and foremost within families and articulating a spatial orientation of children that erases them as political knowers and speakers and instead emphasizes their dependence. Indeed, in 2012, the government formally changed the Women's Ministry name, again, to the "Ministry of Women and Vulnerable Populations."

A Spatial Reimagining of Children's Rights in Peru

In Peru, children are dominantly understood to be contained not just within the nation-state, but most commonly, as individuals within families. Even though children, as MANTHOC members reveal, are rights holders, and talked about in the public domain as such, their collective political subject-hood has been hard fought. Much of that is because the spatial "locality" of children is most dominantly understood as embedded both within a country and often within a home. Children's voice and agency, even with the new emergence of rights language, is largely seen as bound, translated, and mediated through and with adults.[21]

When I first began this research over ten years ago, I interviewed adult policymakers, NGO directors, and governmental officials in Lima to better understand the landscape of children's rights in Peru. Nearly all of them started with the same premise: the challenges of implementation of children's rights because of Peru's culture of "institutional fragmentation." Categorizing the shortcomings of the children's rights system to bureaucratic "culture" rather than structure has a long history in human rights discourse. Many even showed me the same hand gestures, with the rights being the hand on top, and the local reality being that on the bottom. The "gap" they told me, is between the global and the local, the top and the bottom.

Many authors have written about the dangers of false binaries of culture versus modernity and local versus global.[22] One of the dangers, as scholar Makau Mutua has pointed out, is for such metaphors to downplay and erase state accountability. "The state itself is [presented as] a neutral, passive instrumentality—a receptacle or an empty vessel—that conveys savagery by implementing the project of the savage culture" (2001: 86). Critical approaches to such problematic, yet not always evident, binary logics have helped elucidate how deep-seated and prevalent such dualism is, especially within liberal frameworks.[23]

Children's rights policymakers and NGO directors in Peru expressed some of these dichotomous cultural and spatial logics in their interviews. A previous program officer at UNICEF Peru, for example, stated:

> This is not a culture of coordination. Coordination will not be born here voluntarily. This doesn't exist. Because of this we can't have a hope that without hierarchy, there will be coordination. This will not occur. This is not a culture like that.[24]

Similarly, a former director of a national policy network reflected:

> This is a permanent problem in Peru. The tendency for the fragmentation of politics is much higher than in other countries. . . . This is because of the diversity, the history, the culture. . . . The system doesn't function as a system. Every institution does what it wants.[25]

A long-time consultant on children's rights within the state remarked that this problem of coordination is not only specific to children's rights:

> The environmental system doesn't work, the water system doesn't work, the system for children doesn't work, and really, they're not going to work because people in general have so many problems with coordination that it costs them to work in collaboration. It's part of the culture—everyone has their own space, their area, and they work in isolation.[26]

In their unison is clarity that coordination at a national level is not "voluntary" in Peru. These quotes reveal a core aspect of state logics and loyalty: It is the culture, not the structures, that render such systems inadequate. Policymakers attributing this lack of coordination to the "culture" of Peru imply that culture is immutable and reflecting an overarching sense that the lack of coordination is static and permanent. Such narratives align with a dominant description of the relationship between policy and practice as fixed and as lived experiences of laws, primarily in terms of disjuncture between rights and reality.

Scholars of Latin America and beyond have long problematized the metaphorical language or framing of legality as a "gap."[27] They note how distance of policy and practice is often described as a void, which, as a metaphor, is prone to sidestep difficult questions about economic interests, structural inequality, or historical policy legacies of austerity (Li 2005). That is, one of the dangers with analyzing rights and realities or policy and practice as two separate concepts is that it lends itself to a dehistoricized reading and depoliticized analysis. In this case, treating the "culture" of Peru as separate from specific policies and historical context obscures how the state itself treats children and childhood in depoliticized ways.[28] While it may be true that Peru's political structure lacks coordination and its institutions are fragmented, it is also true that the legal and political storyline of the system of children's rights reveals a number of carefully crafted decisions, each with political implications. The category of childhood has long been embedded with great meaning by politicians, often to symbolize the future and to emphasize "the local."

The danger with using children to underscore the distinction between the local and the global is what such metaphors can obscure. Legal scholar Charis Kamphuis has found that one of the results of neoliberalism, starting in the 1990s under Fujimori, was a series of legislative choices that increased the privatization of social services and "the restructuring of the country's legal regimes to create favorable conditions for foreign investors" (2012: 530). Most notably, she writes about private mining companies in Peru and how these corporations have hired private security guards (often ex-military officers) largely to protect the (foreign-owned) mining industry. This has resulted in a decrease in public police officers. This example, on the surface, may seem far from the lives of children and children's rights. Yet, it is just one instance where technical policies of austerity are made to look "natural" and where there are notable material and everyday implications. What may be felt at a "local" level (the Lomas kids' observations that there are no police in their neighborhood) are importantly tied to global, transnational systems of inequity.

In a similar way that the young people of Lomas, as discussed in Chapter 2, treat the educational system in Peru as an imagined fair playing ground, adult interviewees within the state and civil society in Lima pre-

The Politics of Children's Participation in Peru 179

dominantly relied on an analysis where the state was presented in largely neutral ways. Interviewees referred to "cultural" reasons to explain what they feel is a non-functioning children's rights system, in that it doesn't reflect the cohesion it is legally mandated to fulfill. Their descriptions of such failures fit dominant, rational policy language about a "culture of fragmentation"—a reflection of depoliticization at play. This is a spatial scheme in which the local, cultural, or individual is imagined to be at odds with the global, the universal, and the legal. What the young people of Lomas and MANTHOC reveal, however, is that such a logic of distancing is incomplete at best, and often obscures rather than clarifies everyday lived conditions of inequality.

Imagined Futures in a Depoliticized State

The young people interviewed for this book vividly described their dreams and ambitions for the future in different ways. The children of Lomas spoke of wanting to become "professionals"; they aspired to stay in school, to contribute to their families. The girls of Lomas tended to depict dreams of having their own families one day and finishing school, whereas the boys focused on their professional aims. Elena revealed her dreams for the future:

> Have my house. To work hard, study and then have my house with my brothers and sisters, my mom and dad and everyone that I wanted to have. . . . I want to be able to buy something for my mom, so that she can be here and not working.[29]

Lela shared Elena's dream of making life easier for her mother. Lela said she hoped that,

> If my father continues to have money and can pay for me to go to school, I think I can be a great professional. If I work really hard . . . [m]y dream would be to study accounting and to be a great professional so that I could put my mom in her own home. To be able to live better.[30]

José spoke of wanting to go to college and then "become somebody."

180   Looking for the State

These are just a few of the examples from the young people of Lomas as they recounted their most intimate and familiar relationships and their hopes to make those around them proud. In these quotes are affective presentations of imagined progress and creating different lives for their parents than what they currently have. But they also point to the ways young people in Lomas are invested in, and have been taught to be invested in, a story of statehood and development as one of imagined future progress: They believe that it is possible to create better lives through their own efforts. While critical of the state as absent in terms of services and institutional presence, when speaking of their futures, the Lomas young people depict the state as playing a neutral role and thus often put the onus on themselves for future individual success.

The ways the members of MANTHOC discussed their futures also highlighted the complex and malleable ways young people depoliticized the state when speaking about the future. The young people of MANTHOC spoke about the importance of relationships as they imagined their futures, but they meant a different kind of relationship. Almost all spoke of wanting to go into politics. Girls and boys alike had political ambitions, awakened by the teachings of MANTHOC, and declared their plans to use their understandings about children's rights to influence (governmental) change. Activism for them was something tangible and best realized in the public sphere.

Juan, in an interview when he was 15, noted that before coming to MANTHOC he could not speak in public. Through the workshops and community at MANTHOC, he cultivated skills he would otherwise not have. When speaking about MANTHOC, he used the word *desenvolverse* ("MAN-THOC *me desenvuelve*"), a self-reflexive verb that roughly translates to self-development. For Juan, being part of MANTHOC had developed not just his skills but also himself.

The collective organizing and teachings of MANTHOC cultivate in the young people a public identity, a sense of confidence and voice, and an imagined future of effecting change. The children of MANTHOC, unlike the young people in Lomas, are visible and legible to state actors. Indeed, their organizing is *seen* and recognized by the state. They have regular platforms to express their views, and they are an organized and collective movement. But a potential complexity for such platforms, and part of the politics of what it means to see children as protagonists, is a paradox in which they use a language of universal human rights, which renders them subjects for technocratic intervention. The focus then goes to the individual voices of the young people. For them, developing their voices becomes associated with having an audience. Change becomes understood as something that happens in the public, governmental realm and that emphasizes the individual citizen. In such logics, the state is grounded primarily in the public sphere, in formal state politics, and in the use of voice. This stance treats the state as neutral and largely technical.

In discussing their hopes and dreams for the future, the children from Lomas and the members of MANTHOC show various ways that logics of state depoliticization operate, particularly in terms of the daily workings of state power. In doing so, both groups disrupt the ways children are often viewed as primarily apolitical. While the language the girls and boys of Lomas use to articulate everyday violence and disparity is not based on rights language, their perceptions of the state's absence (of services, clean water, adequate sewage system, and working domestic violence shelters) is nonetheless an implicit critique about the use of state resources and power. At the same time, their descriptions of longing for progress and seeking to develop better futures echoes a formulation of a neutral state.

MANTHOC sheds light on this dynamic in a different way: They speak of a country that renders their labor and economic contributions invisible and doesn't provide the opportunity for dignified work. While they claim status as political subjects, the children of MANTHOC have to negotiate doing so in terms that are recognizable and legible to the state. In the context of increased neoliberalism across Latin America, MANTHOC members show how the discourse of individual rights and citizens is a key translation that is legible as an organizing tactic. MANTHOC members face the challenge of framing their political agency in terms that expand the very category of citizenship in Peru, while simultaneously not necessarily disrupting a narrative of what citizenship has traditionally been. While representatives of MANTHOC refer to inequality in their discussions of dignified work, they don't necessarily approach the state as the key source or producer of this inequality. The state is thus often presented as a technical site with which to engage in the public sphere, rather than as part of a larger story about the complex negotiations of capitalist and colonial logics.[31] Eligibility

182 Looking for the State

for MANTHOC to the public sphere, in some ways, depends on treating equality as a key framework through which to engage.

The Lomas children rely on an inductive reading of politics: their first-hand experiences of government officials, followed by an articulation of the neglect they see. The young people of MANTHOC use a deductive reading of politics; they strategically package their arguments in relation to the public sphere, in the language of citizenship, equality, and rights. Both groups, in their own ways, shed light on the logics of everyday state power in Peru.

Looking for the State Beyond Its Institutions

When trying to understand how everyday state violence is manifested and experienced in the lives of particular groups of children, especially those made most marginal, it is necessary to move beyond only an institutional analysis (i.e., identifying a state either as weak or strong based on its institutions) or one that conceptualizes inequality happening primarily at the local level. Both groups of young people discussed in this book upset and complicate the social demarcations of what constitutes acceptable political action, political subjecthood, and political knowledge about the state. They reveal in different ways how state power is often rendered invisible and yet is always present. That is, the young people in this book describe a state that invokes their participation, creates conditions of inequity that depend on their labor, but does not treat them as political subjects or knowers. Such a dynamic reveals the complexities, contradictions, and sources of friction that arise when "local" actors are imagined as divorced or "far from" from global structures of inequity (Luttrell-Rowland et al. 2021).[32] But it also shows that even within the local and the national, certain configurations of power and policies reinforce ideas of political subjecthood, as well as of the depoliticized subject.

Children's rights, and child participation in particular, are susceptible to a spatial categorization that relies on the state's depoliticization of children. This depoliticization relies on the same logics that depoliticize state power and that imagine "the political" as far from and separate from children's everyday life. The emergence, therefore, of the public embrace of children's rights and child participation should be read cautiously, as it is not exempt from the logics of austerity and neoliberalism—an ideology that ensures that such an embrace is conducted, first and foremost, through economic objectives. By reimaging what it might mean to listen to young people—particularly those who have been made vulnerable through structures of injustice, those leading social justice movements, and those whose resistance work is perhaps less visible—it becomes necessary to listen to the context, affect, and histories that surround and shape their lives.

The young people in Lomas and the members of MANTHOC also underscore the need to move beyond thinking of the state primarily as its institutions; these young people demonstrate the fluid and expansive nature of "the state." They illustrate how state power is also taken up by non-state actors. This chapter has outlined some examples of this, such as the practices and discourses of participatory budgeting, government children advisory boards, and also Peru's National System for Children's Rights. These examples defy narratives of the state as a fixed or solely technical site. Instead, the state's power is present in the depoliticization of children (even if wrapped in narratives of participation), in children's rights, and in social movements. In these examples, the state largely drops out of focus and is often treated as a site of neutrality, eluding certain forms of critique and making state power invisible. While the seduction and power of such a framing has been widely noted, what has been less studied, and where further research needs to be done, is on new ways to center and take seriously the knowledge, and knowing, of those most impacted by state violence and its consequences.

When a state uses paternalistic understandings of children primarily as vulnerable subjects—while at the same time deepening such vulnerability through economic, environmental, and political choices—it creates some of the core conditions that underscore why "listening" to marginalized young people as commentators of the state (or even about rights, beyond tokenism) remains so elusive. However, the voices in this book demonstrate how children, particularly those who are directly impacted by state violence and systems of inequality, are constantly negotiating the politics and imaginary of state power in their lives. Their stories, insights, and articulations about how the state is able to make young people marginal through sustained disparity, while at the same time undermining their positions as political subjects, emphasize the urgent need to reimagine not just who, and what, constitute holders of political knowledge, but also the very claims themselves.

AFTERWORD

IN 2018, I RETURNED TO Lomas to visit Elena and see her family. When I first met Elena in 2007, she was 17 years old. When I see her on this visit, she is 28. That day, I join Elena at her house. Elena now has a young son, and she is telling him to sit down. He is playing with several other little kids, and she is trying to cook their dinner and doesn't want them to knock over the pot. The space is small, and the joyful noises of the children playing fill it so that Elena and I mostly speak in between squeals of laughter. On the wall of the living room, there is a large picture of Anna, Elena's mother. In the image, Anna is looking directly at the camera with a large red knapsack on her back. Elena's mother died unexpectedly three years before, and the picture is a reminder of her strong presence in the house.

I ask Elena about her life and about the other young people in the neighborhood. She tells me about each of them, their lives, how they are managing. Now some have children of their own, and they have a variety of jobs. She relates stories of loss, achievements, perseverance, and everyday survival. Elena tells me she is selling Avalon makeup to get by and to be able to stay with her son. "I can't leave my son," she says.

186   Afterword

The neighborhood of Lomas looks largely unchanged. Although a few of the murals in the neighborhood have changed, many are still there, faded from years past.

I remember José telling me over ten years ago, "the people around here, we are very forgotten." Those words ring through my ears as I walk through the neighborhood now. I still carry the young people in my mind's eye from years ago, and now I see how they have aged, and how their lives have changed, even as the physical place seems to have stayed in many ways the same.

Similar to how the young members of MANTHOC demand to have their subjectivity recognized, the community in Lomas (mostly the adults, but some of the teenagers too) have organized in recent years for running water and a sewage system. Their demands to the state have been specific and material, a call for a shift in the current everyday realties of the neighborhood. Elena plays with her young son, gazing at him with admiration and love, just beside the blue bin of water that still sits outside her house. That blue bin, symbolic of so many of the environmental challenges and daily violence that the people in Lomas face, has sat there for over a decade. That this is still the way that Elena gets her water after all these years highlights how the "development of infrastructure" of the area is not just about a linear story of improved material conditions, but rather about structural violence, social and political organizing, and specific unjust conditions. Something as fundamental as water, which many of the Lomas young people spoke about for years, is not divorced from global, translocal, and historical currents of power.[1]

Indeed, coming back all these years later makes vivid why the young people in Lomas speak of how such legacies of violence play out in their bodies and everyday lives. They make urgent the need for young people who have direct experience of state violence to be treated as political subject and knowers, and to be able to strive for greater ways for their knowledge—including emotion, affect, context, and history—to be treated as insights about the state and state violence. Members of MANTHOC show that such listening for state processes of power should not just be understood as only about individuals, but rather also about collective movements and intersectional approaches to identity politics and identity in politics.[2] The lessons offered by these young people emerge from their distinct histories and site-specific knowledge—a knowing that is particular, and yet shared.

As such, I focus this afterword on the image of the blue bin of water in part because it speaks to some of what it means to be writing this book, nearly fifteen years after first beginning this project. This book describes how two groups of working children in Peru understand and make meaning of everyday contradictions, lived inequality, and lingering historical inheritances of state violence. The long experience of doing research and developing the ideas and methodologies behind this book was a process of learning, and unlearning, and has changed the ways I approach my current work as a scholar, activist, teacher, and writer.[3] The world is different today than it was when I started this book. Peru is different, the United States is different. Many things are the same, however, including the perpetual violence that has long persisted in both countries. Global inequality and organized abandonment of those made most marginal is still here, arguably even more pronounced than when I began this project.[4] In this moment of global crisis, with the COVID-19 pandemic still raging, Peru has had the highest death rate per capita of all the countries in the world. Like many places, certain bodies and communities are impacted by state violence more than others.

But one thread that has become more visible in national and international news since beginning to write this book is the significance of young people as political actors and thinkers. Multiple solidarity movements, many led by or centered around young people, have emerged more clearly in the public eye and in the media, critiquing and naming the role of state violence. Youth environmental justice movements, the global movement of Black Lives Matter, and gender justice movements have been at the forefront of popular consciousness and are making explicit conceptual links that media outlets previously haven't covered.

For example, in 2015, the global movement Ni Una Menos (Not One Less) grew out of coalitions of women in Argentina. It was sparked by the murder of 14-year-old Chiara Páez, who was found buried in the garden of her boyfriend's house. This came on the heels of two other killings of young women, gruesomely murdered through gendered violence. Marcela Ojeda, a radio journalist, tweeted: "They are killing us, aren't we going to do anything?" Feminist leaders and organizers led an outpouring of mass mobilizations and protests and created the hashtag #NiUnaMenos. The movement, largely driven by young women and focused on the normalcy of gendered violence and femicide, strengthened across Latin America and

188   Afterword

beyond.[5] Ni Una Menos has made specific and broad-reaching demands of the state (for example, budgets to enforce the anti-violence laws in Argentina and a registry of femicide) and centers its analysis on the interconnected nature and drivers of gendered violence: exposing links between normalized, everyday gendered violence; discriminatory policies against trans and queer women; systems of mass incarceration; and current forms of capitalism and neoliberalism.

The scope of the Ni Una Menos claims, as well as the role of intergenerational participation, are examples of how many transnational movements point to a larger reconsideration of young people's political subjectivity in these times. Until recently, much of the framing of young people's participation in social and political movements has largely downplayed the role of state violence as a prompt for such organizing; nor has this framing emphasized sufficiently the gendered, racialized, classed, and geographically located ways that young people think about and understand themselves. But, given the current conditions, and the range of movements being led by and with young people, there is perhaps reason to believe frames for analysis are changing. That is, to hear the claims made by movements like Ni Una Menos or Black Lives Matter—with attention to the specific commentary they are making about the state, state power, and interlocking systems of state violence—reveals the centrality and significance of particular groups of young people's organizing and knowledge at this historical moment.

The political nature and contributions by those most impacted by structural violence are made clear by both the young people in Lomas and the members of MANTHOC. Working young people in Lima—speaking about their everyday lives, their dreams, their anxieties, and their rights—show how their voices are critical for a broad understanding of the political processes in which they are both embedded and help shape. Listening to the ideas and observations of these two distinct groups of working young people brings into relief how they are not just vulnerable subjects who are slotted into statehood and systems of state power, but rather are political thinkers and knowers. Actively engaged in describing, navigating, and grappling with these everyday global and local conditions, they expose deeply violent structures and currents of power in Peru and beyond.

Notes

Introduction

1. See *"Plan de Desarrollo Concertado de Lomas de Carabayllo 2004–2015,"* a community action plan that is one of the few documents to outline a historical analysis of Lomas and that has been written collectively by local community leaders, families, and NGO workers.

2. Elena interview, 2012. All names in this manuscript have been changed for anonymity, and all translations are my own.

3. See http://www.carabayllo.net/lima-norte/distritos/carabayllo/6971-ollanta-huma la-inauguró-las-obras-de-agua-de-san-pedro-y-las-lomas-de-carabayllo.html

4. While there are expansive examples of this, some works that have influenced my thinking on this point include: Ennew 2002; Invernizzi et al. 2017; Malkki 2010; Malkki 2015; Pupavac 2001; Ross and Solinger 2017; White 2007.

5. While much of the discourse around children's rights focuses on the importance of the interconnection of rights, only a select handful of authors directly engage in discussions that link the everyday, material conditions of children's lives and wider structural and societal analysis. As Cindi Katz (2004) powerfully shows in her longitudinal, ethnographic study of children growing up in Sudan and New York, this often means that particular political ecologies are overlooked in discussions of children's rights.

6. The majority of this book is based on fieldwork I conducted between 2007–2009 in Lima, Peru. I then made additional trips in 2010, 2012, 2014, and 2016, which included archival research, interviews, focus groups, and participatory and visual research.

7. Most of the young people of Lomas did not identify as "Indigenous," and so I don't name them as such in this book. Part of my argument, however, is that the young people of Lomas have specific political knowledge based on their experience being descendants of families who migrated from the highlands of Peru.

190   Notes to the Introduction

8. This point has been a major feature of social movements as well as critical theory. See Anzaldúa 1987; Brown 2013; Bueno-Hansen 2015; Chua 2018; Collins 2000; Collins 2019; Crenshaw 1991; Hernández 2016; Incite! 2017; Katz 2008; Leinaweaver 2008; Perry 2018; Taylor 2016.

9. I use the term "made marginal" to highlight the multiple ways state violence shapes people's lives and experiences with living in conditions of marginality or poverty. I share Kathleen Millar's overarching critique, and caution against, those who write of "scarcity as a persistent paradigm for understanding lives lived in precarious conditions" (Millar 2018: 8).

10. See Sara Ahmed (2014) *The Cultural Politics of Emotion* in which she describes how emotions "should not be regarded as psychological states, but as social and cultural practices" (9). Jennifer Nash's scholarship on love and emotion in Black feminism has also shaped this idea. See Nash 2013.

11. For a robust discussion of interrelated crisis and a political economy approach that attends to both the local and the global, see Britton-Purdy et al. 2020.

12. Details of this conflict will be discussed in Chapter 1, along with the ways human rights language came to be framed since that report. See Bueno-Hansen 2015; CVR 2003.

13. See Boesten 2010; Drinot 2006; Ewig 2010; Thorp and Paredes 2010.

14. See Rosa-Linda Fregoso and Cynthia Bejarano (2010) *Terrorizing Women: Feminicide in the Americas.* See also Cecilia Menjívar (2011) *Enduring Violence: Ladina Women's Lives in Guatemala.*

15. One of the co-directors of the Peruvian feminist organization *Flora Tristan* stated in a 2011 interview with me: "The problem here [in Peru] is that children's rights are used to justify religious ideological positions that go against, in this case, the rights of women. So this is a very brutal use of what is, in reality, a holistic conception of the rights of people."

Much of the public policy discourse treats women's rights and children's rights as basically compatible policy enterprises. However, in Peru children's rights begin at conception, making the very concept of children's rights already a complex one given how it clashes with women's reproductive rights. One question in the classification of childhood is the age at which it ends. My study uses the same standards as the CRC, where "childhood" is understood to end at 18 years of age. Another question, often overlooked by academics, is when the concept of childhood *begins.* While the CRC classifies childhood beginning at birth, the Inter-American Convention on the Rights of the Child that is used in Peru distinguishes childhood as beginning at conception. This is a loaded issue, and international state parties deeply disagree about when the rights of a child should begin. Obviously, therefore, in speaking of experiences of "childhood," the range of who is imagined in this terminology can span from unborn fetuses to 18-year-olds depending on the reader and context.

The framework of "reproductive justice" developed by women of color scholars and activists in the United States has had a crucial and often overlooked contribution to these discussions. They suggest that the individualistic rhetoric of "choice" is often meaningless for many women of color and marginalized groups and argue for a need to

Notes to the Introduction   191

move beyond the familiar pro-life/pro-choice binary. For a history and discussion of the reproductive justice movement see Loretta Ross and Rickie Solinger (2017) *Reproductive Justice*.

16. See Qvortrup et al. 2009. For a general overview of this topic, see Nick Lee (2001) *Childhood and Society: Growing up in an Age of Uncertainty*. See also Hart and Boyden 2018; Invernizzi et al. 2017; White 2002a.

17. Much of the discussion about children's rights has been located within the academic literature called "the sociology of childhood" (see, for example, Mayall 2000; James and Prout 1997). This literature emerged roughly around the same time as the CRC and positioned itself as emphasizing children's agency and participation, which these authors juxtaposed against classic understandings of children as passive and vulnerable. Indeed, the sociology of childhood aims to understand the category of childhood as a "social construction" (James and Prout 1997: 8). Key themes such as child participation and child voice were developed in this literature, along with the notion of child standpoint and representation. While Parsons and Piaget have important differences in their views, they both believe that the child develops from "disorder, instability, and confusion to order, stability, and confidence by transcending their mere biologically classifiable human body. In both cases the process of supplementation allows the child to come into possession of and control over themselves" (Lee 2001: 42).

18. Robin Bernstein's critical book *Racial Innocence* (2011) traces the history of such presentations of the "neutrality" of childhood, and argues that in the U.S. context, such presentations of innocence played a pivotal role in all major racial projects, including slavery and abolition, but also anti-Black violence. The general international performance, or widespread consensus, of childhood as a time and place far from, or outside the polity, is wrapped up in both national and international systems of power. Barry Mayall (2000: 246) notes:

> The spaces and times of childhood are proposed as, ideally, protected from politics. Children are to be protected, in an a-political arena of thought and practice. Just as women have been assigned to the private and the domestic, so we are taught to think of children as growing up there, too, in a happy domain which enables them to develop, unmolested by the stresses of public life. Children therefore are presented to us as pre-people, outside the polity.

I am interested in both the spatial logics needed to imagine children as "outside the polity," but also, as Bernstein notes, the historical and place-specific stakes in doing so.

19. By 2003, an unprecedented 191 countries had ratified the CRC, making it the most ratified treaty in history. Under the CRC, children are entitled to rights that are encapsulated by four overarching principles: nondiscrimination, the best interest of the child, survival and development, and the right to child participation. These overarching principles combine and include the civil, political, and social rights of children. While the integration of rights (civil, political, and social) is one of the primary goals of all human rights treaties, the CRC proved to be a departure from previous international declarations regarding children (namely the 1924 and 1959 Declaration of the Rights of the Child) because of the shift from a primarily welfare framework to a participatory one.

192 Notes to the Introduction

Further, it is distinct because of the ways the overarching principles (particularly that of child participation) are presented as being interconnected with one another, making it not only a right but also a framework for the realization of other rights. The global historical shift from "needs" discourse to "rights" discourse with regards to children, as well as the way children's rights are now viewed as interconnected, are two features of the historical shift in how children themselves were viewed and understood in human rights law. For information on how the "child" is understood in international law, see Bernstein 2011; Van Bueren 1995. See also Holzscheiter 2010; Linde 2016; Rehfeld 2011.

20. Cynthia Enloe (1990) noted in her analysis of the Persian Gulf War that "women" and "children" were so often placed together that the phrase rings as though it were only one word: "womenandchildren." Recent research has shown that this dyad is not just an elision that only happens during wartime but can also be central to state making and state policy (see Luttrell-Rowland 2012).

21. The emergence of Black girlhood studies as a field has been critical to the making visible of this erasure—how certain bodies and people are made more invisible than others. For some influential work who speak to this from both a historical and social perspective, see scholarship by Brown 2013; hooks 1997; Ibrahim 2021; Webster 2021; Wright 2016.

22. There are robust discussions on this point from a range of disciplines; some authors that have shaped my thinking on this include: Abrams 1988; Alvarez 1999; Alvarez et al. 2017; Bhandar 2018; Blackett 2019; Chowdhury 2011; Escobar and Alvarez 1992; Eslava et al. 2017; Hernández et al. 2019; Quijano 2000; Santos 2005; Sharma and Gupta 2006.

23. See Engle 2020; Ewick and Silbey 1998; Levitsky 2014; McCann 2014; Merry 2006a.

24. Colonization and colonial legal frameworks that rely on particular notions of the state and Euro-American law is one example of this. The scholarship of Lila Abu-Lughod, Elora Chowdhury, Kiran Asher, Sonia Alvarez, Cheryl Harris, K.-Sue Park, Aída Hernández Castillo, Akhil Gupta, and Max Liboiron among others is useful here in lodging both the critique and alternative views of understanding.

25. For this critical and relational approach, I draw inspiration from critical race scholars, decolonial scholars, and feminist scholars. See Abu-Lughod 2013; Bhandar 2018; Bhandar and Ziadah 2020; Campt 2017; Chatterjee 2001; Collins 2000; Collins 2019; Enloe 2014; Fine 2017; Fujii 2018; Heathcote 2017; Heathcote and Otto 2014; hooks 1989; Lugones 2010; Mignolo and Walsh 2018; Naples 2003; Smith 2012; Van Vleet 2020.

26. Here I join a long line of critical and interpretative social science researchers and those who understand and think of their interpretative work fundamentally as relational. Some of these authors include, for example, Bacchetta et al. 2018; Bejarano et al. 2019; Cheesman 2018; Fujii 2018; Schwartz-Shea and Yanow 2011; Wedeen 2009; Wiebe 2016.

27. Patricia Hill Collins (2019) *Intersectionality as Critical Social Theory* lays out an expansive and comprehensive history for why an intersectional approach should be thought about not just as a lens for analysis, but also as a critical method in and of itself. Such an approach was paramount to the arguments made in this book.

28. There are a wide range of scholars who have informed this line of thinking. For a further discussion of this point, see, for example, Alcalde 2010; Bueno-Hansen 2015; Gilmore 2007; Gilmore 2002; Hartman 2008; Heathcote 2019; Katz 2004; Paulson 2015; Paulson and Bellino 2017; Perry 2018.

29. Fregoso and Bejarano (2010), along with others who use feminist approaches towards violence and state studies, note a relational understanding the state. Marianne Constable notes that turning towards silence can be a tool to engage "possibilities of relations between law and justice that are not articulated or articulable in the terms of legal positivism" (2005: 11). Further, she writes, turning towards silence is not meant "to discard or dismiss positive law, which is indeed modern law, but to explore openings and possibilities of law and justice that sociological positivism, in its commitment to the social and empirical character of law and language, does not recognize" (ibid.). Cecilia MacDowell Santos, in her 2005 study of women's police stations in Brazil, also notes the various ways feminist scholars of Latin America have changed the field of understanding the state and the ways it is "contingent upon the historical and political conjuncture" rather than as static and essentialized (7). Such expanded ways of seeing and understanding state processes therefore may also require new ways, and possibilities, for listening. See also Campt 2017; Heathcote 2019; Otto 2017.

30. See Collins 2019; Fine 2017; Fujii 2018; Torre 2009; Smith 2012.

31. See, for example Anzaldúa 1987; Chowdhury 2011; Mignolo 2009.

32. National System of Integrated Attention for Children and Adolescents (Sistema Nacional de Atención Integral al Niño y al Adolescente or SNAINA) was established in 1993 through the Children and Adolescent National Code. It was then implemented by Ley del Sistema Nacional de Atención Integral al Niño y el Adolescente, law 26518, August 8, 1995: https://docs.peru.justia.com/federales/leyes/26518-aug-4-1995.pdf

33. There is robust discussion of this in Latin America and comparatively; for some of the authors who have influenced my thinking on this point see Bhandar 2018; Bueno-Hansen 2015; McKittrick 2015; Quijano 2000; Quijano 2007.

34. For important contextual analysis see, for example, Cadena 1998; Graubart 2017; Penry 2019; Premo 2005; Walker 2017a.

35. Latin American feminist theorists have also put forward this challenge in terms of women's movements and the need to look to collective knowledges promoted by communities rather than through the solo individual. See Lugones 2010.

36. In this, my work aligns with a large body of scholars who seek to illuminate hidden or normative power dynamics in their own research design and who strive to find and articulate particular methodological tools to illuminate power. See, for example, Ackerly 2008; Alcalde 2010; Bejarano et al. 2019; Bueno-Hansen 2015; Chowdhury 2015; Collins 2019; Lugones 2010; Pahuja 2011; Smith 2012; Torre 2009; Van Vleet 2020.

37. In Chapter 1, I discuss this concept as it relates to some of the particular ways that slow violence plays out in the bodies and lives of those living in Lomas.

38. Jason Hart (2008) has written about how much of the children's rights participation model relies on and puts forward a visual image in which the child is placed in the center, surrounded sequentially by family, community, school, and so forth: "This schema is depicted in the form of a child figure nested within concentric circles of rela-

194 Notes to the Introduction

tionship that extend from those kin closest to the child to an abstract 'society' furthest away" (410). Such spatial schema often become a way "intended or otherwise, to produce compliant subjects of the state and producers/consumers within the global market" (ibid.).

Scholars and international development agencies of children's rights often unwittingly reinforce the same exclusions as rights discourse itself in two ways. First, they tend to focus on contemporary patterns of violation, abuse, or empowerment without examining the historical or contextual evolution of such patterns. Second and interrelated, rights discussions have the danger to obscure rather than illuminate the lived experiences of those they claim to represent. Much of the children's rights and children's participation literature focuses on the politics of (age) recognition, while neglecting the specifics and politics of suffering. Dominant discussions of children's rights focus on individual actors and legality as an imagined relationship between rights holders and rights granters. In doing so, the state often drops out of focus as a producer of rights violation. Its apparent absence, in other words, is often where it is most present. See, for example, Bernstein 2011; Hart 2008; Hart 2012; Malkki 2010; Pupavac 2001.

39. Davis (2006) notes that Peru is the seventh in the world with the highest amount of people living in urban slums (68%). There is a marked spatial dimension to Peru's inequality; poverty is more pronounced in rural areas than in urban ones. See also Balarin 2011.

40. United Nations 2015.

41. Drinot writes: "The current economic orthodoxy in Peru holds that economic growth, fueled by exports of raw materials and agricultural commodities, will produce economic benefits that will 'trickle down' to the poor" (2006: 11). While Drinot isn't explicit about children in this discussion, they are often imagined as embedded in families and therefore part of the dominant economic orthodoxy.

42. Here I am influenced by David Kazanjian's historical work and his discussions of comparative interpretations. He writes "typically, comparative projects presume stable terms against which objects of analysis can be compared (the historian, the anthropologist, the cultural critic) as well as universal units of comparison (kinship, literature, gender, race, class, nationality), and so is also implicated in the exercise of colonial power" (2016: 8).

43. For examples of a range of ways others have addressed this aspect of research with movements, see Assis 2021; Chua 2018; Escobar and Alvarez 1992; Hernández 2016.

44. In *Pollution Is Colonialism*, Max Liboiron writes of the politics of "method-ethics" and how the two should be thought of together. For this book, part of my ethics was influenced by the recent significant body of literature that suggests it is useful to do research *with* children as compared to solely *about* children. This scholarship claims that children are not just objects to be studied, but also subjects in their own right. Some of these authors (Alderson and Morrow 2020; Brown 2013; Crivello et al., 2009; Fine 2017; Fine and Weis 2003; Morrow 2007; among others) argue in various ways for a child-centered approach and that using children's voices and experience is essential, as is finding appropriate method-ethics to do so.

Notes to Chapter 1   195

45. I agree here with anthropologist Lila Abu-Lughod that "focusing on individuals encourages familiarity rather than distance and helps to break down 'otherness' for it not only corresponds to the way we ordinarily think about those close to us in our everyday world, but also actively facilitates identification with and sympathy towards others" (1993: 29).

46. On about the discourse of tolerance in North America, Wendy Brown (2006: 5) writes:

> What kind of social subject does it produce? What kind of citizen does it hail, with what orientation to politics, to the state, and to fellow citizens? What kind of state legitimation might it supply and in response to what legitimation deficits? What kind of justice might it promise and what kinds might it compromise or displace?

While this body of work by Brown mainly focused on questions about adult subjects, her theoretical contributions on the point of imagined subjecthood and depoliticization was influential to the core questions in this book. I use the term "depoliticized state" throughout the book with these core questions of state legitimation in mind.

Chapter 1

1. This was a crucial moment in my own fieldwork experience of standing witness to the material effects of everyday poverty and extreme inequality. Andrea and Julian (the parents of Clara and Eva) confided in me about how the medicines Julian had to take would cause nausea. Julian felt it would be impossible to take medicines regularly, and due to taking the medicine intermittently, he had developed drug resistant TB. Even though they knew they should not sleep in the same room, their living space was small, and they did not have the funds to make a separate room. I contacted the local chapter of Partners in Health in Peru, Socios en Salud, and even though they did not work in that particular section of Lomas de Carabayllo, they agreed to meet the family. Socios en Salud provided medicine, treatment, and support for the entire family and built a new roof for a section of the house so that they could sleep separately until the father recovered. I watched the holistic and comprehensive layers of support Socios en Salud provided Andrea and Julian's family over time and until the family was healthy. It was support that, according to Andrea and Julian, was a "life-changing" intervention for their family.

2. In 2010 Peru had the highest number of drug resistant cases of TB across the Americas. The local chapter of Partners in Health, Socios en Salud, began to work in Peru in 1997 and focused their work in Lomas de Carbayallo because of the high levels of TB cases. See Mineo 2015.

3. King and Mutter (2104) note some important parallels between how scholars often frame environmental disasters and violent conflicts that include a temporality that focus on crisis and emergency, and often avoid discussions about culpability and causes.

4. Colonization and colonial legal frameworks that rely on particular notions of the state and Euro-American law are examples of the depoliticization I am referring to.

196   Notes to Chapter 1

Bianca Premo (2005) notes how one feature in particular of Spanish colonial rule of Peru in the sixteenth and seventeenth centuries was the use of law and legality as tools for the state.

5. Sociologist Philip Abrams (1988) in his published talk "Notes on the Difficulty of Studying the State" notes how this belief, or "state-idea" is partly how the state itself works, through a de-historicized lens, which leads to reification.

6. Dominant and familiar narratives about law and legality as embedded in entities or sites tends to be state-centric as well as Euro-American centric. This narrative has deep historical roots and is certainly not limited to Peru. See also Asher 2009; Darian-Smith 2013; Goldberg-Hiller and Silva 2011; Pahuja 2011; Penry 2019; Quijano 2000; Quijano 2007; Sassen 2007; Walker 2017a.

7. Rob Nixon notes that one of the very features of what he calls "slow violence" is the fact that so much of it "remain largely unobserved, undiagnosed, and untreated" (2011: 6), particularly as it plays out in the bodies and lives of poor people.

8. The young people's insights illustrate that politics is not just about state action; it is also about state inaction and what is made invisible. Sundhya Pahuja notes how the "secret" of international law's authority lay in the erasing of the very categories of what is law. "This erasure is in large measure effected by law's claim to *be* 'law'" (2011:27). See also Allen 2003; García 2005; Leinaweaver 2007.

9. Pascha Bueno-Hansen describes the roots of Spain's colonization of Peru as lasting into present-day state policies: "The colonizers considered themselves as civilized in contrast to the natives. Through the nineteenth and twentieth centuries, the Peruvian nation-state adapted this social hierarchy into an understanding of what it means to be modern" (2015: 8).

10. Geographer Claudia Leal (2018) in *Landscapes of Freedom* notes how important it is not understand space and geography not just through a physical understanding, but also a racialized lens. Her book notes the relationships between environmental conditions and expressions of freedom.

11. See "*Plan de Desarrollo Concertado de Lomas de Carabayllo 2004–2015.*"

12. It was not until 1998 that this recognition was accorded a basis in written law and that the state established the exact boundaries of the Lomas residential zone.

13. Lomas de Carabayllo's latest local state action plan describes the history this way: "These territories were occupied under the modality of 'invasions' and were subsequently acquired legally" ("*Plan de Desarrollo Concertado de Lomas de Carabayllo 2004–2015*").

14. For more details of this history, see "*Plan de Desarrollo Concertado de Lomas de Carabayllo 2004–2015.*"

15. See Fernández-Maldonado 2006.

16. The areas surrounding Lomas are comprised of brick and lead factories and various mines.

17. The work done by the parents of the young people in Lomas is quite gendered. A study conducted in 2006 by CESIP found that 60% of families interviewed in Lomas had mothers who stayed at home to take care of the children ("*Plan de Desarrollo Concertado de Lomas de Carabayllo 2004–2015*").

Notes to Chapter 1   197

18. For important discussion of these lived contradictions and tensions, see Ferreira da Silva 2009; Katz 2004; Li 2007; Millar 2018; Weeks 2011; Weeks 2018; Wiebe 2016.

19. Focus group interview, Lima, 2008. I have purposefully included long quotes from the transcripts of the interviews with the children. This is a methodological stance to provide a sense of the rhythm and interaction among the young people and to let their insights stand on their own. For discussion on this, see Ackerly 2008; Fine 2017; Morrow 2007; Morrow and Richards 1996. Additionally, the rhythm and flow of these exchanges was built up over years of relationship with Enrique, the interviewer. While I was present for each of these exchanges, and asked additional questions if they arose, having Enrique run the focus groups put the young people at ease in critical ways.

20. Interview, Lima, 2008.

21. Other work that has been done with young people in Latin America shows that children recognize the importance of environmental degradation. In their book *Flammable*, for example, Javier Auyero and Débora Alejandra Swistun (2009) write of the residents of an Argentine shantytown, including children, and the complex and layered ways they speak of everyday toxins and place.

22. Ironically, this dynamic has been most clearly brought to public attention through recent examples of children advocates and children activists, who have been fighting for years for the need to make necessary linkages between environmental justice. Some of those young people, particularly in the Global South, and including the young people of MANTHOC discussed later in this book, have been fighting for the centrality of environmental justice in their movements for years.

23. Geographer Cindi Katz (2004) outlines this point in her comparative ethnography about young people living in the Sudanese village of Howa and a group in Harlem in New York City:

> All modes of production produce and are enabled by particular political ecologies. This fact is so obvious that it often goes unremarked, but the environmental toll of centuries of capitalist production, and its increasingly global nature, has been enormous. The widespread and serious environmental problems that are symptomatic of capitalist relations of production have received plenty of public attention, but not necessarily as problems of social reproduction. (21)

24. Interview, Lima, 2008.

25. See Mervin 2015.

26. Jessica Leinaweaver (2007) "Choosing to Move: Child Agency on Peru's Margins" influenced my thinking on being explicit about this clarification. See also Das and Poole 2004; Escobar 2011; Millar 2018; Ticktin 2011; and Van Vleet 2002, among others, for critical discussions exploring this tension.

27. Part of my methodological commitment of using visual images and drawings as prompts for dialogue was that I didn't see the drawings as objects for me to interpret or read as an expert. Rather, they were prompts for curiosity, for engagement, for exchange. Because of this, when I include the drawings or visual images in this book, I follow what anthropologist Tom Cliff calls the need to "leave something in the image

198   Notes to Chapter 1

that the word does not say" (2016: 18). That is, by treating drawings or images in this book as part of the flow of the argument, I join others who are committed to a way of working with the visual by "layering up ideas and imagery that are not entirely controlled and that move towards the conceptual" (ibid.). I'm not using the images solely to extract my own meaning or to factually demonstrate a statement I have given, but rather, like my exchanges with the young people, to use the visual as part of the wider lens for co-interpretation and dialogue.

28. Claudia Mitchell's important work on visual methodologies showcases the range of visual practices used in social sciences, as well as a number of reasons to use visual methodologies. Mitchell (2011) notes how useful visual methods can be when there is interest not just for technical prompts for research participants, but rather to spark and highlight participants themselves as interpreters, curators, and narrators.

29. I draw here on the broad and intersectional work of Brown 2006; Bueno-Hansen 2015; Campt 2017; Collins 2019; Crenshaw 1991; Enloe 2004; Hartman 2008; Perry 2018; Spade 2015; Tsing 2005; Tsing 2009, among others. While these authors don't necessarily take up children or visual methods as their focus, they lay foundational ideas in terms of notions of marginality and what is both seen and unseen.

30. Here I am influenced by and indebted to Saidiya Hartman (2008) "Venus in Two Acts" in which she calls for "a critical reading" of the archive. She writes:

> The archive of slavery rests upon a founding violence. This violence determines, regulates and organizes the kinds of statements that can be made about slavery and as well it creates subjects and objects of power. The archive yields no exhaustive account of the girl's life, but catalogues the statements that licensed her death. (10)

The young people of Lomas were offering notations on their images, stories of violence that were off the page, but that helped organize and shape the content of their drawings.

31. Finding methods and tools that allow for such nuance is critical, particularly because as Lois Weis and Michelle Fine (2012) note: "structures produce lives at the same time as lives across the social class spectrum produce, reproduce, and, at times, contest these same social/economic structures" (175). The contradictions the young people struggle with are the same contradictions they see play out around them in everyday, lived ways.

32. See Auyero and Swistun 2009; Millar 2018; Scheper-Hughes 1993 for nuanced discussions of ethnographies of communities in Latin America existing in toxic spaces, and the number of ways they interpret, understand, and make sense of creating lives there.

33. Linda Tuhiwai Smith (2012) *Decolonizing Methodologies: Research and Indigenous People* lays out what she identifies as some of the core colonial and imperial assumptions present in dominant research methods; and some ways to challenge or reimagine such approaches. One aspect she names is contextualizing knowledge within larger political, social, and cultural contexts. In this case, the young people's drawings are a form of knowledge, story-telling, and political narrative.

34. See Maxine Greene (2000) *Releasing the Imagination: Essays on Education, the Arts, and Social Change,* Anna Tsing (2005) *Friction: An Ethnography of Global Connection,* and Habiba Ibrahim (2021) *Black Age: Oceanic Lifespans and the Time of Black Life* for a range of ways this point is engaged and theorized.

35. See Gupta and Ferguson 1997; Leinaweaver 2007; Leinaweaver 2008; Malkki 2010; Mignolo 2012; Millar 2018; West 2005.

36. As discussed above, it's possible that the descriptions of the burning of trash or contamination could have equally been said with a sense of what the young people thought would made a "good" answer for a white, North American outsider. One way I aimed to avoid this, at least to some extent, was to have Enrique, who they knew and felt comfortable with, be the primary interviewers in the focus groups. Elena also enjoyed coming to the focus group discussions and being part of the informal times together. Having Enrique and Elena present and asking questions, too, created conditions that allowed the children to feel that the questions were not out of the ordinary or meant to be performative, but that as much as possible, these conversations were to be similar to ones they would regularly have about their everyday lives.

37. For more about this history, see Karen Graubart (2007) *With Our Labor and Sweat: Indigenous Women and the Formation of Colonial Society in Peru, 1550–1700.*

38. Historian Bianca Premo (2005) notes: "Spanish colonizers imagined the indigenous inhabitants of the Americas to be infantlike Others who possessed a protected, diminished status within political society. In addition, a great number of slaves of African descent inhabited Lima, and their conditions as chattel redoubled categories of legal subjugation based on color and social class" (12). Lima's colonial history of racial and ethnic subordination, and of legal subjugation of those who were treated as childlike Others, has lasting implications of everyday life.

39. For a discussion of this, see Theidon 2013.

40. For more of this history, see Degregori 1996; Gandolfo 2009; Henríquez and Ewig 2013; Starn 1999.

41. See Alcalde 2010; Bueno-Hansen 2015.

42. See Burt 2009.

43. International Commission of Jurists, Report on the Administration of Justice in Peru (published in Spanish by Instituto de Defensa Legal, Lima, 1993: 45) (citing law 25475).

44. One human rights report about that time period notes:

> Under these laws, the police are granted exceptional powers, many freedoms are restricted, and arbitrary deadlines and time periods are imposed. The opportunities to present *habeas corpus* or *amparo* petitions are limited and the measures are draconian, including life imprisonment, the criminal prosecution of minors, conviction in absentia, and bench warrants that do not expire. (Villarán de la Puenta 2007: 111)

45. Fujimori resigned from office by fax from Japan in 2000 and was later arrested in Chile for human rights abuses. He was sentenced to twenty-five years on murder and corruption charges.

200 Notes to Chapter 1

46. See Nick Cheesman (2015) *Opposing the Rule of Law: How Myanmar's Courts Make Law and Order* for an important discussion of how the concept of law and order animated everyday justice in another country context.

47. This outcome was remarkable for transitional justice cases in Latin America. Jo-Marie Burt (2009) has written about the significance of the trial and outcome of Fujimori's case and why it was so meaningful—and rare—to convict a head of state.

48. Salomón Lerner, CVR chairman, noted:

> Can a system be considered fair or effective if, on the one hand, it convicted and ordered the well-deserved confinement of many guilty people, while on the other, it consigned hundreds of innocent individuals to the same fate? How to comprehend that the same State that issued the harshest of sentences should find itself obliged to create an Ad Hoc Commission for pardons that would find . . . nearly six hundred prisoners who were innocent of all crimes? Peru has been living in a state of denial of justice. (cited in Villarán de la Puente 2007: 113)

49. As Pascha Bueno-Hansen (2015) argues, these patterns reflect the historical devaluation of these populations that extend back to Peru's colonial history.

50. As Kimberly Theidon (2013) has documented, women gave testimonies in the commission process about the gendered challenges of everyday life amongst a backdrop of fear and uncertainty:

> Women offered insights into the gendered dimensions of war and the ways in which the violence permeated all spheres of life. They spoke about the challenges of keeping children fed, homes intact, livestock safe, the search for missing loved ones, the lacerating sting of ethnic insults in the cities in which they sought refuge: women spoke about familial and communal suffering and about the quotidian aspects of armed conflict. When people go to war, caregiving can become a dangerous occupation. (192)

51. See CVR 2003: 162. Translation of original Spanish text from Laplante and Theidon 2007: 234.

52. The CVR strongly recommended that all secondary schools teach the history of the recent civil war and political violence, and how the complexities of structural inequalities contributed and led to wide-reaching violence.

53. Interview, Lima, 2014.

54. Interview, Lima, 2014.

55. Clara transitioned from working part time at the factory to full time as a housekeeper for a family in the center of Lima the year before she would enter fifth grade.

56. Even though the young people of Lomas were not alive during the time of the internal armed conflict, the violence and terror shaped the consciousness of their parents. In Lima, for example, in 1992,

> Maria Elena Moyano, a thirty-two-year-old Afro-Peruvian feminist organizer and the deputy mayor of Villa El Salvador district, defied Sendero by publicly condemning its terrorist methods and continuing her work to provide the people

in her community with basic necessities. In February of that year, senderistas gunned down Moyano and dynamited her body in front of her two young sons and dozens of other people at a public event in Villa El Salvador. Her funeral was attended by thousands. (Alcalde 2010: 61)

57. Interview, Lima, 2014.

58. Navaro-Yashin's argument in *The Make-Believe Space* is "that institutions have a life (or liveliness) of their own that goes further than, and beyond, human life. Institutions exceed, and are excessive of, human potential" (2012: 32). She ethnographically makes this case through studying everyday state practices, objects, and administrative actions. Her theoretical approach challenges and disrupts traditional ideas about how state practice is understood and limited to (rational) government agents.

59. For examples of discussions of the tension between a focus on the "local" in international development and international law and the ways such discussions can displace more complex histories and relational understandings, see Abu-Lughod 2013; Alvarez et al. 2014; Asher 2009; Canfield 2018; Chatterjee, 2001; Darian-Smith 2013; Eslava 2015; Eslava et al. 2017.

60. For a cross-country comparison of this point, see Mikaela Luttrell-Rowland (2016), "The Recession as the Site of the Exceptional: Young People, Self-Determination and Social Mobility."

Chapter 2

1. See Tara Cookson (2018) *Unjust Conditions: Women's Work and the Hidden Cost of Cash Transfer Programs* for an important discussion of this point.

2. For a further discussion, see Altamirano et al. 2004; Crabtree 2006; Drinot 2014.

3. See White 2002b.

4. This is a broad and important literature on this point. For some comparative discussions, see Dehm 2021; Escobar 2011; Ferguson 1990; Han 2012; Krupa and Nugent 2015; Li 2007.

5. There is an interesting literature on spectral state presences in a range of country contexts. See Krupa and Nugent 2015; Navaro-Yashin 2002.

6. See Abrams 1988; Navaro-Yashin 2002.

7. See, for example, Cook 2020; Eslava 2015; Fine and Ruglis 2009; Han 2012; Hart and Boyden 2018; Katz 2004; Luttrell-Rowland 2012; White 2007.

8. Listening to young people as commentators of the state—largely in terms of how the observe and narrate daily life—allows for an emergence of patterns and a way of seeing young people able to be commentators, even in what sometimes could be partial, or fantastical, or affective descriptions. This chapter suggests both can be true. That is, their descriptions and "reporting" of insights can be partial, contradictory, even not factual, and still offer insight and generative details of the state. Two examples of this dynamic—namely how the young people of Lomas describe and understand their (state) schools and how they understand the (state) police—embody this tension. These two sites of state processes in their lives—and how they see, describe, and understand such interventions—provide critical evidence, not just of the working of the Peruvian state

202   Notes to Chapter 2

itself, but also of how rarely we actually take young people seriously as commentators of the state.

9. Focus group interview, Lima, 2008.

10. Interview, Lima, 2014.

11. Interview, Lima, 2014.

12. Interview, Lima, 2014.

13. Interview, Lima, 2014.

14. María Balarin's study of a group of youth living in one of the shantytowns in Lima, for example, notes:

> Participants expressed very high personal aspirations, in many cases unrealistic because of their unlikely fulfillment, which were always mediated by deep trust in the possibilities of personal success through education. While this myth of education is betrayed by the stark reality of an extremely poor public education system that has been compared to an "educational apartheid" . . . and by a neoliberal political system that is deeply implicated in the generation of social inequalities, participants never appeared to question it, and focused only on discussing the difficulties of accessing educational opportunities in a context where these, particularly at the tertiary level, are highly privatized. (Balarin 2011: 363; citation omitted)

See also Crivello 2011; Leinaweaver 2008.

15. For a wide range of important discussions about this, both in terms of Peru and across Latin America, see Balarin 2008; Drinot 2014; García 2005; Oglesby 2004; Oglesby 2007; Rousseau 2009; Schild 2000; Shever 2012.

16. See, for example, Kamphuis 2012.

17. For a discussion of this in terms of current inequalities and schooling in Peru, particularly for Indigenous children, see Ames 2012.

18. Carlos Newland (1994) defines the Teaching State as a set of institutions in Latin America aiming to create discipline and consistent curricular content.

19. For a cross-country analysis of this point, see Sandra Balagopalan (2014) *Inhabiting "Childhood": Children, Labour and Schooling in Postcolonial India.*

20. The legacies of Spanish colonial systems of domination, and their continuing influence on everyday inequality in Peru, are stark. See, for example, Madrid 2011; Penry 2019; Quijano 1972; Quijano 2007.

21. Recent scholarship by Peruvian educational experts Tamia Portugal Teillier and Francesca Uccelli Labarthe (2018) confirm this finding. They note in their study that the classroom was not typically where there was teaching and discussion about internal armed conflict. Instead, they found, like the young people in Lomas, most young people today have instead heard through family members or those who recounted direct experience.

22. Interview, Lima, 2010.

23. Interview, Lima, 2010.

24. Interview, Lima, 2010.

25. Interview, Lima, 2009.

Notes to Chapter 2   203

26. For a range of discussions of this point, see for example, Eslava 2015; Ferreira de Silva 2009; Heathcote 2019; Kapur 2018; Otto 1999; Pahuja 2011.

27. For some historical context, see, for example, Oliant 2017; Paulson 2015; Teillier and Uccelli Labarthe 2018; Uccelli et al. 2017.

28. Education scholar Michelle Bellino, for example, has documented the flattening of history in Guatemala's national curriculum, which relies on a narrative of human rights to frame the history of the armed conflict. She finds that Guatemalan textbooks disproportionally focus on post-war peace rather than conflict. Human rights are illustrated as a triumph and as a frame to shape the nation's "best story." For comparative discussions of the complexities of this point, see Bellino 2015; Oglesby 2007.

29. In 2000, the Peruvian Truth and Reconciliation Commission (Comisión de la Verdad y Reconciliación, CVR), drew on testimony of 17,000 people and produced a nine-volume Truth Commission Report (CVR 2003). They found that nearly 70,000 women, men, and children were killed or disappeared during the conflict. For a discussion of the Peruvian transitional justice initiatives after the conflict, as well as some methodological and conceptual challenges in the Peruvian case, see Bueno-Hansen 2010.

30. In her work on Peru's internal armed conflict, Kimberly Theidon (2013) found that any suggestion that a person sympathized with Sendero Luminoso justified denying them rights and committing violence against them. She says that the armed forces as well as the APRA political party, and the members of the conservative Catholic Church, have used this logic extensively to deny their own culpability for violence actions. She found the phrase "only the 'innocent' have rights in Peru" to be true "both in the past and in the present" (389). See also Paulson 2015; Uccelli et al. 2017.

31. For more details about this history, see Degregori 1996; Henríquez and Ewig 2013; Starn 1999.

32. For context to this important history, see Paulson 2010; Theidon 2013.

33. Guzmán was a philosophy professor in Ayacucho who often appeared wearing glasses and dressed in the suit of a university professor. The image of Guzmán as a professor in a suit echoed "the standard Peruvian association of wisdom and leadership with the white, the urban and the educated" (Starn et al. 1995: 407).

34. Commissioner Paloma Noceda, a member of Congress who led a major national campaign, passed a law to change all school textbooks without any mention of violence by the armed forces. Noceda is a member of Fuerza Popular, the political party that was in power from 1990–2000 during much of the internal armed conflict, under then-president Fujimori. Noceda and Fuerza Popular felt the portrayal of Fujimori in the textbooks didn't do justice to his presidency and proposed even refraining from using the term "internal armed conflict." The historical narrative of the internal armed conflict in Peru and how this history is taught and passed on to children remains, even as of this writing, highly contested.

35. See for example Teillier and Uccelli Labarthe 2018.

36. Dominant narratives of violence often reflect a simplification and polarization that reinforce particular types of violence as "natural." This is perhaps particularly true in contexts of state power and state violence. Such frames often implicitly and sometimes explicitly rely on particular temporal and spatial presentations of legality and law.

204   Notes to Chapter 2

See Cynthia Milton (2018) *Conflicted Memory: Military Cultural Interventions and the Human Rights Era in Peru* for a rich discussion of this point.

37. Focus group interview, Lima, 2008.

38. Sociologist and legal scholar Patricia Ewick (2014) writes:

> Imagination necessarily involves projecting a future or invoking a past, since that too involves an act of creative reconstruction. At the heart of imagination, in other words, is a counterfactual—what might have been; what might be. But whether it is retrospective or prospective, to imagine is always and necessarily to transcend the present. (162)

In the case of the young people of Lomas, this transcending took the form of both present-day description but also normative agreements about who the police "should be."

39. Focus group interview, Lima, 2009.

40. Interview, Lima, 2011.

41. Jelke Boesten (2010) has written about the ways that the police in Lima are notoriously unresponsive to women reporting domestic violence and notes that the domestic shelter offices often do not even have the necessary material needs (paper, computers, electricity, etc.) to help.

42. Nearly all the parents of the young people I spoke to in Lomas mentioned in some form present-day social and political isolation and their lack of access to state services. Some of the Lomas mothers spoke about this in terms of domestic violence in their lives and their neighbors' lives. Rates of domestic violence in Peru are comparatively high for Latin America. In two separate studies of domestic violence in Lima, 51% of women interviewed had experienced physical and sexual violence, and 88% percent of women interviewed knew someone who had experienced intimate violence in the previous twelve months (Alcalde 2010). While Peru became the first country in Latin America to pass laws specifically about domestic violence, everyday practices for justice often remain elusive. Domestic violence cases that get reported to the police rarely lead to convictions (see Boesten 2010).

43. Denise Ferreira da Silva (2009) writes about this in the context of Rio de Janeiro and offers relevant insights regarding the implications for theorizing the political and the police not being experienced by the community as a protective force.

44. See Leinaweaver 2008; Orlove 2002; Rasmussen 2017 for discussions of a range of ways the term "abandonment" has been a common framing used in the Peruvian Andes. These discussions in imagined conversation with Gilmore's (2008) discussion of "organized abandonment" have informed my thinking, and relational listening, for this chapter.

45. Focus group interview, Lima, 2008.

46. Focus group interview, Lima, 2008.

47. Interview, Lima, 2010.

48. Legal scholar Charis Kamphuis has found one of the outcomes of neoliberalism in Peru has been the choice by the government to weaken expenditure of the police and increase private security guards—for the sake of and paid for by private mining com-

Notes to Chapter 2   205

panies. The decrease of public police officers, as felt and described by the young people in Lomas, has been observed across the country. Kamphuis (2012) notes: "The United Nations ('UN') study estimated that in 2008 there were 100,000 private security guards in Peru, outnumbering the 92,000 public police officers. It also concluded that approximately half of the private security guards in Peru work for companies in the informal sector" (535).

49. For Peru, an important element of this shifting of state responsibility was also the shift towards neoliberalism in the 1990s and the presidency of Alberto Fujimori. "Fujimori introduced a radical program of liberalization that focused on removing subsidies, privatizing state-owned companies, and reducing the role of the state in the economy. This restructuring program followed the neoliberal guidelines established by the International Monetary Fund and the World Bank as a precondition for receiving loans and technical assistance" (Li 2015: 16).

50. Interview, Lima, 2009.

51. Neoliberal and structural adjustment policies and programs in Latin America often rely on women and motherhood for their success in ways that are both visible and invisible (Molyneux 2006).

52. For discussions of this in comparative perspectives, see Arias and Goldstein 2010; Goldstein 2003; Marquardt 2012; Santos 1977; Smith 2019.

53. Christina Ewig (2010) writes about health:

As the state retracted social policy commitments on health funding, it turned to "emergency" social policies such as those that funnelled international food donations to women's groups in poor communities. As a hedge against the worsening economy, the government encouraged the proliferation of communal soup kitchens run by women volunteers in poor communities, kitchens originally funded by the Catholic Church. (66)

54. I see this insight from the young people of Lomas in conversation with Clarissa Rile Hayward's notion about power and the ways all social actors are situated in relations of power, but not equally. Hayward's *De-Facing Power* is an ethnographic study of critical power relations based on two different schools in the United States. Hayward argues "power relations enable and constrain participants' freedom, to varying degrees and in varying ways" (2000: 8); therefore, a critical account of power has to attend "to the ways in which power's mechanisms enable and disable this capacity for 'action on' power'" (ibid.). In the case of Lomas, the mechanisms of power certainly include law and dominant understandings of legality.

55. American geographer Ruth Wilson Gilmore writes about the concept of "organized abandonment" (building on David Harvey's discussion in *The Limits to Capital*) as a critical feature of the ways contemporary systems of racial capitalism and neoliberalism work. Rather than just categorizing poor places as marginalized, or forgotten, or even abandoned, with the insertion of "organized," Gilmore (2008) draws attention to the role of states, as well as systems of capital and labor: "Abandoned places are also planned concentrations or sinks—of hazardous materials and destructive practices that are in turn sources of group-differentiated vulnerabilities to premature death" (36).

206 Notes to Chapter 3

Gilmore's point is not to flatten the people who live and work in such places, but rather to give attention to some of the many consequences.

Chapter 3

1. Interview, Lima, 2008.

2. For a discussion of this, see Ben Orlove (2002) *Lines in the Water: Nature and Culture at Lake Titicaca*.

3. The district that José refers to (Santa Patricia de Retama) is on the other side of the main road. The name of the district has been changed.

4. Focus group interview, Lima, 2008. In this group, Elena was present and asked to participate in running the discussion. Having Enrique and Elena in the focus groups with the young people changed the dynamics and quality of the early years of research exchange.

5. Lomas de Carabayllo consists of eighty-two smaller settlements. All have been formally recognized by the state, but at different historical moments. This billboard marks that moment. The characterization of "promised land" is particularly ironic given that Lomas was only recognized by the state in 2003, despite having been occupied from at least 1960. Unsurprisingly, recognition of ownership and occupation have been, and continue to be, key sites of contestation.

6. See the discussion by Charis Kamphuis (2010), "The Convergence of Public and Corporate Power in Peru: Yanacocha Mine, Campesino Dispossession, Privatized Coercion," regarding how colonialism, and later state law, were used as tools for dispossession of Indigenous land in Peru.

7. The way that land and dispossession was used as a colonial state strategy in Peru was similar in much of the world. K-Sue Park (2016) writes about this in terms of colonial America and what she notes as contact economy in the United States—the ways negotiations about land—particularly debt and loss—were used by colonizers as a tool of "indigenous dispossession," shaping not just the material realities of space and land. By contact economy, Park means "a market whose dynamics are determined by negotiations and transactions between groups that approach one another with fundamentally different premises concerning trade and the value of the objects that they nonetheless exchange" (1006). The negotiation of land rights, in Lomas and elsewhere, as part of the history of colonialism in Peru, is important context for this kind of framing of legality and "promised land" as seen in the billboard.

8. In his ethnography of China's Han settlers in the Xinjiang region, Tom Cliff notes his inclusion of everyday images throughout his 2016 book. For him, "incorporating image and text as communicative equals" serves not "simply as evidence for something which has already been stated in the text." Instead, "visual images demand the subconscious intellectual participation of the reader" (18). I echo this sentiment in this chapter and argue that these images and messages, from both state and non-state actors, carry weight.

9. See Das and Poole 2004; Poole 1997.

10. Tamara Walker's scholarship on the multiple ways slaves, particularly African slaves, used clothing in Peru to express "ideas about their status, and, in the process

challenged the social, economic, and—most importantly—legal boundaries of slavery" (2017b: 13) has informed my approach to reading everyday artifacts of life in Lomas. Her use of the visual and multiple sources of historical documents to study "the world of social and transactional relationships" in Peru's colonial history make an important contribution to the type of multimethod approach needed to better understand and contextualize the young people's understandings of state violence in Peru.

11. For wider context about this, see Cant 2012, Cant 2021.

12. Talía Dajes (2011) notes: "Both the revolution and the agrarian reform were organised by the government but they were conceived as mechanisms the population could use to gain greater political control and to channel the spirit of rebellion that had been unleashed by successive administrative failures" (136).

13. For a comparative discussion of the employment of visual culture across Latin America, see David Craven (2002) *Art and Revolution in Latin America, 1910–1990*.

14. For more on this topic, see Carlos Aguirre and Paulo Drinot (2017) *The Peculiar Revolution: Rethinking the Peruvian Experiment Under Military Rule*.

15. For a discussion of this point, see Espinoza 2013; Oliart 2017.

16. Even if not overtly discussed, we know children are, and have been, active members of communities—as observers, as participants in everyday life, and even as members of the (social, political, economic) economy. See Tobias Hecht (2002) *Minor Omissions: Children in Latin American History and Society*.

17. In a comparative context, the field of Black girlhood studies in the United States has been influential in the illustration of this point. See, for example, Brown 2013; Ibrahim 2021; Simmons 2015; Webster 2021; Wright 2016.

18. Using imagery of children in this way is not unique, to Peru or to the past. Karen Strassler (2006) writes about this dynamic in terms of Indonesia and notes "in post-Suharto Indonesia, children served as both a symbol of the nation's future and as the actual objects of the struggle to render the violence of the reform movement meaningful within a teleology of national progress" (54).

19. Christina Ewig notes these messages were often targeted towards poor, rural women with messages about family planning and infant health. They "used women to achieve their population goals, but also appropriated national and global feminist discourses to legitimize their actions" (2006: 635).

20. For important history and context of forced sterilization of women in Peru, see the digital archive of documents and images at Archivo PNSRPF at https://1996pnsrpf2000 .wordpress.com/ and the edited volume by Alejandra Ballón (2014).

21. For comparative discussions of this, see Bernstein 2011; Ross and Solinger 2017.

22. "The origins of the *retablo* date back to Spanish missionaries' efforts to convert indigenous peoples to Christianity through the use of images" (Ulfe 2014: 117).

23. The "Constructing Peru" campaign was initiated by the passing of law 29035.

24. See Kiran Asher (2009) *Black and Green: Afro-Colombians, Development, and Nature in the Pacific Lowlands* for more on how narratives of progress and modernity often play a part of the colonial project.

25. The history and politics of the shift from clientelism to rights language in terms of elections is important and interesting in Peru. Scholars have noted the ways clientelism

208 Notes to Chapter 3

has been used to shape elections, but also the ways politicians have advanced rights language as a clientelist technique (see Schneider and Zúniga-Hamlin 2005: 582). In Lomas, by holding the promises at arm's length, the orientation toward the future as embodied by the youth is continually invoked—as a means toward political incorporation.

26. Somos Perú is a center-right Christian democratic political party that first formed in 1995 under the name Somos Lima (We Are Lima). It began as a party to support the mayoral candidate Alberto Andrade, who was Lima's mayor from 1996–2002. In 2011, Somos Perú joined the Possible Peru Alliance (Alianza Electoral Perú Posible) and won 14.8% of the congressional election.

27. For a discussion of clientelism in Peru, see Paula Muñoz (2014), "An Informational Theory of Campaign Clientelism: The Case of Peru."

28. Paulo Drinot points out that a feature of state policies in Peru has been "a sustained human de-capitalization. As physical and financial capital (whether it be new infrastructural investment or international reserves) expands significantly in Peru, the under-investment in human capital is all the more striking" (2014: 173). The call from Lomas residents for roads and sidewalks therefore fits into a narrative of marginalization, where people in the "center" of Lima are perceived as receiving state infrastructure when those in Lomas feel they are not.

29. For a critical orientation to this point in a comparative perspective, see Cheryl Harris (1993) "Whiteness as Property." For a discussion of this point more broadly within Latin America, I have been heavily influenced by the scholarship of Tamara Walker (2017a, 2017b).

30. See Michael Freeman (2020) *A Magna Carta for Children? Rethinking Children's Rights.*

31. Jelke Boesten (2010) has written about the ways that the police are notoriously unresponsive to women reporting domestic violence in Lima and notes that the domestic shelter offices often do not even have the necessary material needs (paper, computers, electricity, etc.) to help.

32. María Balarin has conducted research with young people in Lima in similar marginalized areas about young people's perceptions of citizenship. She finds narratives that

> were highly individualistic and de-solidarized, where people appear to be on their own and have to cater for their well-being and find individual opportunities for advancement. What prevails is a paradoxical combination of a meritocratic imagination of citizenship, one in which personal effort and, very often, chance are seen as the only ways to well-being, in a nonmeritocratic contest, where opportunities of access and especially of outcomes are scares and unequally distributed. (2014: 139)

For discussions of this point beyond Peru, see Goodale and Postero (2013) *Neoliberalism, Interrupted: Social Change and Contested Governance in Contemporary Latin America.*

33. For a robust discussion of a range of comparative examples of theorizing of the translocal in everyday practice, see Alvarez et al. 2014; Canfield et al. 2021; Dehm 2021; Lima and Alvarez 2014; Luttrell-Rowland et al. 2021.

Notes to Chapter 4   209

34. Ruth Wilson Gilmore's discussion of forgotten places and "organized abandonment" as a critical feature of the ways contemporary systems of racial capitalism and neoliberalism work is relevant here. See Gilmore 2008.

Chapter 4

1. MNNATSOP includes a coalition of organizations and movements from across Peru and represents 10,000 working young people ages 8–17 as members. MNNATSOP is explicitly secular in its approach but otherwise shares the fundamental values of MANTHOC, one of its base movements. For further reading on the principles of MNNATSOP, see Taft 2019.

2. "*Colaboradores*" is a Spanish word the MANTHOC children use to speak about the role adults can play; it roughly translates to "allies."

3. MANTHOC members have been strategic in outlining the contours of what kind of state recognition they seek. Partly this is about the entry of children workers' voices into what they call "public space" (as discussed later in this chapter), but it's also about the changing of laws, codes, and legal norms. For example, one specific campaign they pushed for was the changing of the children's rights code in Peru to lower the minimum working age. This point about recognition from the state, and what exactly recognition looks like, is interesting in relation to larger conversations about what constitutes a worker. Julia Tomassetti (2012) raises relevant questions within the U.S. context and notes the importance of paying attention to the rationales used by lawmakers within the rapidly expanding and changing configurations of who is considered a worker.

4. While statistics about working children are often unreliable and underrepresentative, one recent statistic from the International Labor Organization suggest that there were approximately 2 million child and adolescent workers in Peru, and 168 million worldwide. This number is quite different from findings from Rodriguez and Vargas (2009) with data collected by the National Institute for Statistics and Information (INEI), in which they found 3.3 million Peruvians between the ages of 5–17 working, a number which is 42% of the national population See Jessica Taft (2013) *Nothing About Us, Without Us: Critiques of the International Labor Organization's Approach to Child Labor from the Movements of Working Children* for a range of responses about the framing of normative statistics by the ILO.

5. See Spyrou et al. (2018), *Reimagining Childhood Studies*.

6. MANTHOC is just one of multiple movements of working children in Latin America. For a history and discussion of the emergence of these movements, see Cussiánovich and Méndez Quintana 2008.

7. Sonia Alvarez has done relevant work about what she termed the NGO-ization that happened with some social movements throughout Latin America in the early 1990s. This trend was also part of a larger historical moment where mainstreaming of identity politics was happening in Peru, a point that is critical not to look over when understanding the core principles of MANTHOC. See Alvarez 1999; Alvarez 2009; Alvarez et al. 2017.

8. While MANTHOC has chapters throughout Lima, they do not have a chapter in Lomas de Caraballyo as of 2022.

210   Notes to Chapter 4

9. In the context of the United States, Jennifer Nash writes about Black feminist love-politics that are grounded in movement work and that serve to produce "new forms of political communities as a kind of affective politics" (2013: 3). There are important links to make about the role of emotions in movement and organizing work and that MANTHOC shows to be important beyond only identity politics.

10. He explains that when MANTHOC began in 1976 out of the Young Christian Workers (Joventud Obrera Cristiana, JOC), the young people did not articulate or use the language of "tenderness" but rather spoke of working with "dignity." As the movement grew, and as its leaders worked to create a local school for child workers in the 1980s, Cussiánovich and the working young people formed a language of tenderness and also a theoretical framework.

11. This point supports Sally Merry's body of work, in her book *Human Rights and Gender Violence: Translating International Law into Local Justice* (2006a) and her article *"Transnational Human Rights and Local Activism: Mapping the Middle"* (2006b), which both show how the language of rights can offer global legitimacy in the face of violence and inequality.

12. I went to IFEJANT for the first time in 2007 and began interviewing Cussiánovich thereafter. In one of our early interviews, as I arrived with pages of handwritten notes and questions, he humored me and took my questions seriously. But he ended the interview by suggesting I had it wrong to focus on him: It was actually the young people of MANTHOC with whom I should meet, speak, and work. They are the leaders and creators of this movement. Knowing about his life and ideas are critical for context of the MANTHOC movement, but I take his point seriously that it is not a movement about him.

13. While this point may seem obvious on the surface, I emphasize it to underscore the ways that reading MANTHOC should not just be seen in terms of resistance of the larger political and social happenings in Peru during the time of the armed conflict, but rather also the ways that resistance could be interpreted for its constative features.

14. For more on this point, see Cynthia Milton (2014) *Art from a Fractured Past: Memory and Truth-Telling in Post–Shining Path Peru.* She describes the layered and complex ways that "In Peru, memory is not synonymous with human rights" (37).

15. Dianne Otto (2015) notes:

[I]ncreased acceptability of executive law-making and reliance on economic, technocratic, and military experts to solve global problems. Crisis governance has fostered neoliberal expansionism by legitimating the adoption of short term, quick fix responses that ignore the larger historical context of causation and individualize responsibility, dismissing analytical and critical perspectives, shutting out democratic everyday structural inequalities and injustices as given. (116)

See also Charlesworth 2002; Cheesman 2015; Rajah 2012.

16. For a rich discussion of what it may mean to listen to multitudes, in the U.S. context, see Jennifer Nash (2019) *Black Feminism Reimagined: After Intersectionality.*

17. For an important comparative discussion on holding space for tensions and within movements, see Alondra Nelson (2011) *Body and Soul: The Black Panther Party and the Fight Against Medical Discrimination.*

18. Interview, Lima, 2014.

19. Field notes, Lima, 2014.

20. For a further discussion of this, see Manfred Liebel (2020) *Decolonizing Childhoods: From Exclusion to Dignity.*

21. See Alderson and Morrow 2020; Crivello et al. 2009; Fine 2017; Hart and Tyrer 2006; Morrow and Richards 1996; Ridge 2011.

22. For more on this point, see Benporath 2003.

23. See Jennifer Nash's (2019) discussion of intersectionality and debates around if it should be read not just in terms of individuals, but towards and with structures.

24. Participatory observation field notes, Lima, 2014.

25. Interview, Lima, 2014.

26. While not fully explored in this chapter, the members of MANTHOC and their ideas about their work and identities offer insights to the literatures on the concept of recognition. Nancy Fraser and Axel Honneth (2003) have debated the politics of recognition in *Redistribution or Recognition? A Political-Philosophical Exchange,* and Honneth notes in his critique of Fraser the need for labor itself to be coded as a form of recognition.

27. In her work on informal female workers in India, Rita Agarwala (2012) notes how informal workers have created a movement that privileges the role of the state, while simultaneously pressing to address their needs. She writes:

> Because their ultimate goal is to attract the Indian state's attention, informal workers' transnational efforts have not veered away from local issues and a commitment to empowerment. On the contrary, informal workers' organizations in India go out of their way to yield voice to their members and appear as links to the mass vote bank of informal workers, who are key pegs in the state's neoliberal agenda. It is this link that attracts state attention. Informal workers' transnational efforts in India's democratic context yield important insights into the prospects of Southern leadership in transnational efforts and the impact of transnational labor alliances on domestic class relations. (445)

Agarwala's work argues that as a pragmatic tool, there can be much to be gained by placing the nation-state as a central focus. I'm not suggesting, therefore, that MANTHOC members exhibit false consciousness or even lack sophistication in their organizing. Indeed, as Agarwala shows with the Self-Employed Women's Association (SEWA), other informal workers use such techniques as tactical and innovative organizing strategies.

28. Personal communication, 2014.

29. Here I am indebted to many for discussions of ethical tensions, dilemmas, and practices in ethnographic fieldwork, and the role of power and standpoint in discerning those tensions. See, for example, Brown 2013; Chowdhury 2011; Chua 2012; Chua 2018; Collins 2019; Darian-Smith and McCarty 2017; Edelman 2009; Fine 2017; Fujii 2011; Fujii 2018; Mohanty 2003; Schwartz-Shea & Yanow 2011; Torre 2009; White and Choudhury 2007; Wiebe 2016.

30. There is much written about the complexities of this point. Some discussions

212   Notes to Chapter 5

that have influenced my thinking on this include Collins 2019; Incite! 2017; Nash 2013; Nash 2019.

31. This obscuring for political purposes was particularly true before 2013 when the organization only spoke of child leadership and a child-centered constitution. Their new constitution includes adult supporters in a more overt way; the movement is still trying to clarify what that means for them.

32. See Hart 2008; Lundy 2007.

33. Discussing child participation in Bangladesh, Sarah White and Shyamol Choudhury (2007) point out that a common feature of child participation in development organizations is the "strong element of show, or theatricality." They write about the complexities of testimony of children as forms of spectacle. They note participation as spectacle:

> blurs the picture with respect to agency: who is authorizing action, and on whose terms does it take place. Children who are posed as subjects in giving voice to their experiences simultaneously became objects of the gaze of others. . . . This makes it difficult to accept them at face value as the unmediated insertion of an authentic "child voice" in the development arena. On the contrary, the timbre of the voice seems to change with the context in which it sounds. (530)

34. See Alvarez 1999; Smith 2012; White and Choudhury 2007.

35. See Bejarano et al. 2019.

36. For a discussion of this with regard to other social movements, see Mark Goodale and Sally Engle Merry (2007) *The Practice of Human Rights: Tracking Law Between the Local and the Global.*

37. Much normative research to date about child labor focuses largely on the need to protect individual child workers. MANTHOC's goals to speak from a collective standpoint of organized consciousness is therefore provocative not only because of the specific claims they make, but also because of their wish to speak for more than individual children.

38. Both Marx and Habermas have argued that democracy and capitalism fundamentally depend on the functioning of a public sphere separate from both state and market. While MANTHOC's interpretation of politics relies on core ideas about the exchange of ideas, participation, and voice (i.e., what they term "child protagonism"), the use of "public space" by MANTHOC differs from the public sphere as defined by Habermas.

Chapter 5

1. Nancy Fraser makes an argument that the politics of "recognition," "representation," and "redistribution" can and must be understood relationally. Fraser believes core to the justice process is the requirement for "social arrangements that permit all to participate as peers in social life" (2008: 16). For Fraser, this means people have access to participate in the political process in decisions that will affect their lives. In many ways, MANTHOC is a good example of a movement that is calling for new forms of recognition claims.

Notes to Chapter 5   213

2. See Bourdillon 2010; Liebel 2020; Taft 2019.

3. See Rehfeld 2011 for an interesting discussion of children's limited political participation.

4. For other discussions of new possibilities of child subjectivity, see Hart and Boyden 2018.

5. María Balarin's ethnographic research with young people in Lima about citizenship is a good example of how young people in Peru internalize messages about statehood as linked to discourses of citizenship. Balarin (2014) found that one of the main themes to emerge among the young people she worked with was

> one where individual effort is seen to be the only way forward, mainly through education and amidst a generally hostile spatial, communal and institutional context that leaves them to their own devices to find their ways through a highly privatized and unregulated system of education, and with little opportunities for fair employment. (56)

The end result, she found, was a "very precarious imagination of citizenship" because of an absence of a "collective idiom of claims making" (Balarin 2014, describing Wacquant). For a larger discussion of this both within Peru and comparatively, see, for example, Bhandar 2018; Bueno-Hansen, 2015; Ewig 2010; García 2003; García 2005; Lugones 2003; Perry 2018.

6. See Cussiánovich and Quintana 2008; Hernández 2016; Levitt and Merry 2009.

7. Public mission statement on the MANTHOC website in 2009.

8. Jessica Taft (2019) writes:

> With the growing investment of the ILO's program to end child labor and the changes in Peruvian law that prohibited work, Peru's working children in the 1990s found themselves facing criminalization, including the threat of being removed from their families, and increasing stigmatization as they were discussed as a visible maker of both poverty and national "underdevelopment." (25)

9. In 1999 the ILO put forward the "decent work" agenda as a key overarching discourse of the organization. One of the core pillars of this discourse is core labor standards that include the prohibition of child labor. As pointed out by Leah Vosko (2002), however, the other pillar of the decent work agenda at the ILO is its commitment to marginalized workers. Vosko, as such, reveals the power for groups who have been made marginalized by using the discourse of decent work. For a contemporary example of the mobilization of the discourse of decent work and everyday justice, see Adelle Blackett (2019) *Everyday Transgression: Domestic Workers' Transnational Challenges to International Labor Law.*

10. Personal communication, MNNATSOP, 2009.

11. Interview, Lima, 2008.

12. Interview, Lima, 2007.

13. The National Movement of Organized Working Children and Adolescents of Peru (Movimiento Naccional de Niños y Adolescentes Trabajadores Organizados del Peru, MNNATSOP) is the larger coalition of child workers organizations in Peru, of which MANTHOC is a part.

214   Notes to Chapter 5

14. Verónica Schild's definition of the neoliberal state is useful here. She defines it as emerging institutional practices and discourses for empowering people for the market and making them responsible for their own selves, including their own failures, and ultimately their own poverty (Schild 2000: 282).

15. A key contribution that critical legal scholarship has offered over the last decade has been to question the boundaries around the "who" question of law. Whose voices are counted in law, as legal subjects, and whose voices are discounted? Whose concerns resonate within the very structure and imaginary of "law" and who gets left in the margins? These debates and discussions remain relevant to the challenges MANTHOC faces.

16. Interview, Lima, 2014.

17. Interview, Lima, 2014.

18. Interview, Lima, 2014.

19. See Gilmore 2007; Gilmore 2008; and Harvey 2018 for important discussions of the notion of organized state abandonment.

20. See Darian-Smith 2015.

21. See also Bueno-Hansen 2015; Ewig 2006; García 2003; García 2005; Leinaweaver 2008; Stepputat 2005.

22. For more on this subject across country contexts, see Goodale 2008; Goodale 2013; Goodale and Merry 2007; Sarat and Ewick 2015.

23. One of the basic problems with this singular formulation in terms of identity politics is how easily certain rights and identities can be made invisible (see Collins 2000; Collins 2019; Chenshaw 1991; Nash 2019). Kimberle Crenshaw's work on intersectionality, for example, has been critical in showing the ways law needs greater conceptual tools for understanding multiple identities around citizenship, rights, and vulnerabilities. Indeed, when women sought equality in terms of citizenship, it was equality with white, European, middle-class, able-bodied heterosexual men. In other words, the imagined male citizen was himself imbued with hierarchal norms and assumptions.

24. In the context of the United States, Inderpal Grewal (2017) writes that in the face of neoliberalism, "divisions of public and private become difficult to sustain, as sovereignty is claimed by white male power and privilege, and as corporations carry out the work of the military and as nongovernmental organizations take over the welfare function of the state" (5).

25. There exists decades-long feminist conversation about the pitfalls of the dichotomous formula of sameness/difference built into discussions of recognition and citizenship. One of the major critiques by feminists has been the denial of genuine citizenship for women, or the reliance on legal structures that work to exclude women.

26. As explained by Pascha Bueno-Hansen (2015), Peruvian decolonial theorist Anibal Quijano has written extensively on "the intersubjective relations of domination," which is a system of domination in Peru that

> trap[s] the colonized population in the past along a linear temporal trajectory that glorifies Europe as modern. Indigenous languages were deemed inferior to Spanish. This systematic control of social relations and communications func-

tions through to the present day and continues to serve Euro-centered capitalism and the European *criollo* descendants in Peru. The dehumanization and exploitation of colonial subjects blocks the radical redistribution of power and full citizenship through the valorization of all peoples. (144)

27. Looking at this point across movements is interesting. Keeanga-Yamahtta Taylor traces the history of the Black Lives Matter movement and the intentional ways the messaging has centered and named state violence, rather than solely police brutality (Taylor 2016).

28. Interview, Lima, 2016.

29. Interview, Lima, 2016.

30. The idea of citizenship as something to linked to the public sphere is a conception that furthers a dichotomous understanding of public/private and active/passive spheres: a feature of traditional discussions of citizenship that grows out of a long history in Peru. See García 2005.

31. Sonia Alvarez and others have done critical work on the need to move beyond the binary of "good" versus "bad" NGOs and their relationship with the adaptation of state language. See Alvarez 2009; Hernández 2016; Liebel 2020.

32. There is an important literature on this by scholars who have noted the role activists have played around the world to show peace is not just the absence of war. See Gina Heathcote and Dianne Otto (2014), *Rethinking Peacekeeping, Gender Equality and Collective Security*.

33. See also Stéphanie Rousseau (2009), *Women's Citizenship in Peru: The Paradoxes of Neopopulism in Latin America*.

Chapter 6

1. For a discussion of this history, see Ballón 2014; Boesten 2010; Ewig 2010.

2. Wendy Brown (2006) notes:

Depoliticization involves removing a political phenomenon from comprehension of its historical emergence and from a recognition of the powers that produce and contour it. No matter its particular form and mechanics, depoliticization always eschews power and history in the representation of its subject. (2006: 15)

Here I drawn on Brown's ideas of depoliticization to ask what a depoliticized state looks like, and also what kinds of subjectivities it both produces and reflects.

3. As of 2020, at the national level of Peru, there were 569 CCONNA boards throughout the country. To read more about these participatory spaces, see https://www.mimp .gob.pe/direcciones/dgnna/contenidos/articulos.php?codigo=30

4. See Zapata 2019.

5. For a broad discussion of this point in terms of Peru's history of education reform, see Oliart 2017.

6. Melinda Cooper (2017) *Family Values: Between Neoliberalism and the New Social Conservatism* shows how the preservation of the unit of "the family" is a rational partner

216 Notes to Chapter 6

to neoliberalism more broadly, in the ways the logics to roll back social services comply with having a strong family unit.

7. See Rosa Linda Fregoso and Cynthia Bejarano's 2010 edited volume, *Terrorizing Women: Feminicide in the Americas*, for an example with regard to women's rights and violence against women, on this point.

8. Sanborn and Paredes 2014: frontispiece in Spanish.

9. See, for example, Alvarez et al. 2017; Baiocchi and Ganuza 2017; McNulty 2011.

10. For details of the challenges implementing *consulta previa* in the case of Peru, see Sanborn et al. 2016.

11. One example of this is that Indigenous peoples of Peru have not been consulted, or given permission, for state-led land extraction practices over natural resources, particularly in mining regions in Peru. See Fabiana Li's important 2015 book, *Unearthing Conflict: Corporate Mining, Activism, and Expertise in Peru*, to read more on this point.

12. See Cornwall and Coelho 2007; McNulty 2011.

13. For rich discussions on this in a range of contexts, see Alcalde 2010; Boesten 2010; Bueno-Hansen 2015, Collins 2000; Collins 2019; Nash 2019.

14. See Verónica Schild (2019) "Feminisms, the Environment and Capitalism: On the Necessary Ecological Dimension of a Critical Latin American Feminism." Schild discusses the newest wave of feminist organizing across Latin America that ties together critical movements and that is "explicitly linking gender demands to the end of a neoliberal capitalist model of development and its devasting social, economic and ecological effects on Latin America's overwhelming majority" (24).

15. Interview, Lima, 2008.

16. See *Ley del Sistema Nacional de Atención Integral al Niño y el Adolescente*, law 26518.

17. Interview, Lima, 2009.

18. Interview, Lima, 2009.

19. Interview, Lima, 2009.

20. Interview, Lima, 2008.

21. See Spyrou et al. (2018), *Reimagining Childhood Studies*.

22. My thinking on this point has been influenced by the wide range of literature on the dangers and meanings of dichotomous logics used in international development endeavors. See, for example, Abu-Lughod 2013; Bhandar 2018; Chowdhury 2011; Eslava et al. 2017; Gupta and Ferguson 1992; Lugones 2010; Tsing 2005; West 2006.

23. For a wider discussion of this, see Ratna Kapur (2018) *Gender, Alterity and Human Rights: Freedom in a Fishbowl*.

24. Interview, Lima, 2008.

25. Interview, Lima, 2008.

26. Interview, Lima, 2009.

27. See Alvarez 2009; Darian-Smith 2013; Escobar and Alvarez 1992; Klug 2000.

28. Law professor Sundhya Pahuja (2011) notes:

Certain concepts are typically understood to be the foundation or grounds of international law; "the nation state," "the international" and "legality" are all categories which, to paraphrase Herzog, seem undeniable, immune to revision and located outside the operation of international law, if not outside society and politics. This remains true even when these foundational terms are contested normatively, as being, for instance, too limited in their scope. But as we shall see in detail in each telling instance, when international law operates in the world, it does not simply meet a set of pre-existing categories that must be slotted into its logic. Rather it produces its own subjects, as well as the objects of its rule. (26)

29. Interview, Lima, 2016.

30. Interview, Lima, 2016.

31. For examples of this with regard to economic projects, packaged as about equity, in Latin America, see Cookson 2018; García 2005; Goodale and Postero 2013; Schild 2015; Quijano 2000.

32. For some discussions that have influenced my thinking on this point, see Darian-Smith 2013; Canfield et al. 2021; Eslava 2015; Ferreira da Silva 2009; Merry 2006a; Ticktin 2011; Tsing 2005.

Afterword

1. For important scholarship on this point, see Bueno-Hansen 2015; Canfield et al. 2021; Dehm 2021; Kazanjian 2016; Li 2007; Lima and Alvarez 2014; Sassen 2002; Sharma and Gupta 2006; Tsing 2005.

2. See, for example, Assis 2021; Bhandar and Ziadah 2020; Collins 2019; Mignolo 2012.

3. See Cerwonka and Malkki's critical 2007 book *Improvising Theory: Process and Temporality in Ethnographic Fieldwork* for a discussion of this point of making and unmaking in the research process.

4. For a discussion of organized abandonment, see Gilmore 2008; Harvey 2018.

5. Seven of the ten countries in the world with the highest rate of female murder are in Latin America; feminist activists created the Ni Una Menos movement to decry its core causes and continuities.

Works Cited

Abrams, Philip. 1988. "Notes on the Difficulty of Studying the State." *Journal of Historical Sociology* 1 (1): 58–89.

Abu-Lughod, Lila. 1993. *Writing Women's Worlds: Bedouin Stories.* Berkeley: University of California Press.

———. 2013. *Do Muslim Women Need Saving?* Cambridge, MA: Harvard University Press.

Ackerly, Brooke A. 2008. *Universal Human Rights in a World of Difference.* Cambridge, UK, and New York: Cambridge University Press.

Agarwala, Rina. 2012. "The State and Labor in Transnational Activism: The Case of India." *Journal of Industrial Relations* 54 (4): 443–458.

Aguirre, Carlos, and Paulo Drinot. 2017. *The Peculiar Revolution: Rethinking the Peruvian Experiment Under Military Rule.* Austin: University of Texas Press.

Ahmed, Sara. 2014. *The Cultural Politics of Emotion.* New York: Routledge.

Albarrán, Elena Jackson. 2104. *Seen and Heard in Mexico: Children and Revolutionary Cultural Nationalism.* Lincoln: University of Nebraska Press.

Alcalde, M. Cristina. 2010. *The Woman in the Violence: Gender, Poverty, and Resistance in Peru.* Nashville: Vanderbilt University Press.

Alcoff, Linda. 1991. "The Problem of Speaking for Others." *Cultural Critique* 20 (Winter): 5–32.

Alderson, Priscilla, and Virginia Morrow. 2020. *The Ethics of Research with Children and Young People.* New York: Sage.

Allen, Barbara L. 2003. *Uneasy Alchemy: Citizens and Experts in Louisiana's Chemical Corridor Disputes.* Cambridge, MA: MIT Press.

Altamirano, TeóFilo, James Copestake, Adolfo Figueroa, and Katie Wright-Revolledo. 2004. "Universal and Local Understanding of Poverty in Peru." *Global Social Policy* 4 (3): 313–336.

220 Works Cited

Alvarez, Sonia E. 1999. "Advocating Feminism: The Latin American Feminist NGO 'Boom.'" *International Feminist Journal of Politics* 1 (2): 181–209.

———. 2009. "Beyond NGO-Ization?: Reflections from Latin America." *Development* 52: 175–184.

Alvarez, Sonia E., Claudia de Lima Costa, Verónica Feliu, Rebecca J. Hester, Norma Klahn, and Millie Thayer, eds. 2014. *Translocalities/Translocalidades: Feminist Politics of Translation in the Latin/a Americas*. Durham and London: Duke University Press.

Alvarez, Sonia E., Jeffrey W. Rubin, Millie Thayer, Gianpaolo Baiocchi, and Agustín Laó-Montes, eds. 2017. *Beyond Civil Society: Activism, Participation, and Protest in Latin America*. Durham: Duke University Press.

Ames, Patricia. 2002. *Para ser iguales, para ser distintos: Educación, escritura y poder en el Perú*. Lima: IEP.

———. 2012. "Language, Culture and Identity in the Transition to Primary School: Challenges to Indigenous Children's Rights to Education in Peru." *International Journal of Educational Development* 32 (3): 454–462.

———. 2013. "Constructing New Identities? The Role of Gender and Education in Rural Girls' Life Aspirations in Peru." *Gender and Education* 25 (3): 267–283.

Anzaldúa, Gloria. 1987. *Borderlands / La Frontera: The New Mestiza*. San Francisco: Aunt Lute Books.

Archivo PNSRPF. "Proyecto de Archivo e Investigación Crítica Acerca Del «Programa Nacional de Salud Reproductiva y Planificación Familiar»." https://1996pnsrpf2000.wordpress.com/

Arias, Enrique Desmond, and Daniel M. Goldstein, eds. 2010. *Violent Democracies in Latin America*. Durham: Duke University Press.

Asher, Kiran. 2009. *Black and Green: Afro-Colombians, Development, and Nature in the Pacific Lowlands*. Durham: Duke University Press.

Assis, Mariana Prandini. 2021. "Strategic Litigation in Brazil: Exploring the Translocalisation of a Legal Practice." *Transnational Legal Theory* 12 (3): 360–389.

Auyero, Javier. 2012. *Patients of the State: The Politics of Waiting in Argentina*. Durham: Duke University Press.

Auyero, Javier, and Débora Alejandra Swistun. 2009. *Flammable: Environmental Suffering in an Argentine Shantytown*. Oxford: Oxford University Press.

Bacchetta, Paola, Sunaina Maira, and Howard Winant, eds. 2018. *Global Raciality: Empire, Postcoloniality, Decoloniality*. New York: Routledge.

Baiocchi, Gianpaolo, and Ernesto Ganuza. 2016. *Popular Democracy: The Paradox of Participation*. Stanford: Stanford University Press.

Balagopalan, Sarada. 2014. *Inhabiting "Childhood": Children, Labour and Schooling in Postcolonial India*. Basingstoke and New York: Palgrave Macmillan.

Balarin, María. 2008. "Promoting Educational Reforms in Weak States: The Case of Radical Policy Discontinuity in Peru." *Globalisation, Societies and Education* 6 (2): 163.

———. 2011. "Global Citizenship and Marginalisation: Contributions Towards a Political Economy of Global Citizenship." *Globalisation, Societies and Education* 9 (3–4): 355–366.

———. 2014. "Laclau's Theory of Hegemony: Between Sociocultural Politics and a Political Economy of Citizenship." In *Peru in Theory*. Edited by Paulo Drinot, pp. 125–142. New York: Palgrave Macmillan.

Ballón, Alejandra, ed. 2014. *Memorias Del Caso Peruano de Esterilización Forzada*. Colección Las Palabras Del Mudo. Lima: Biblioteca Nacional del Perú, Fondo Editorial.

Bejarano, Carolina Alonso, Lucia López Juárez, Mirian A. Mijangos García, and Daniel M. Goldstein. 2019. *Decolonizing Ethnography: Undocumented Immigrants and New Directions in Social Science*. Durham: Duke University Press.

Bellino, Michelle J. 2015. "The Risks We Are Willing to Take: Youth Civic Development in 'Postwar' Guatemala." *Harvard Educational Review* 85 (4): 537–561.

———. 2017. *Youth in Postwar Guatemala: Education and Civic Identity in Transition*. New Brunswick, Camden, and Newark: Rutgers University Press.

Benporath, Sigal R. 2003. "Autonomy and Vulnerability: On Just Relations Between Adults and Children." *Journal of Philosophy of Education* 37 (1): 127–145.

Bernstein, Robin. 2011. *Racial Innocence: Performing American Childhood from Slavery to Civil Rights*. New York: NYU Press.

Bhandar, Brenna. 2018. *Colonial Lives of Property: Law, Land, and Racial Regimes of Ownership*. Durham: Duke University Press.

Bhandar, Brenna, and Rafeef Ziadah. 2020. *Revolutionary Feminisms: Conversations on Collective Action and Radical Thought*. New York: Verso Books.

Birla, Ritu. 2009. *Stages of Capital: Law, Culture, and Market Governance in Late Colonial India*. Durham: Duke University Press Books.

Blackett, Adelle. 2019. *Everyday Transgressions: Domestic Workers' Transnational Challenge to International Labor Law*. Ithaca: ILR Press/Cornell University Press.

Boesten, Jelke. 2003. "Poor Women in Peru: Reproducers of Poverty and Poverty Relievers." *Women's Studies Quarterly* 31(3–4): 113–128.

———. 2010. *Intersecting Inequalities: Women and Social Policy in Peru, 1990–2000*. University Park: Pennsylvania State University Press.

———. 2014. *Sexual Violence During War and Peace: Gender, Power, and Post-Conflict Justice in Peru*. New York: Palgrave Macmillan.

Bourdillon, Michael, ed. 2010. *Rights and Wrongs of Children's Work*. New Brunswick: Rutgers University Press.

Britton-Purdy, Jedediah, David Singh Grewal, Amy Kapczynski, and K. Sabeel Rahman. 2020. "Building a Law-and-Political-Economy Framework: Beyond the Twentieth-Century Synthesis." *Yale Law Journal* 129 (6): 1784–1835.

Brown, Ruth Nicole. 2013. *Hear Our Truths: The Creative Potential of Black Girlhood*. Urbana, Chicago, and Springfield: University of Illinois Press.

Brown, Wendy. 2006. *Regulating Aversion: Tolerance in the Age of Identity and Empire*. Princeton: Princeton University Press.

Bueno-Hansen, Pascha. 2010. "Engendering Transitional Justice: Reflections on the Case of Peru." *Journal of Peacebuilding and Development* 5 (3): 61–74.

———. 2015. *Feminist and Human Rights Struggles in Peru: Decolonizing Transitional Justice*. Urbana, Chicago, and Springfield: University of Illinois Press.

222   Works Cited

Burt, Jo-Marie. 2009. "Guilty as Charged: The Trial of Former Peruvian President Alberto Fujimori for Human Rights Violations." *International Journal of Transitional Justice* 3 (3): 384–405.

Cadena, Marisol de la. 1998. "Silent Racism and Intellectual Superiority in Peru." *Bulletin of Latin American Research* 17 (2): 143–164.

Campt, Tina M. 2017. *Listening to Images.* Durham: Duke University Press.

Canfield, Matthew C. 2018. "Disputing the Global Land Grab: Claiming Rights and Making Markets Through Collaborative Governance." *Law & Society Review* 52 (4): 994–1025.

Canfield, Matthew C., Julia Dehm, and Marisa Fassi. 2021. "Translocal Legalities: Local Encounters with Transnational Law." *Transnational Legal Theory* 12 (3): 335–359.

Cant, Anna. 2012. "'Land for Those Who Work It': A Visual Analysis of Agrarian Reform Posters in Velasco's Peru." *Journal of Latin American Studies* 44 (1): 1–37.

———. 2021. *Land Without Masters: Agrarian Reform and Political Change Under Peru's Military.* Austin: University of Texas Press.

Cerwonka, Allaine, and Liisa H. Malkki. 2007. *Improvising Theory: Process and Temporality in Ethnographic Fieldwork.* Chicago: University of Chicago Press.

Charlesworth, Hilary. 2002. "International Law: A Discipline of Crisis." *Modern Law Review* 65 (3): 377–392.

Chatterjee, Piya. 2001. *A Time for Tea: Women, Labor, and Post/Colonial Politics on an Indian Plantation.* Durham: Duke University Press.

Cheesman, Nick. 2015. *Opposing the Rule of Law: How Myanmar's Courts Make Law and Order.* Cambridge, UK: Cambridge University Press.

———. 2018. "Rule-of-Law Ethnography." *Annual Review of Law and Social Science* 14 (1): 167–184.

Chowdhury, Elora Halim. 2011. *Transnationalism Reversed: Women Organizing Against Gendered Violence in Bangladesh.* Albany: SUNY Press.

Chua, Lynette J. 2012. "Pragmatic Resistance, Law, and Social Movements in Authoritarian States: The Case of Gay Collective Action in Singapore: Pragmatic Resistance." *Law & Society Review* 46 (4): 713–748.

———. 2018. *The Politics of Love in Myanmar: LGBT Mobilization and Human Rights as a Way of Life.* Stanford: Stanford University Press.

Cliff, Tom. 2016. *Oil and Water: Being Han in Xinjiang.* Chicago and London: University of Chicago Press.

Cole, Jennifer, and Deborah Durham, eds. 2006. *Generations and Globalization: Youth, Age, and Family in the New World Economy.* Bloomington: Indiana University Press.

Collins, Patricia Hill. 2019. *Intersectionality as Critical Social Theory.* Durham: Duke University Press.

———. 2000. *Black Feminist Thought: Knowledge, Consciousness, and the Politics of Empowerment,* 2nd edition. New York: Routledge.

Constable, Marianne. 2005. *Just Silences: The Limits and Possibilities of Modern Law.* Princeton: Princeton University Press.

Cook, Daniel Thomas. 2020. *The Moral Project of Childhood.* New York: NYU Press.

Works Cited 223

Cookson, Tara Patricia. 2018. *Unjust Conditions: Women's Work and the Hidden Cost of Cash Transfer Programs*. Oakland: University of California Press.

Cooper, Melinda. 2017. *Family Values: Between Neoliberalism and the New Social Conservatism*. Cambridge, MA: MIT Press.

Cornwall, Andrea, and Vera Schatten Coelho. 2007. *Spaces for Change?: The Politics of Citizen Participation in New Democratic Arenas*. London and New York: Zed Books.

Crabtree, John, ed. 2006. *Making Institutions Work in Peru: Democracy, Development and Inequality Since 1980*. London: Institute for the Study of the Americas.

Craven, David. 2002. *Art and Revolution in Latin America, 1910–1990*. New Haven: Yale University Press.

Crenshaw, Kimberle. 1991. "Mapping the Margins: Intersectionality, Identity Politics, and Violence Against Women of Color." *Stanford Law Review* 43 (6): 1241–1299.

Crivello, Gina. 2011. "'Becoming Somebody': Youth Transitions Through Education and Migration in Peru." *Journal of Youth Studies* 14 (4): 395–411.

———. 2015. "'There's No Future Here': The Time and Place of Children's Migration Aspirations in Peru." *Geoforum* 62 (June): 38–46.

Crivello, Gina, Laura Camfield, and Martin Woodhead. 2009. "How Can Children Tell Us About Their Wellbeing? Exploring the Potential of Participatory Research Approaches Within Young Lives." *Social Indicators Research* 90 (1): 51–72.

Cussiánovich, Alejandro. 2001. "What Does Protagonism Mean?" In *Working Children's Protagonism: Social Movements and Empowerment in Latin America, Africa, and India*. Edited by Manfred Liebel, Bernd Overwien, and Albert Recknagel, pp. 157–169. Frankfurt: IKO.

———. 2006. *Ensayos sobre infancia: sujeto de derechos y protagonista*. Lima: IFEJANT.

———. 2007. *Aprender La Condición Humana. Ensayo Sobre Pedagogía de La Ternura*. Lima: IFEJANT.

———. 2010. *Ensayos sobre infancia: sujeto de derechos y protagonista II. Primera edición*. Lima: Ifejant.

———. 2015. *Ensayos II sobre Pedagogía de la Ternura. Aprender la condición humana*. Lima: IFEJANT.

Cussiánovich, Alejandro, and Ana María Márquez. 2002. *Hacia una participación protagónica de los niños, niñas y adolescentes. Documento de discusión elaborado por Save the Children Suecia*. https://www.sename.cl/wsename/otros/Hacia%20una%20participacion%20protagonica-savethechildren.pdf

Cussiánovich, Alejandro, and Donald Méndez Quintana. 2008. *Movimientos Sociales de Nats En América Latina: Análisis Histórico y Balance Político en Los Ultimos Treinta Años—Red de Desarrollo Social de América Latina y el Caribe (ReDeSoc)*. Lima: IFEJANT.

CVR (Comision de la Verdad y la Reconciliacion). 2003. *Informe final* [Final Report]. http://www.cverdad.org.pe/ifinal/index.php

Dajes, Talía. 2011. "From Pop to Populism: Jesús Ruiz Durand's Agrarian Reform Posters." In *Seeing in Spanish: From Don Quixote to Daddy Yankee—22 Essays on Hispanic Visual Cultures*. Edited by Ryan Prout and Tilmann Alternberg, pp. 129–142. Newcastle upon Tyne: Cambridge Scholars Publishing.

224 Works Cited

Darian-Smith, Eve. 2013. *Laws and Societies in Global Contexts: Contemporary Approaches.* New York: Cambridge University Press.

———. 2015. "New Modalities of Nationality, Citizenship, Belonging and Being." In *The Handbook of Law and Society.* Edited by Austin Sarat and Patricia Ewick, pp. 351–366. Malden: Wiley-Blackwell.

Darian-Smith, Eve, and Philip C. McCarty. 2017. *The Global Turn: Theories, Research Designs, and Methods for Global Studies.* Oakland: University of California Press.

Das, Veena, and Deborah Poole. 2004. *Anthropology in the Margins of the State.* Santa Fe: School of American Research Press.

Davidson, Russ, and David Craven. 2006. *Latin American Posters: Public Aesthetics and Mass Politics.* Santa Fe: Museum of New Mexico Press.

Davis, Mike. 2006. *Planet of Slums.* New York: Verso Books.

Degregori, Carlos Iván, ed. 1996. *Las Rondas Campesinas y La Derrota de Sendero Luminoso* (Estudios de La Sociedad Rural). Lima: IEP Ediciones.

———. 2007. *Del Mito de Inkarri al Mito Del Progreso: Poblaciones Andinas, Cultura e Identidad Nacional.* Lima: IEP Ediciones.

———. 2012. *How Difficult It Is to Be God: Shining Path's Politics of War in Peru, 1980–1999.* Edited by Steve J. Stern; translated by Nancy Appelbaum, Joanna Drzewieniecki, Héctor Flores, Eric Hershberg, Judy Rein, and Kimberly Theidon. Madison: University of Wisconsin Press.

Dehm, Julia. 2021. *Reconsidering REDD+: Authority, Power and Law in the Green Economy.* New York: Cambridge University Press.

Drinot, Paulo. 2006. "Nation-Building, Racism, and Inequality: Institutional Development in Peru in Historical Perspective." In *Making Institutions Work in Peru: Democracy, Development, and Inequality Since 1980.* Edited by John Crabtree. London: University of London Press, Institute for the Study of the Americas.

———. 2011. *The Allure of Labor Workers, Race, and the Making of the Peruvian State.* Durham: Duke University Press.

———. 2014. *Peru in Theory.* New York: Palgrave Macmillan.

Edelman, Marc. 2009. "Synergies and Tensions Between Rural Social Movements and Professional Researchers." *Journal of Peasant Studies* 36 (1): 245–265.

Engle, Karen. 2020. *The Grip of Sexual Violence in Conflict: Feminist Interventions in International Law.* Stanford: Stanford University Press.

Ennew, Judith. 2002. "Outside Childhood: Street Children's Rights" (revised version). In *The Handbook of Children's Rights: Comparative Policy and Practice.* Edited by Bob Franklin, pp. 201–215. London: Routledge.

Enloe, Cynthia. 1990. "Womenandchildren: Making Feminist Sense of the Persian Gulf Crisis." *Village Voice* 25 (9).

———. 2004. *The Curious Feminist: Searching for Women in a New Age of Empire.* Berkeley: University of California Press.

———. 2014. *Bananas, Beaches and Bases: Making Feminist Sense of International Politics, 2nd edition.* Berkeley: University of California Press.

Escobar, Arturo. 2011. *Encountering Development: The Making and Unmaking of the Third World*, rev. edition. Princeton: Princeton University Press.

Works Cited   225

Escobar, Arturo, and Sonia E. Alvarez, eds. 1992. *The Making of Social Movements in Latin America: Identity, Strategy, and Democracy*. Boulder: Westview Press.

Eslava, Luis. 2015. *Local Space, Global Life: The Everyday Operation of International Law and Development*. Cambridge, UK: Cambridge University Press.

Eslava, Luis, Michael Fakhri, and Vasuki Nesiah, eds. 2017. *Bandung, Global History, and International Law: Critical Pasts and Pending Futures*. Cambridge, UK: Cambridge University Press.

Espinoza, G. Antonio. 2013. *Education and the State in Modern Peru: Primary Schooling in Lima, 1821–c. 1921*. New York: Palgrave Macmillan.

Ewick, Patricia. 2014. "Afterword: Time, Imagination, and Punishment." In *The Punitive Imagination: Law, Justice, and Responsibility*. Edited by Austin Sarat, pp. 158–173. Tuscaloosa: University of Alabama Press.

Ewick, Patricia, and Susan S. Silbey. 1998. *The Common Place of Law: Stories from Everyday Life*. Chicago: University of Chicago Press.

Ewig, Christina. 2006. "Hijacking Global Feminism: Feminists, the Catholic Church, and the Family Planning Debacle in Peru." *Feminist Studies* 32 (3): 633–659.

———. 2010. *Second-Wave Neoliberalism: Gender, Race, and Health Sector Reform in Peru*. University Park: Pennsylvania State University Press.

Ferguson, James. 1990. *The Anti-Politics Machine: "Development," Depoliticization, and Bureaucratic Power in Lesotho*. New York: Cambridge University Press.

Fernández-Maldonado, Ana María. 2006. "Barriadas and Elite in Lima, Peru: Recent Trends of Urban Integration and Disintegration." In *Cities Between Integration and Disintegration: Opportunities and Challenges*. Edited by International Society of City and Regional Planners (ISoCaRP), pp. 132–145. Rome: ISOCARP. https://www.iso carp.net/Data/case_studies/848.pdf

Ferreira da Silva, Denise. 2009. "No-Bodies: Law, Raciality and Violence." *Griffith Law Review* 18 (2): 212–236.

Fine, Michelle. 2017. *Just Research in Contentious Times: Widening the Methodological Imagination*. New York: Teachers College Press.

Fine, Michelle, and Jessica Ruglis. 2009. "Circuits and Consequences of Dispossession: The Racialized Realignment of the Public Sphere for U.S. Youth." *Transforming Anthropology* 17 (1): 20–33.

Fine, Michelle, and Lois Weis. 2003. *Silenced Voices and Extraordinary Conversations: Re-Imagining Schools*. New York: Teachers College Press.

Fraser, Nancy. 2008. *Scales of Justice: Reimagining Political Space in a Globalizing World*. New York: Columbia University Press.

Fraser, Nancy, et al. 2014. *Transnationalizing the Public Sphere. Edited by Kate Nash. Cambridge, UK*: Polity.

Fraser, Nancy, and Axel Honneth. 2003. *Redistribution or Recognition? A Political-Philosophical Exchange*. London: Verso Books.

Freeman, Michael. 2020. *A Magna Carta for Children? Rethinking Children's Rights*. Cambridge, UK: Cambridge University Press.

Fregoso, Rosa Linda, and Cynthia L. Bejarano, eds. 2010. *Terrorizing Women: Feminicide in the Americas*. Durham: Duke University Press.

226 Works Cited

Fujii, Lee Ann. 2011. *Killing Neighbors: Webs of Violence in Rwanda*. Ithaca and London: Cornell University Press.

———. 2018. *Interviewing in Social Science Research: A Relational Approach*. New York: Routledge.

Gandolfo, Daniella. 2009. *The City at Its Limits: Taboo, Transgression, and Urban Renewal in Lima*. Chicago: University of Chicago Press.

García, María Elena. 2003. "The Politics of Community: Education, Indigenous Rights, and Ethnic Mobilization in Peru." *Latin American Perspectives* 30 (1): 70–95.

———. 2005. *Making Indigenous Citizens: Identities, Education, and Multicultural Development in Peru*. Stanford: Stanford University Press.

Gilmore, Ruth Wilson. 2002. "Fatal Couplings of Power and Difference: Notes on Racism and Geography." *The Professional Geographer* 54 (1): 15–24.

———. 2007. *Golden Gulag: Prisons, Surplus, Crisis, and Opposition in Globalizing California*. Berkeley: University of California Press.

———. 2008. "Forgotten Places and the Seeds of Grassroots Planning." In *Engaging Contradictions: Theory, Politics, and Methods of Activist Scholarship*. Edited by Charles Hale, pp. 31–61. Berkeley: University of California Press.

Goldberg-Hiller, Jonathan, and Noenoe K. Silva. 2011. "Sharks and Pigs: Animating Hawaiian Sovereignty Against the Anthropological Machine." *South Atlantic Quarterly* 110 (2): 429–446.

Goldstein, Daniel M. 2003. "'In Our Own Hands': Lynching, Justice, and the Law in Bolivia." *American Ethnologist* 30 (1): 22–43

Goodale, Mark. 2008. *Dilemmas of Modernity: Bolivian Encounters with Law and Liberalism*. Stanford: Stanford University Press.

———, ed. 2013. *Human Rights at the Crossroads*. Oxford: Oxford University Press.

Goodale, Mark, and Sally Engle Merry, eds. 2007. *The Practice of Human Rights: Tracking Law Between the Global and the Local*. Cambridge and New York: Cambridge University Press.

Goodale, Mark, and Nancy Grey Postero, eds. 2013. *Neoliberalism, Interrupted: Social Change and Contested Governance in Contemporary Latin America*. Stanford: Stanford University Press.

Graubart, Karen B. 2007. *With Our Labor and Sweat: Indigenous Women and the Formation of Colonial Society in Peru, 1550–1700*. Stanford: Stanford University Press.

———. 2017. "Shifting Landscapes. Heterogeneous Conceptions of Land Use and Tenure in the Lima Valley." *Colonial Latin American Review* 26 (1): 62–84.

Greene, Maxine. 2000. *Releasing the Imagination: Essays on Education, the Arts, and Social Change*. Princeton: Jossey-Bass.

Grewal, Inderpal. 2017. *Saving the Security State: Exceptional Citizens in Twenty-First-Century America*. Durham: Duke University Press.

Gupta, Akhil. 2012. *Red Tape: Bureaucracy, Structural Violence, and Poverty in India*. Durham: Duke University Press.

Gupta, Akhil, and James Ferguson. 1992. "Beyond 'Culture': Space, Identity, and the Politics of Difference." *Cultural Anthropology* 7 (1): 6–23.

————, eds. 1997. *Culture, Power, Place: Explorations in Critical Anthropology*. Durham: Duke University Press.

Gutiérrez, Gustavo. 1973. *A Theology of Liberation: History, Politics, and Salvation*. New York: Orbis Books.

Han, Clara. 2012. *Life in Debt: Times of Care and Violence in Neoliberal Chile*. Berkeley: University of California Press.

————. 2021. *Seeing Like a Child: Inheriting the Korean War*. New York: Fordham University Press.

Han, Clara, and Andrew Brandel. 2020. "Genres of Witnessing: Narrative, Violence, Generations." *Ethnos* 85 (4): 629–646.

Harris, Cheryl I. 1993. "Whiteness as Property." *Harvard Law Review* 106 (8): 1707–1791.

Hart, Jason. 2008. "Children's Participation and International Development: Attending to the Political." *International Journal of Children's Rights* 16: 407–418.

————. 2012. "The Spatialisation of Child Protection: Notes from the Occupied Palestinian Territory." *Development in Practice* 22 (4): 473–485.

Hart, Jason, and Jo Boyden. 2018. "Childhood (Re)Materialized: Bringing Political-Economy into the Field." In *Reimagining Childhood Studies*. Edited by Spyros Spyrou, Rachel Rosen, and Daniel Thomas Cook, pp. 75–91. London: Bloomsbury Academic.

Hart, Jason, and Bex Tyrer. 2006. *Research with Children Living in Situations of Armed Conflict: Concepts, Ethics, & Methods*. Oxford: University of Oxford.

Hartman, Saidiya. 2008. "Venus in Two Acts." *Small Axe* 12 (2): 1–14.

Harvey, David. 2018. *The Limits to Capital*. New York: Verso Books.

Hayward, Clarissa Rile. 2000. *De-Facing Power*. New York: Cambridge University Press.

Heathcote, Gina. 2017. "Women and Children and Elephants as Justification for Force." *Journal on the Use of Force and International Law* 4 (1): 66–85.

————. 2019. *Feminist Dialogues on International Law: Successes, Tensions, Futures*. Oxford and New York: Oxford University Press.

Heathcote, Gina, and Dianne Otto, eds. 2014. *Rethinking Peacekeeping, Gender Equality and Collective Security*. New York: Palgrave Macmillan.

Hecht, Tobias. 2002. *Minor Omissions: Children in Latin American History and Society*. Madison: University of Wisconsin Press.

Henríquez, Narda, and Christina Ewig. 2013. "Integrating Gender into Human Security: Peru's Truth and Reconciliation Commission." In *Gender, Violence, and Human Security: Critical Feminist Perspectives*. Edited by Aili Mari Tripp, Myra Marx Ferree, and Christina Ewig, pp. 260–282. New York: NYU Press.

Hernández Castillo, R. Aída. 2016. *Multiple InJustices: Indigenous Women, Law, and Political Struggle in Latin America*. Tucson: University of Arizona Press.

Hernández Castillo, R. Aída, Suzi Hutchings, and Brian Noble, eds. 2019. *Transcontinental Dialogues: Activist Alliances with Indigenous Peoples of Canada, Mexico, and Australia*. Tucson: University of Arizona Press.

Holzscheiter, Anna. 2010. *Children's Rights in International Politics: The Transformative Power of Transnational Discourse*. New York: Palgrave Macmillan.

228   Works Cited

hooks, bell. 1989. "Choosing the Margin as a Space of Radical Openness." *Framework: The Journal of Cinema and Media*, no. 36: 15–23.

———. 1997. *Bone Black: Memories of Girlhood*. New York: Holt Paperbacks.

Ibrahim, Habiba. 2021. *Black Age: Oceanic Lifespans and the Time of Black Life*. New York: NYU Press.

Incite! Women of Color Against Violence. 2017. *The Revolution Will Not Be Funded: Beyond the Non-Profit Industrial Complex*. Durham: Duke University Press.

Invernizzi, Antonella, Manfred Liebel, Brian Milne, and Rebecca Budde, eds. 2017. *"Children Out of Place" and Human Rights: In Memory of Judith Ennew*. New York: Springer.

James, Allison, and Alan Prout. 1997. *Constructing and Reconstructing Childhood: Contemporary Issues in the Sociological Study of Childhood*. London: RoutledgeFalmer.

Kamphuis, Charis. 2010. "The Convergence of Public and Corporate Power in Peru: Yanacocha Mine, Campesino Dispossession, Privatized Coercion." *Comparative Research in Law & Political Economy*. https://digitalcommons.osgoode.yorku.ca/clpe/318

———. 2012. "Foreign Investment and the Privatization of Coercion: A Case Study of the Forza Security Company in Peru." *Brooklyn Journal of International Law* 37 (2). https://brooklynworks.brooklaw.edu/cgi/viewcontent.cgi?article=1089&context=bjil

Kapur, Ratna. 2018. *Gender, Alterity and Human Rights: Freedom in a Fishbowl*. Cheltenham: Edward Elgar.

Katz, Cindi. 2004. *Growing up Global: Economic Restructuring and Children's Everyday Lives*. Minneapolis: University of Minnesota Press.

———. 2008. "Cultural Geographies Lecture: Childhood as Spectacle: Relays of Anxiety and the Reconfiguration of the Child." *Cultural Geographies* 15 (1): 5–17.

Kazanjian, David. 2016. *The Brink of Freedom: Improvising Life in the Nineteenth-Century Atlantic World*. Durham: Duke University Press.

King, Elisabeth, and John C. Mutter. 2014. "Violent Conflicts and Natural Disasters: The Growing Case for Cross-Disciplinary Dialogue." *Third World Quarterly* 35 (7): 1239–1255.

Klug, Heinz. 2000. *Constituting Democracy: Law, Globalism and South Africa's Political Reconstruction*. Cambridge, UK: Cambridge University Press.

Krupa, Christopher, and David Nugent, eds. 2015. *State Theory and Andean Politics: New Approaches to the Study of Rule*. Philadelphia: University of Pennsylvania Press.

Laplante, Lisa, and Kimberly Theidon. 2007. "Truth with Consequences: Justice and Reparations in Post-Truth Commission Peru." *Human Rights Quarterly* 29 (1): 228–250.

Leal, Claudia. 2018. *Landscapes of Freedom: Building a Postemancipation Society in the Rainforests of Western Colombia*, 3rd edition. Tucson: University of Arizona Press.

Lee, Nick. 2001. *Childhood and Society: Growing up in an Age of Uncertainty*. Maidenhead: Open University Press.

Leinaweaver, Jessaca. 2007. "Choosing to Move: Child Agency on Peru's Margins." *Childhood* 14 (3): 375–392.

———. 2008. *The Circulation of Children: Kinship, Adoption, and Morality in Andean Peru*. Durham: Duke University Press.

Levitsky, Sandra R. 2014. *Caring for Our Own: Why There Is No Political Demand for New American Social Welfare Rights*. New York: Oxford University Press.

———. 2018. "Law and the Building Blocks of the Familiar." *Law & Social Inquiry* 43 (1): 258–66.

Levitt, Peggy, and Sally Merry. 2009. "Vernacularization on the Ground: Local Uses of Global Women's Rights in Peru, China, India and the United States." *Global Networks* 9 (4): 441–61.

Li, Fabiana. 2015. *Unearthing Conflict: Corporate Mining, Activism, and Expertise in Peru*. Durham: Duke University Press.

Li, Tania Murray. 2005. "Beyond the State and Failed Schemes." *American Anthropologist* 107 (3): 383–394.

———. 2007. *The Will to Improve: Governmentality, Development, and the Practice of Politics*. Durham: Duke University Press.

Liboiron, Max. 2021. *Pollution Is Colonialism*. Durham: Duke University Press.

Liebel, Manfred. 2001. "Strengthen Children's Rights! Approaches to Participation byWorking Children." In *Working Children's Protagonism: Social Movements and Empowerment in Latin America, Africa and India*. Edited by Manfred Liebel, Bernd Overwien, and Albert Recknagel, pp. 171–180. Frankfurt am Main and London: IKO.

———. 2012. *Children's Rights from Below: Cross-Cultural Perspectives*. Basingstoke: Palgrave Macmillan.

———. 2020. *Decolonizing Childhoods: From Exclusion to Dignity*. Bristol: Bristol University Press.

Lima, Claudia de Costa, and Sonia E. Alvarez. 2014. "Dislocating the Sign: Toward a Translocal Feminist Politics of Translation." *Signs: Journal of Women in Culture and Society* 39 (3): 557–563.

Linde, Robyn. 2016. *The Globalization of Childhood: The International Diffusion of Norms and Law Against the Child Death Penalty*. New York: Oxford University Press.

Lugones, María. 2003. *Pilgrimages/Peregrinajes: Theorizing Coalition Against Multiple Oppressions*. Lanham: Rowman & Littlefield.

———. 2010. "Toward a Decolonial Feminism." *Hypatia* 25 (4): 742–759.

Lundy, Laura. 2007. "'Voice' Is Not Enough: Conceptualising Article 12 of the United Nations Convention on the Rights of the Child." *British Educational Research Journal* 33 (6): 927–942.

Luttrell-Rowland, Mikaela. 2012. "Ambivalence, Conflation, and Invisibility: A Feminist Analysis of State Enactment of Children's Rights in Peru." *Signs* 38 (1): 179–202.

———. 2016. "The Recession as the Site of the Exceptional: Young People, Self-Determination and Social Mobility." *British Journal of Sociology of Education* 37 (3): 335–349.

Luttrell-Rowland, Mikaela, Jessica Engebretson, Puleng Segalo, and the Women, Peace and Security Collective. 2021. "Shaping Policy, Sustaining Peace: Intergenerational Activism in the Policy Ecosystem. *Agenda* 35 (1): 109–119.

Madrid, Raúl L. 2011. "Ethnic Proximity and Ethnic Voting in Peru." *Journal of Latin American Studies* 43 (2): 267–297.

230   Works Cited

Malkki, Liisa. 2010. *"Children, Humanity, and the Infantilization of Peace." In In the Name of Humanity: The Government of Threat and Care. Edited by Ilana Feldman and Miriam Ticktin, pp. 55–85.* Durham: Duke University Press.

———. 2015. *The Need to Help: The Domestic Arts of International Humanitarianism.* Durham: Duke University Press.

MANTHOC (Movimiento de Adolescentes y Niños Trabajadores Hijos de Obreros Cristianos). 2016. MANTHOC: *40 años de pensamiento, visa y acción de los niños, niñas, y adolescentes trabajadores por el ejercicio de sus derechos y dignidad.* Lima: MANTHOC.

Marquardt, Kairos M. 2012. "Participatory Security: Citizen Security, Participation, and the Inequities of Citizenship in Urban Peru." *Bulletin of Latin American Research* 31 (2): 174–189.

Mayall, Barry. 2000. "The Sociology of Childhood in Relation to Children's Rights." *International Journal of Children s Rights* 8 (3): 243–259.

Mayer, Enrique. 2009. *Ugly Stories of the Peruvian Agrarian Reform.* Durham: Duke University Press.

McCann, Michael. 2014. "The Unbearable Lightness of Rights: On Sociolegal Inquiry in the Global Era." *Law & Society Review* 48 (20): 245–273.

McClintock, Cynthia. 1984. "Why Peasants Rebel: The Case of Peru's Sendero Luminoso." *World Politics* 37 (1): 48–84.

McKittrick, Katherine. 2015. *Sylvia Wynter: On Being Human as Praxis.* Durham: Duke University Press.

McNulty, Stephanie. 2011. *Voice and Vote: Decentralization and Participation in Post-Fujimori Peru.* Stanford: Stanford University Press.

Menjívar, Cecilia. 2011. *Enduring Violence: Ladina Women's Lives in Guatemala.* Berkeley: University of California Press.

Merry, Sally Engle. 2006a. *Human Rights and Gender Violence: Translating International Law into Local Justice.* Chicago: University of Chicago Press.

———. 2006b. "Transnational Human Rights and Local Activism: Mapping the Middle." *American Anthropologist* 108 (1): 38–51.

Mervin, John. 2015. "Water Is a High for Lima's Poor." *BBC News* (October 9), sec. Business.

Mignolo, Walter D. 2009. "Epistemic Disobedience, Independent Thought and Decolonial Freedom." *Theory, Culture and Society* 26 (7–8): 159–181.

———. 2012. *Local Histories/Global Designs: Coloniality, Subaltern Knowledges, and Border Thinking,* rev. edition. Princeton and Woodstock: Princeton University Press.

Mignolo, Walter D., and Catherine E. Walsh. 2018. *On Decoloniality: Concepts, Analytics, Praxis.* Durham: Duke University Press.

Millar, Kathleen M. 2018. *Reclaiming the Discarded: Life and Labor on Rio's Garbage Dump.* Durham and London: Duke University Press.

Milton, Cynthia E., ed. 2014. *Art from a Fractured Past: Memory and Truth-Telling in Post–Shining Path Peru.* Durham: Duke University Press.

———. 2018. *Conflicted Memory: Military Cultural Interventions and the Human Rights Era in Peru.* Madison: University of Wisconsin Press.

Mineo, Liz. 2015. "In Peru, Progress Against TB." *Harvard Gazette* (blog) (August 31).

Ministerio de Educación, Republica del Perú. 2006. *Diseño curricular nacional*. Lima: Ministerio de Educación. http://www.minedu.gob.pe/normatividad/reglamentos/DisenoCurricularNacional2005FINAL.pdf

Mitchell, Claudia. 2011. *Doing Visual Research*. London: SAGE.

Mitchell, Timothy. 1990. "Everyday Metaphors of Power." *Theory and Society* 19 (5): 545–577.

Mohanty, Chandra Talpade. 2003. *Feminism Without Borders: Decolonizing Theory, Practicing Solidarity*. Durham: Duke University Press.

Molyneux, Maxine. 2006. "Mothers at the Service of the New Poverty Agenda: Progresa/Oportunidades, Mexico's Conditional Transfer Programme." *Social Policy & Administration* 40 (4): 425–449.

Morrow, Virginia. 2007. "Editorial: At the Crossroads." *Childhood* 14 (1): 5–10.

Morrow, Virginia, and Martin Richards. 1996. "The Ethics of Social Research with Children: An Overview." *Children & Society* 10 (2): 90–105.

Muñoz, Paula. 2014. "An Informational Theory of Campaign Clientelism: The Case of Peru." *Comparative Politics* 47 (1): 79–98.

Mutua, Makau. 2001. "Savages, Victims, and Saviors: The Metaphor of Human Rights." *Harvard International Law Journal* 42: 201.

Naples, Nancy A. 2003. *Feminism and Method: Ethnography, Discourse Analysis and Activist Research*. New York and London: Routledge.

Nash, Jennifer C. 2013. "Practicing Love: Black Feminism, Love-Politics, and Post-Intersectionality." *Meridians* 11 (2): 1–24.

———. 2019. *Black Feminism Reimagined: After Intersectionality*. Durham: Duke University Press.

Navaro-Yashin, Yael. 2002. *Faces of the State: Secularism and Public Life in Turkey*. Princeton: Princeton University Press.

———. 2012. *The Make-Believe Space: Affective Geography in a Postwar Polity*. Durham: Duke University Press.

Nelson, Alondra. 2011. *Body and Soul: The Black Panther Party and the Fight Against Medical Discrimination*. Minneapolis: University of Minnesota Press.

Newland, Carlos. 1994. "The Estado Docente and Its Expansion: Spanish American Elementary Education, 1900–1950." *Journal of Latin American Studies* 26 (2): 449–467.

Nixon, Rob. 2011. *Slow Violence and the Environmentalism of the Poor*. Cambridge, MA: Harvard University Press.

Oglesby, Elizabeth. 2004. "Corporate Citizenship? Elites, Labor, and the Geographies of Work in Guatemala." *Environment and Planning D: Society and Space* 22 (4): 553–572.

———. 2007. "Educating Citizens in Postwar Guatemala: Historical Memory, Genocide, and the Culture of Peace." *Radical History Review* 2007 (97): 77–98.

Oliart, Patricia. 2017. "Politicizing Education: The 1972 Reform in Peru." In *The Peculiar Revolution Rethinking the Peruvian Experiment Under Military Rule*. Edited by Carlos Aguirre and Paulo Drinot, pp. 123–147. Austin: University of Texas Press.

Orlove, Ben. 2002. *Lines in the Water: Nature and Culture at Lake Titicaca*. Berkeley: University of California Press.

232   Works Cited

Otto, Dianne. 1999. "Postcolonialism and Law." *Third World Legal Studies* 15 (1): vii–xviii.

———. 2015. "Decoding Crisis in International Law: A Queer Feminist Perspective." In *International Law and Its Discontents: Confronting Crises.* Edited by Barbara Stark, pp. 115–136. Cambridge, UK: Cambridge University Press.

———. 2017. "Beyond Legal Justice: Some Personal Reflections on People's Tribunals, Listening and Responsibility." *London Review of International Law* 5 (2): 225–249. https://doi.org/10.1093/lril/lrx007

Pahuja, Sundhya. 2011. *Decolonising International Law: Development, Economic Growth and the Politics of Universality.* Cambridge, UK: Cambridge University Press.

Park, K-Sue. 2016. "Money, Mortgages, and the Conquest of America." *Law & Social Inquiry* 41 (4): 1006–1035.

Paulson, Julia. 2010. "History and Hysteria: Peru's Truth and Reconciliation Commission and Conflict in the National Curriculum." *International Journal for Education Law and Policy* 2010 Special Issue: 132–146.

———. 2011. *Education, Conflict and Development.* Oxford: Symposium Books.

———. 2015. "'Whether and How?' History Education About Recent and Ongoing Conflict: A Review of Research." *Journal on Education in Emergencies* 1 (1): 14–47.

Paulson, Julia, and Michelle J. Bellino. 2017. "Truth Commissions, Education, and Positive Peace: An Analysis of Truth Commission Final Reports (1980–2015)." *Comparative Education* 53 (3): 351–378.

Penry, S. Elizabeth. 2019. *The People Are King.* New York: Oxford University Press.

Perry, Imani. 2018. *Vexy Thing: On Gender and Liberation.* Durham: Duke University Press.

"Plan de Desarrollo Concertado de Lomas de Carabayllo: 2004–2015." Lima: CIDAP-AGIDELCA. https://cidap.org.pe/wp-content/uploads/63148230-Plan-de-Desarrollo-Concertado-de-Lomas-De-Carabayllo-al-2015.pdf

Poole, Deborah. 1997. *Vision, Race, and Modernity: A Visual Economy of the Andean Image World.* Princeton: Princeton University Press.

Premo, Bianca. 2005. *Children of the Father King.* Chapel Hill: University of North Carolina Press.

Pupavac, Vanessa. 2001. "Misanthropy Without Borders: The International Children's Rights Regime." *Disasters* 25 (2): 95–112.

Quijano, Anibal. 1972. *Nationalism and Capitalism in Peru: A Study in Neo-Imperialism.* Translated by Helen R. Lane. New York: Monthly Review Press.

———. 2000. "Coloniality of Power, Eurocentrism, and Latin America." *Nepantla: Views from South* 1 (3): 48.

———. 2007. "Coloniality and Modernity/Rationality." *Cultural Studies* 21 (2–3): 168–178.

Qvortrup, Jens., ed. 2005. *Studies in Modern Childhood: Society, Agency, Culture.* Basingstoke: Palgrave Macmillan.

Qvortrup, Jens, William A. Corsaro, and Michael-Sebastian Honig, eds. 2009. *The Palgrave Handbook of Childhood Studies.* Basingstoke: Palgrave Macmillan.

Rajah, Jothie. 2012. *Authoritarian Rule of Law: Legislation, Discourse, and Legitimacy in Singapore.* New York: Cambridge University Press.

Rasmussen, Mattis. 2017. "Tactics of the Governed: Figures of Abandonment in Andean Peru." *Journal of Latin American Studies: Cambridge* 49 (2): 327–353.

Rehfeld, Andrew. 2011. "The Child as Democratic Citizen." *Annals of the American Academy of Political and Social Science* 633: 141–66.

Ridge, Tess. 2011. "The Everyday Costs of Poverty in Childhood: A Review of Qualitative Research Exploring the Lives and Experiences of Low-Income Children in the UK." *Children & Society* 25 (1): 73–84.

Rodríguez, José, and Silvana Vargas. 2009. "*Trabajo Infantil En El Perú. Magnitud y Perfiles Vulnerables. Informe Nacional 2007–2008.*" *Departamento Académico de Economía.* https://departamento.pucp.edu.pe/economia/libro/trabajo-infantil-en-el-peru-magnitud-y-perfiles-vulnerables-informe-nacional-2007-2008/

Ross, Loretta, and Rickie Solinger. 2017. *Reproductive Justice: An Introduction.* Oakland: University of California Press.

Rousseau, Stéphanie. 2009. *Women's Citizenship in Peru: The Paradoxes of Neopopulism in Latin America.* New York: Palgrave Macmillan.

———. 2020. "Antigender Activism in Peru and Its Impact on State Policy." *Politics & Gender* 16 (1).

Ruddick, Sue. 2003. "The Politics of Aging: Globalization and the Restructuring of Youth and Childhood." *Antipode* 35 (2): 334–362.

Sanborn, Cynthia A., Verónica Hurtado, and Tania Ramírez. 2016. *La Consulta Previa en el Perú: Avances y Retos.* Lima: Universidad del Pacífico.

Sanborn, Cynthia A., and Álvaro Paredes. 2014. "Consulta previa: Perú." *Americas Quarterly Special Report.* https://centroderecursos.cultura.pe/sites/default/files/rb/pdf/Consulta%20Previa%20Peru.pdf

Santos, Boaventura de Sousa. 1977. "The Law of the Oppressed: The Construction and Reproduction of Legality in Pasargada Law." *Law and Society Review* 12: 5–126.

Santos, Cecilia MacDowell. 2005. *Women's Police Stations—Gender, Violence, and Justice in Sao Paulo, Brazil. New York*: Palgrave Macmillan.

Sarat, Austin, and Patricia Ewick, eds. 2015. *The Handbook of Law and Society.* Chichester, UK, and Malden, MA: Wiley-Blackwell.

Sassen, Saskia, ed. 2002. *Global Networks, Linked Cities.* New York: Routledge.

———, ed. 2007. *Deciphering the Global: Its Scales, Spaces and Subjects.* New York: Routledge.

Scheper-Hughes, Nancy. 1993. *Death Without Weeping: The Violence of Everyday Life in Brazil.* Berkeley: University of California Press.

———. 2008. "A Talent for Life: Reflections on Human Vulnerability and Resilience." *Ethnos* 73 (1): 25–56.

Schibotto, Giangi, and Alejandro Cussiánovich. 1994. *Working Children: Building an Identity.* Lima: MANTHOC.

Schild, Verónica. 2000. "Neoliberalism's New Gendered Market Citizens: The 'Civilizing' Dimension of Social Programmes in Chile." *Citizenship Studies* 4 (November): 275–305.

———. 2015. "Emancipation as Moral Regulation: Latin American Feminisms and Neoliberalism." *Hypatia* 30 (3): 547–563.

234 Works Cited

———. 2019. "Feminisms, the Environment and Capitalism: On the Necessary Ecological Dimension of a Critical Latin American Feminism." *Journal of International Women's Studies; Bridgewater* 20 (6): 23–43.

Schneider, Aaron, and Rebeca Zúniga-Hamlin. 2005. "A Strategic Approach to Rights: Lessons from Clientelism in Rural Peru." *Development Policy Review* 23 (5): 567–84.

Schwartz-Shea, Peregrine, and Dvora Yanow. 2011. *Interpretive Research Design*. New York: Routledge.

Scott, James C. 1999. *Seeing Like a State: How Certain Schemes to Improve the Human Condition Have Failed*. New Haven: Yale University Press.

Sharma, Aradhana, and Akhil Gupta, eds. 2008. *The Anthropology of the State: A Reader*. West Sussex: Wiley-Blackwell.

Shever, Elana. 2012. *Resources for Reform: Oil and Neoliberalism in Argentina*. Stanford: Stanford University Press.

Simmons, LaKisha Michelle. 2015. *Crescent City Girls: The Lives of Young Black Women in Segregated New Orleans*. Chapel Hill: University of North Carolina Press.

Smith, Linda Tuhiwai. 2012. *Decolonizing Methodologies: Research and Indigenous Peoples*. London: Zed Books.

Smith, Nicholas Rush. 2019. *Contradictions of Democracy: Vigilantism and Rights in Post-Apartheid South Africa*. Oxford: Oxford University Press.

Soule, Emily Berquist. 2015. "Review of *Education and the State in Modern Peru: Primary Schooling in Lima, 1821–c. 1921 (Historical Studies in Education)*, by G. Antonio Espinoza." *American Historical Review* 120 (1): 305–306.

Spade, Dean. 2015. *Normal Life: Administrative Violence, Critical Trans Politics, and the Limits of Law*. Durham: Duke University Press.

Spyrou, Spyros, Rachel Rosen, and Daniel Thomas Cook, eds. 2018. *Reimagining Childhood Studies*. London and New York: Bloomsbury Academic.

Starn, Orin. 1999. *Nightwatch: The Making of a Movement in the Peruvian Andes*. Durham: Duke University Press.

Starn, Orin, Carlos Iván Degregori, and Robin Kirk, eds. 1995. *The Peru Reader: History, Culture, Politics*. Durham: Duke University Press.

Stephens, Sharon. 1995. *Children and the Politics of Culture*. Princeton: Princeton University Press.

Stepputat, Finn. 2005. "Violence, Sovereignty, and Citizenship in Postcolonial Peru." In *Sovereign Bodies: Citizens, Migrants, and States in the Postcolonial World*. Edited by Thomas Blom Hansen and Finn Stepputat, pp. 61–81. Princeton: Princeton University Press.

Stern, Steve J., ed. 1998. *Shining and Other Paths: War and Society in Peru, 1980–1995*. Durham: Duke University Press.

Strassler, Karen. 2006. "Reformasi Through Our Eyes: Children as Witnesses of History in Post-Suharto Indonesia." *Visual Anthropology Review* 22 (2): 53–70.

Taft, Jessica K., ed. 2013. *Nothing About Us, Without Us: Critiques of the International Labor Organization's Approach to Child Labor from the Movements of Working Children*. Lima: IFEJANT.

———. 2019. *The Kids Are in Charge: Youth Activism and Political Power.* New York: NYU Press.

Taylor, Keeanga-Yamahtta. 2016. *From #BlackLivesMatter to Black Liberation.* Chicago: Haymarket Books.

Teillier, Tamia Portugal, and Francesca Uccelli Labarthe. 2018. "Memorias, temores y silencios: el conflicto armado interno y su tratamiento en la escuela." *Tarea* (Diciembre). https://repositorio.iep.org.pe/bitstream/handle/IEP/1156/Tamia-Portugal_Francesca-Uccelli_Memorias-temores-silencios.pdf?sequence=1&isAllowed=y

Theidon, Kimberly. 2013. *Intimate Enemies: Violence and Reconciliation in Peru.* Philadelphia: University of Pennsylvania Press.

Thorp, Rosemary, and Maritza Paredes. 2010. *Ethnicity and the Persistence of Inequality: The Case of Peru.* Basingstoke: Palgrave Macmillan.

Ticktin, Miriam Iris. 2011. *Casualties of Care Immigration and the Politics of Humanitarianism in France.* Berkeley: University of California Press.

Tomassetti, Julia. 2012. "Who Is a Worker? Partisanship, the National Labor Relations Board, and the Social Content of Employment." *Law & Social Inquiry* 37 (4): 815–847.

Torre, María Elena. 2009. "Participatory Action Research and Critical Race Theory: Fueling Spaces for Nos-Otras to Research." *Urban Review* 41 (1): 106–120.

Tsing, Anna. 2005. *Friction: An Ethnography of Global Connection.* Princeton: Princeton University Press.

———. 2009. "Supply Chains and the Human Condition." *Rethinking Marxism* 21 (2): 148–176.

Uccelli, Francesca, Tamia Carolina Portugal Teillier, Maria Angelica Pease Dreibelbis, and José Carlos Agüero Solórzano. 2017. *Atravesar el silencio: Memorias sobre el conflicto armado interno y su tratamiento en la escuela.* Lima: IEP.

Ulfe, María Eugenia. 2014. "Narrating Stories, Representing Memories: Retablos and Violence in Peru." In *Art from a Fractured Past: Memory and Truth Telling in Post–Shining Path Peru.* Edited by Cynthia Milton, *pp. 116–123.* Durham: Duke University Press.

United Nations. 2015. *Human Rights Council. Report of the Working Group on the Issue of Discrimination Against Women in Law and in Practice. Addendum: Mission to Peru,* pp. 1–22. https://digitallibrary.un.org/record/798717?ln=en

Van Bueren, Geraldine. 1995. *International Law on the Rights of the Child.* Dordrecht and Boston: Kluwer Academic.

Van Vleet, Krista E. 2002. "The Intimacies of Power: Rethinking Violence and Affinity in the Bolivian Andes." *American Ethnologist* 29 (3): 567–601.

———. 2020. *Hierarchies of Care: Girls, Motherhood, and Inequality in Peru.* Urbana: University of Illinois Press.

Villarán de la Puente, Susana. 2007. *Victims Unsilenced: The Inter-American Human Rights System and Transitional Justice in Latin America.* Washington, DC: Due Process of Law Foundation. https://dplf.org/sites/default/files/11904038281.pdf

Vosko, Leah F. 2002. "'Decent Work': The Shifting Role of the ILO and the Struggle for Global Social Justice." *Global Social Policy: An Interdisciplinary Journal of Public Policy and Social Development* 2 (1): 19–46

236 Works Cited

Walker, Tamara J. 2017a. "Black Skin, White Uniforms: Race, Clothing, and the Visual Vernacular of Luxury in the Andes," *Souls* 19 (2): 196–212.

———. 2017b. *Exquisite Slaves: Race, Clothing, and Status in Colonial Lima.* Cambridge, UK: Cambridge University Press.

Waylen, Georgina. 1993. "Women's Movements and Democratisation in Latin America." *Third World Quarterly* 14 (3): 573–587.

———. 2007. *Engendering Transitions: Women's Mobilization, Institutions and Gender Outcomes.* Oxford: Oxford University Press.

Webster, Crystal Lynn. 2021. *Beyond the Boundaries of Childhood: African American Children in the Antebellum North.* Chapel Hill: University of North Carolina Press.

Wedeen, Lisa. 2009. *Peripheral Visions: Publics, Power, and Performance in Yemen.* Chicago: University of Chicago Press.

Weeks, Kathi. 2011. *The Problem with Work: Feminism, Marxism, Antiwork Politics, and Postwork Imaginaries.* Durham: Duke University Press.

———. 2018. *Constituting Feminist Subjects.* London and Brooklyn: Verso.

Weis, Lois, and Michelle Fine. 2012. "Critical Bifocality and Circuits of Privilege: Expanding Critical Ethnographic Theory and Design." *Harvard Educational Review* 82 (2): 173–201.

West, Paige. 2005. "Translation, Value, and Space: Theorizing an Ethnographic and Engaged Environmental Anthropology." *American Anthropologist* 107 (4): 632–642.

———. 2006. *Conservation Is Our Government Now: The Politics of Ecology in Papua New Guinea.* Durham: Duke University Press.

White, Sarah. 2002a. "Being, Becoming and Relationship: Conceptual Challenges of a Child Rights Approach in Development." *Journal of International Development* 14 (8): 1095–1104.

———. 2002b. "Thinking Race, Thinking Development." *Third World Quarterly* 23 (3): 407–419.

———. 2007. "Children's Rights and the Imagination of Community in Bangladesh." *Childhood* 14 (4): 505–520.

White, Sarah, and Shyamol A. Choudhury. 2007. "The Politics of Child Participation in International Development: The Dilemma of Agency." *European Journal of Development Research* 19 (4): 529–550.

Wiebe, Sarah Marie. 2016. *Everyday Exposure: Indigenous Mobilization and Environmental Justice in Canada's Chemical Valley.* Vancouver: UBC Press.

Wright, Nazera Sadiq. 2016. *Black Girlhood in the Nineteenth Century.* Urbana: University of Illinois Press.

Zapata, Rossana Mendoza. 2019. "El Consejo Consultivo de Niños y Niñas de Muñoz." *RPP* (blog).

Index

Note: page numbers in italics refer to figures. Those followed by n refer to notes, with note number.

Abrams, Philip, 196n5

Abu-Lughod, Lila, 17, 192n24, 195n45, 201n59, 2016n22

Advisory Board of Girls, Boys, and Adolescents (CCONNA), 167–68, 173, 215n3

Agarwala, Rita, 211n27

agrarian reforms, 28; 82–83, 207n12

Ahmed, Sara, 190n10

air pollution/smoke from burning trash, Lomas' children's expression of concern about, 32–33, 34, 38–39

Alberti, Giorgio, 83

Alcoff, Linda Martín, 13–14

Alvarado, Velasco, 82–83, 112

Alvarez, Sonia, 209–10n7, 192n22, 209n7, 215n31

Ames, Patricia, 57, 58, 202n17

Argentina: oil extraction from public lands, 152; training of citizens to remain temporarily neglected, 101

armed conflict of 1980s–90s: and authoritarian rule, 45, 119; and children's rights, 165–66; heavy toll on Indigenous and Quechua-speaking peoples, 44, 46; legacy of, shaping Lomas de Carabayllo, 44–49, 64, 75, 200n56; MANTHOC's pedagogy of tenderness and, 118, 119, 147, 149–50, 161; and migration of rural population to Lima, 28, 45, 47; number killed and disappeared in, 5, 46; and patterns of social hierarchy, 5; peasant self-defense militias (*rondas campesinas*), 44; presentation in schools, as matter of contention, 203n34; pro-government accounts taught to children, 60–62, 66, 203n30, 203n34; ruthless violence of Sendero Luminoso, 44, 47–48; state narrations of state violence in, 63–66; state's brutal counterinsurgency, 44, 46, 47, 48, 119, 149, 166; testimony on gendered dimensions of, 200n50. *See also* education in Peru, on armed conflict of 1980s–90s; Truth and Reconciliation Commission (CVR)

Auyero, Javier, 101–102, 197n21, 198n32

238   Index

Balarin, María, 194n39, 202n14, 208–9n32, 213n5
Bejarano, Cynthia L., 193n29
Bellino, Michelle, 6, 193n28, 203n28
Bernstein, Robin, 15, 191n18, 194n38, 207n21
Bhandar, Brenna, 193n33, 213n5, 216n22, 217n2
billboard, "Welcome to Lomas de Carabayllo," 77, 79–80, 206n5
binary logics, obscuring of state accountability through, 176–78
Black feminist love-politics, 210n9
Black girlhood studies, 192n21, 207n17
Black Lives Matter movement, 187, 188, 215n27
bodies: impacted by state violence, 14, 26, 33, 187; made invisible, 192n21
Boesten, Jelke, 66, 175, 204n41, 208n31, 215n1
Brazil, "community policing" in, 71
Brown, Wendy, 156, 195n46, 215n2
Brown, Ruth Nicole, 54, 190n8, 192n21
Bueno-Hansen, Pascha, 118, 151, 155, 190n8, 193n28, 196n9, 214–15n26
Burt, Jo-Marie, 200n47

Campt, Tina, 192n25, 193n29, 198n29
Cant, Anna, 83, 207n11
capitalism: and organized abandonment, 205–6n55; as production, 31, 34, 40 197n32; as structural violence, 31; as structural violence in Lomas de Carabayllo, 40–41, 50
CCONNA. See Advisory Board of Girls, Boys, and Adolescents
CESIP (NGO): on health effects of environmental contamination, 33; study on Lomas gendered work, 196n17
child-centered research, 124, 132, 134, 194n44
childhood, definition of start and endpoint of, 190–91n15
child labor: and dominant discourses 94–95, 142, 145; and the ILO 143,

213n9, 212n37, 209n4; laws in Peru: MANTHOC's effort to change, 138, 141–42, 213n8
child protagonism, MANTHOC struggle for: and disruption, 151; and effort to expand categories of recognition, 147; evolution from needs-based to citizenship-based arguments, 139–40, 141, 146; and gender equality, 155–56; importance of categories used to claim political subjecthood, 139; and language of equality, legibility to general public, 158; and legibility at global level, 141; pairing of child worker and child citizen concepts in, 139, 151; pedagogy of tenderness as fundamental to, 172; pragmatic shifting of language for state legibility, 139–41, 147, 151, 157, 160, 181; and state's vision of political subjecthood, 140, 155, 156–57, 215n30
children, Peruvian discourse about: to emphasize "the local," 178; growing inequality despite, 166; increased visibility since Fujimori, 166; to legitimize state spending, 3, 168; nationalism and modernity as real focus of, 166–68; as rhetorical device to create consensus, 173; and state's casting of itself as neutral site, 166–67; state's influence on children's living conditions as rarely discussed, 3, 189n5; to symbolize future, 178
children's rights: beginning at conception, as conflict with women's reproductive rights, 190n15; calls for children's participation in budget process, 170–72; focus on individual voices in discussions of, 171; Indigenous rights as opening for discussion of, 170; institutional fragmentation in Peru as barrier to, 176–78; neoliberal context of, 182–83; omission of environmental justice in discussions of, 34; and prioritization of equality,

obscuring of interlocking systems of oppression by, 172; spatial scheme in, 193n38. *See also* Convention on the Rights of the Child (CRC)

child work: and domestic chores, 33–34, 55; and knowledge/learning, 119, 138, 143, 145, 210; and identity, 109–10, 127–28, 134, 212n37; and recycling, 33, 92, 95; selling items, 25

Christianity: influence on MANTHOC, 121–23; influence on Western law, 121

citizenship, 139, 151–53, 214n25, 208–9n32

Cliff, Tom, 198n27, 206–7n8

Code for Children and Adolescents, 10, 12, 128–29, 145

Collins, Patricia Hill, 54, 131, 190n8, 192n27, 193n30, 198n29, 212n30, 214n23, 216n13

colonialism, legacy of: and assumptions in research methods, 198n33; and children's shared experience of disparity and state violence, 17; as felt by children of Lomas de Carabayllo, 26–27; hierarchical order as, 196n9; legacy of, shaping Lomas de Carabayllo, 43–44, 50; legacy of dispossession as violence, 14–15, 25, 40–41; as structural violence, 14–15, 25, 40–41

colonial Peru, 80, 206n7, 207n10. *See also* Lima, colonial

colonial Spanish America, 14–15

Comisión de la Verdad y Reconciliación (CVR). *See* Truth and Reconciliation Commission

community policing in Peru: children of Lomas de Carabayllo on, 69–70, 71

contamination, 24, 25, 33, 48, 55–56, 58, 92, 200n54. *See also* pollution

Consejo Consultivo de Niñas, Niños, y Adolescentes de Lima Metropolitana (CCONNA). *See* Advisory Board of Girls, Boys, and Adolescents

Constable, Marianne, 193n29

contradiction as insight, 35, 42, 49, 55, 70,

75, 99, 109, 115, 120, 187, 197n18, 198n31

Convention on the Rights of the Child (CRC): and children's rights as politically non-threatening, 7; Fifth Meeting of Working Children criticism of, 153–54; language from, in murals of Lomas de Carabayllo, 95; number of states ratifying, 7, 191n19; Peru as among first signers of, 10; and shift in view of children, 191n19; and views on children's need for protection, 7

Cotler, Julio, 83

COVID-19, 187

CRC. *See* Convention on the Rights of the Child

Crecer (child nutrition program), 175

Crenshaw, Kimberle, 214n23

critical legal scholarship, 214n15

critical analysis, 131, 159, 176–77, 190n8, 192n25, 192n27, 209n34

Crivello, Gina, 6, 194n44, 202n14,

Cussiánovich, Alejandro: career of, 117–18; on child protagonism, 123–24; as MANTHOC theorist and *colaborador*, 110–11, 116, 119, 147, 210n10, 210n12; pedagogy of tenderness of, 116–20, 147, 210n10; on public space as *milieu* conditioning social relations, 127; on role of adult *colaboradores* in MANTHOC, 113; scholarship on working children's protagonism, 110–11

CVR. *See* Truth and Reconciliation Commission

Declaration of the Fifth Meeting of Working Children of Latin America and the Caribbean to the International Community (1997), on UN Convention on the Rights of Children, 153–54

decolonial approaches: 6–7, 13–14, 192n25

Decolonizing Methodologies (Smith), 198n33

Degregori, Carlos Iván, 57, 63

240   Index

dengue fever, 35
depoliticization, 195n46, 215n2
dignified work, 12, 139, 142–43, 145–146,
  151, 158 dogs in Lomas de Carabayllo,
  5, 24, 32, 38–39, 51–52
domestic violence, 25, 67–68, 204nn41–
  42, 208n31
drawings of neighborhood by children
  of Lomas de Carabayllo, 36–43; as
  aspirational images, 42; and children's
  exposure of systemic injustices, 40–43,
  198n31; children's descriptions of contamination outside margins of, 36–40;
  and feminist curiosity about silence
  and margins, 36; and importance of
  materiality of daily lives to children,
  39; interpretation and narration in, 38;
  lack of people in, 39; as prompts for
  engagement, 197–98n27; as typically
  map-like, 36, 39–40
Drinot, Paulo, 5, 194n41, 201n2, 202n15,
  207n14, 208n28

economic development, 16, 194n41
economic inequality, and state violence,
  166
education in Peru: and erasure of Indigenous knowledge and identity, 57,
  58–59; portrayal of Abimael Guzmán
  in textbooks, 65, 65–66; and reproduction of social hierarchies, 59; and
  rise of Myth of Progress, 57; and state
  formation, 58–59; and Teaching State
  (Estado Docente), 58–59; as understood as key to personal success, 55,
  56–57, 58, 59–60, 75, 202n14, unequal
  access to, under neoliberal policies,
  57, 58, 59
emotion, 25, 31, 50, 55, 158, 186, 190n10,
  210n9
Enloe, Cynthia, 36, 192n20, 198n29
environmental contamination: in
  drawings by children of Lomas de
  Carabayllo, 36–40; scholarship on

children's recognition of, 197n21;
  and state violence, 166; as structural
  violence, in Lomas de Carabayllo,
  40–41; as symptomatic of capitalist
  relations of production, 34, 197n23. *See
  also* air pollution/smoke from burning
  trash; health effects of environmental
  contamination; water contamination
environmental justice, 34, 197n22
environmental justice movement, and
  young people as political actors, 187
environmental violence in Lomas de
  Carabayllo: children's descriptions of,
  24–25, 26, 32–34, 49; as state violence,
  25
equality, in Peruvian state discourse:
  citizen-individual as focus of, 168;
  prioritization of, 172
Eslava, Luis, 41, 192n22, 201n59, 203n26,
  217n32
Espinoza, Antonio, 59
Ewick, Patricia, 128, 204n38
Ewig, Christina, 84, 205n53, 207n19

feminists: in Latin America, call for end
  to neoliberal capitalism, 216n14; Latin
  American, on collective vs. individual
  knowledges, 193n35; NGOs of, adaptation of state language, 215n31; on
  state's obligation to provide life free
  from violence, 5–6
*Feminist and Human Rights Struggles in
  Peru* (Bueno-Hansen) 151, 155, 196n9
families, conceptualization of children as
  members of: in neoliberal discourse,
  4, 176; and spatial logics distancing
  children from politics, 7–8, 15, 16–17,
  176, 191nn18–19, 193n38
Ferreira da Silva, Denise, 197n18, 203n26,
  204n43, 217n32
Fine, Michelle, 198n31, 201n7, 212n29
Fraser, Nancy, 211n26, 212n1
Fregoso, Rosa Linda, 190n14, 193n29
Freire, Paolo, 118

Fuerza Popular, 203n34
Fujimori, Albert: antiterrorism campaign of, 45, 119, 149, 199n44; authoritarian rule by, 45, 119; conviction for human rights violations, 46, 199n45, 200n47; family planning campaign, racialized messages of, 84; and *fujishock*, 29; impact of legacy on Peruvians' views on law, 46; and Indigenous rights, 169; and legal penalties for "apologies for terrorism," 64–65; on National Plan of Action for Children, 165; neoliberal reforms of, 57; rewriting of constitution by, 45; sterilization of poor Indigenous women, 165; and Women's Ministry, creation of, 174–75
fujishock, 29
Fujii, Lee-Ann, 54, 192, 193, 212

García, Alan: economic instability under, 45, 63; investigation for corruption, 70
gender hierarchy, and state violence, 166
gendered violence, 66, 75
Gilmore, Ruth Wilson, 102, 193n28, 204n44, 205n55, 209n34, 214n19, 217n4
Gobierno Revolucionario de las Fuerzas Armadas (GRFA). *See* Revolutionary Government of the Armed Forces
Grewal, Inderpal, 214n24
Growing up Global (Katz) 189n5
Gupta, Akhil, 14, 70, 199n35, 217n1
Gutiérrez, Gustavo, 118
Guzmán, Abimael: capture of, 45; and founding of Sendero Luminoso, 44, 63; image as intellectual, 65, 203n33; portrayal in Peruvian textbooks, 65, 65–66

Habermas, Jürgen, 212n38
Hague Global Child Labour Conference, MOLACNATs and, 129–30
Han, Clara, 26–27, 201n4
Hart, Jason, 15, 191n16, 193–94n38, 211n21

Hartman, Saidiya, 193n28, 198n30
Hayward, Clarissa Rile, 205n54
health effects of environmental contamination: children of Lomas de Carabayllo on, 33, 34, 38–39; studies on, 33; as type of violence, 34
Honneth, Axel, 211n26
hooks, Bell, 192n21, 192n25
Humala, Ollanta: graffiti by Lomas de Carabayllo residents demanding services from, *91*, 91–92; and Indigenous rights, 169, 170; investigation for corruption, 70; promises made in speech in Lomas de Carabayllo, 2–3
human rights, 7, 62, 95, 134, 142, 154, 168, 181, 191–192n19

IFEJANT (Training Institute for Educators of Child, Adolescent and Youth Workers of Latin America and the Caribbean), 118, 170, 210n12
ILO. *See* International Labor Organization
India, informal female workers in, 211n27
Indigenous identity: erasure of, in Peruvian education policy, 57, 58–59
Indigenous rights: and Law of the Right to Prior Consultation, 169–70, 216n11; as opening for discussion of child rights, 170
inequality, 5, 179, 182, 187, 195n1, 202n20
injustice, 4, 26, 39, 53, 78, 87, 102, 147, 183
Institute of Popular Education, 118
Instituto de Formación para Educadores de Jóvenes y Niños Trabajadores de America Latina y el Caribe. *See* IFEJANT
Inter-American Commission of Human Rights, 45
International Labor Organization (ILO): Convention, 169, Peru's ratification of, 169; MANTHOC critique of, 130, 141–43, 213n8; standards of "decent work," 213n9

242 Index

international law, 191n19, 196n8, 201n59, 217n28

International Workers' Day march in Lima, 107–8, 122–23; speech by MANTHOC member, 137–38, 139, 151, 152–53, 156–9

intersectionality: as approach, 66, 131–33, 134–36; 192n2, 198n29, 211n16; and identities, 172, 186, 214n23

Intersectionality as Critical Social Theory (Collins), 192n27

JOC. *See* Peruvian Youth Christian Workers

Joventud Obrera Cristiana. *See* Peruvian Youth Christian Workers

Juntos (conditional cash transfer program), 175

Kamphuis, Charis, 178, 205n48

Katz, Cindi, 34, 189n5, 190n8, 197n23

Kazanjian, David, 17, 194n42

knowledge: children as agents of, 6, 8, 9, 49, 55, 74, 82, 140, 186; as co-constituted 9, 12, 193; multiple expressions of, 116, 183; privileging of certain forms,11, 198n33

Krupa, Christopher, 100

Kuczynski, Pedro Pablo, 70

Labarthe, Francesca Uccelli, 202n21, 235n

land dispossession: colonialism and, 14–15, 25, 40–41; and extractive practices 152; and state violence, 166, 170

landfill. *See* Lomas de Carabayllo landfill (El Zapallal)

Landscapes of Freedom (Leal), 196n10

Latin American and Caribbean Working Children and Adolescents Movement. *See* MOLACNATs

law and legality narratives, 52, 74, 80, 134, 144, 178, 19n38, 196n6, 205n54, 206n7

law: authority of, 15, 52, 61, 196n6; colo-

nial conceptions and use of, 11, 15, 20, 43, 80, 99, 192n24, 195n4

law and order discourse, 46, 119; 210n15

Law of the Right to Prior Consultation for Indigenous and Native Peoples, 169–70

Leal, Claudia, 196n10

legal subjects, 140, 193n38, 214n15

Leinaweaver, Jessaca, 6, 58, 196n8, 197n26, 202n14

Lerner, Salomón, 5, 200n48

Levitsky, Sandra, 111

Ley del Derecho a la Consulta Previa a los Pueblos Indigenas u Origiarois. *See* Law of the Right to Prior Consultation for Indigenous and Native Peoples

liberation theology, 118

Liboiron, Max, 192n24, 194n42

Liebel, Manfred, 123, 134, 142, 154, 201n20, 2013n2

Lima, colonial: early founding of, 43; importance as Spanish port, 43; multiethnic diversity, 43; racial paternalism in, 43–44, 199n38; removal of Indigenous inhabitants, 43. *See also* colonialism, legacy of

Lomas de Carabayllo landfill (El Zapallal): and environmental degradation, 29; health effects of children's work in, 33; as source of jobs, 29; types of employment, and pay, 30

Lomas de Carabayllo residents: environmental violence faced by, 24–25, 26, 32–34, 49; gendered work of parents in, 196–97n17; malnutrition in, 29; migration to Lomas from rural areas during armed conflict of 1980s–90s, 47, 48, 49

Lugones, Maria, 192n25, 193n35; 213n5

MANTHOC (Movement of Working Children and Adolescents from Working-Class Christian Families), 127–30; and addressing state violence at collective level, 109, 110; and Advisory Board of Girls, Boys, and Adolescents, 167; and armed conflict of 1980s–90s, 118, 119; as challenge to dominant narrative of childhood, 111; on children's political input as necessary for true democracy, 142; children's rights manifesto of, 110; Christian influence on, 121–23; collective reflection practice, 122–23; and concept of recognition, 211n26; context needed to understand, 111–12; critique of laws made for and not with children, 129, 130; definition of dignified work, 142; on dignified vs. exploitive work, 142–43; early members as youth labor leaders in JOC, 113; education of members within, 146; focus on collectivity and movement building, 119; founding in opposition to violence of armed conflict of 1980s–90s, 147–50; ideological origins of, 113–16, 118–19; insights into state violence provided by, 166; at International Workers' Day march in Lima (2014), 107–8, *108*, 122–23, 137–38, 139, 151, 152–53, 156–57; at International Workers' Day march in Lima (2018), 158; and intersectional approaches to identity in politics, 186; market as fundamental platform for, 136; MO-LACNATs and, 129; as one of oldest youth rights organizations in Peru, 109, 110; and pedagogy of collectivity, 116, 122, 210n10; political conditions at founding, 12, 111–12, 115; political engagement of, 13; and political participation of children, as issue, 138; redistribution claims, 157; relational listening practices with, methodological complexities, 130–35; release of book on history, values and mission, 158–59; support for all poor working children in Peru, 114–15; support for

rallying around identity in politics, 110; teaching of respect, tenderness, and gender equity, 157; and tensions under neoliberalism, emphasis on, 115–16; and "un-crisis" thinking, 120 *See also* child protagonism; pedagogy of tenderness of MANTHOC

MANTHOC, adult *colaboradores* of, 108, 114, 131–32, 133–34, 147, 157–58, 212n31; and authenticity of child voice as issue, 125, 126, 138, 157; Cussiánovich as, 110–11, 116, 119, 147, 210n10, 210n12; former MANTHOC members as, 114; and language of rights derived from union organizers, 12

Marx, Karl, 212n38

Mayer, Enrique, 28

media: coverage of Humala's speech in Lomas de Carabayllo, 3; coverage of state corruption in Peru, 70; invisibility of slow structural violence to, 25, 196n7

Merry, Sally, 210n11, 212n36

methods: as critical and post-colonial, 4, 8, 130–31, 198n31, 198n33; and understanding children on their own terms, 123; visual practices and, 197–98nn27–28, 198n30. *See also* relational listening practices

middle class in Peru, rise of, 5

migration: as a result of internal armed conflict 19, 28; historical patterns shaped by slavery of, 43

Millar, Kathleen, 30–31, 190n9, 197n26, 199n35

mining companies, 178

Ministerio de Promoción de la Mujer y del Desarrollo Humano (PROMU-DEH). *See* Women's Ministry

Ministerio de la Mujer y Poblaciones Vulnerables (MIMPV), 174–75

Ministry of Women and Social Development (MIMDES) 174–75

Mitchell, Claudia, 198n28

244 Index

Mitchell, Timothy, 59
MNNATSOP (National Movement of Organized Working Children and Adolescents of Peru): adult *colaboradores* (allies) supporting, 108; and Advisory Board of Girls, Boys, and Adolescents, 167; and discussion of child rights, 170; forum of child workers, 145; International Workers' Day march in Lima (2014), 107–8; MANTHOC as part of, 107, 109; number of members, 209n1
modernity, 57–58, 86, 166, 176
MOLACNATs (Latin American and Caribbean Working Children and Adolescent Movement), 129–30
Morrow, Virginia, 194n44, 197n19, 211n21
Movement of Working Children and Adolescents from Working-Class Christian Families. *See* MANTHOC
Movimiento de Adolescentes y Niños Trabajadores Hijos de Obreros Cristianos. *See* MANTHOC
Movimiento Naccional de Niños y Adolescentes Trabajadores Organizados del Peru. *See* MNNATSOP
Movimiento Revolucionario Túpac Amaru. *See* MRTA
Moyano, Maria Elena, 200–201n54
MRTA (Túpac Amaru Revolutionary Movement), 28, 44, 62
murals, political, in Lomas de Carabayllo, *86*, 86–92; and children as symbolic props, 97; community improvements promised in, 90–91; government slogans supporting initiatives, *86*, 86–87; graffiti by residents demanding services, *91*, 91–92; hand painting of, as symbolic of local commitment, 88–89; influence on children's views on politics, 80–82, 91; in schoolyards, 92–99; and message that young people are seen by government, 81; political campaign ads, *87–89*,

87–90; promises on, as tool of political incorporation, 208n25; as reminder of unkept promises, 81–82, 86–88, 91–92, 99–102; slogans referencing local issues in, 89; timeless quality of, 88; and visual economy of Lomas, 81; on walls of unfinished construction, 89. *See also* billboard, "Welcome to Lomas de Carabayllo"
Mutua, Makau, 176
Myth of Inkarri in Peru, replacement by Myth of Progress, 57

Nash, Jennifer, 190n10, 210n9
National Movement of Organized Working Children and Adolescents of Peru. *See* MNNATSOP
National Plan of Action for Children (PNAI), 10, 165–66
National System of Integrated Attention for Children and Adolescents (SNAINA): consensus in state action on children as goal of, 173; move to Women's Ministry, 174–76; as nonfunctioning, 173–74; provisions of, 15–16; systems approach of, 16
National System of Support for Social Mobilization (SINAMOS), 83
NATs. *See* Niños y Adolescentes Trabajadores
Navaro-Yashin, Yael, 49, 201n8, 201n58
neoliberalism: and collapsing of public and private, 152, 214n24; depoliticized solutions offered by, 172; and language of participation and empowerment, 172; and organized abandonment, 205n55; and privatization of services, 178; and reduced funding for police, 205n48; and reduced role of government, 205n49
Niños y Adolescentes Trabajadores (NATs), 118, 153–54
Ni Una Menos movement, 187–88
Nixon, Rob, 14, 196n7

Noceda, Paloma, 203n34
Nugent, David, 100

Organization Educational Forum, 118
organized abandonment, 102, 150, 187, 204n44. *See also* Gilmore, Ruth Wilson
Otto, Dianne, 120, 210n15
Oxfam, study on cost of water in Lima, 35

Pahuja, Sundhya, 193n36, 196n8, 203n26, 217n28
Paniagua, Valentín, 46
Park, K-Sue, 192n24, 206n7
Parsons, Talcott, 7, 191n19
participatory budgeting for children, 168, 170–72
Paulson, Julia, 60, 62, 64, 203n26, 203n32
pedagogy of tenderness of MANTHOC: Cussiánovich on, 116–20, 147, 210n10; as fundamental to child protagonism, 172; and Jesus as model child worker, 122; and murals at MANTHOC site, 122; as reaction against violence of armed conflict of 1980s-90s, 119, 147, 149–50, 161
Perry, Imani, 154, 190n8, 198n29, 213n5.
Peru: community policing in marginalized communities, 74; and *fujishock*, 29; high levels of inequality in, 15, 194n39; informal economy in, 74; number of child workers in, 209n4; shift from clientelism to rights discourse in, 208n25
Peruvian Andes, and *pueblos alvidado* (forgotten towns), 78
Peruvian Institute of Education in Human Rights and Peace, 118
Peruvian state: accountability, false binaries obscuring, 176–78; and centrifocal imaginary of state power, 100; child imagined by, vs. hierarchal logic of colonial thought, 11; deepening of

children's vulnerability despite rhetoric to the contrary, 183; and health funding, cuts in, 205n53; hierarchical order in treatment of political subjecthood, 140, 141; influence of MANTHOC on, 128; multiple forms of violence employed by, 4, 5, 11, 190n15; paternalistic view of children, 7, 183; perpetuation of disparity, in children's view, 4, 5; and political subjecthood of young people, move away from, 115; power of, as daily site of negotiation and struggle, 140; spatial logics separating children from politics, 15, 167, 193n38; "systems" understanding of modern childhood, insights missed in, 20; as typically framed in terms of its institutions, 52; underinvestment in human capital, 208n28; view of children as sites of investment in future, 3, 7, 15.
Peruvian Youth Christian Workers (JOC), 112, 113
Piaget, Jean, 7, 191n19
Plan Nacional Acción por la Infancia (PNAI). *See* National Plan of Action for Children
PNAI. *See* National Plan of Action for Children
police, children of Lomas de Carabayllo on, 67–71; absence of, 67, 68, 75, 178; and community policing, 69–70, 71; corruption of, 67, 68–69, 70, 71; as expression of political knowledge, 202n8
political subjecthood, 6, 139–40, 155, 156–57, 182
political violence: colonial violence as root of, 44; founding of MANTHOC amidst, 12, 111–12, 115; influence of, as felt but not articulated by children of Lomas de Carabayllo, 26–27; legacy of, shaping Lomas de Carabayllo, 43–50, 150, 200–201n56. *See also* armed conflict of 1980s–90s

246 Index

pollution, 5, 26, 30, 32, 37. *See also* contamination
Poole, Deborah, 81
popular education movement, 117
poverty, 118, 161, 118, 175, 194n39, 214n14
Premo, Bianca, 14–15, 43, 193n34, 199n38
PROMUDEH. *See* Women's Ministry

Quijano, Anibal, 49, 192n22, 193n33, 202n20, 214n26

racial hierarchy, and state violence, 166
Racial Innocence (Bernstein), 191n18
racial systems of power, and view of children as outside the polity, 191n18
racism, influence on children of Lomas de Carabayllo, 9, 50, 62
relational listening practices, 8–12, 39–40, 100; adult mediations and, 9; and allowing children to set conversational agenda, 18; 124–25; and breaking free from myth of solo individual, 9; and children's exposure of systemic injustices, 36, 40–43, 198n31; and coformation of knowledge, 9; importance of context, affect, and histories in, 183; and intersectional identities of MANTHOC members, 131–33, 134–35, 136; larger context for interpretation of, 55; and long-term engagement, 8–9, 11–12; with MANTHOC, methodological complexities, 130–35; new conceptions of state and, 193n29; recognition of link between children's narratives and larger structural violence, 40–43, 49–50, 53–54, 198n31; and recognition of young people as readers of state power, 50
religion 121-122, 161
Revolutionary Government of the Armed Forces (GRFA), and agrarian reform slogans, 82

Santos, Boaventura de Sousa, 71
Santos, Cecilia MacDowell, 9, 193n29

Scheper-Hughes, Nancy, 42
Schild, Verónica, 214n14, 216n14
Seeing Like a Child (Han), 26–27
Sendero Luminoso (Shining Path), 28, 44, 45, 60–63, 203n30, 203n34
Shever, Elena, 152
SINAMOS. *See* National System of Support for Social Mobilization
Sistema Nacional de Apoyo a la Movilización Social (SINAMOS). *See* National System of Support for Social Mobilization
Sistema Nacional de Atención Integral al Niño y al Adolescente (SNAINA). *See* National System of Integrated Attention for Children and Adolescents
Smith, Linda Tuhiwai, 41, 198n33, 212n34
SNAINA. *See* National System of Integrated Attention for Children and Adolescents
social justice, 149, 183, 209n7, 213n1
sociology of childhood, on children's rights, 191n19
Somos Perú, *89*, 89–90, 208n26
spatial imagining of rights, 8
spatial logics of Peruvian state distancing children from politics, 6, 15, 17, 193n38; and children's location in families, 15, 16–17, 176, 193n38; as disservice to children, 16–17; and invisibility of state power, 182–83; location of SNAINA in Women's Ministry as, 174
state power: immaterial and affective expressions of, 52; invisibility of, 182; nature of, scholarship on, 7–8
Strassler, Karen, 207n18
structural violence, slow forms of, 14; absence of government action on contaminated water and land as, 35; colonial legacy as, 14–15, 25, 40–41; distraction from, in Peruvian education, 66; environmental contamination as, 40–41; health effects of environmental contamination as, 34;

as often undiagnosed and untreated, 196n7; as often unrecognized by scholars, media, and international organizations, 25, 196n7; as still pervasive globally, 187

subjecthood, 12, 44, 82, 139, 145, 195n46

Taft, Jessica, 6, 110, 113, 126, 135, 141, 209n4, 213n8

Taylor, Keeanga-Yamahtta, 215n27

Teillier, Tamia Portugal, 202n21

Theidon, Kimberly, 7, 44, 199n39, 200n50, 203n30

A Theology of Liberation (Gutiérrez), 117

To Learn of the Human Condition (Cussiánovich), 116–17

Toledo, Alejandro, 70

tolerance, discourse of, 195n46

Truth and Reconciliation Commission (CVR): goals of, 46; hearings on Fujimori's antiterrorism laws, 46, 200n48; on number of deaths in armed conflict of 1980s–90s, 46, 84, 203n29; on ongoing structural violence by state, 47; on psychosocial impact of conflict, 46; recommendations on teaching about armed conflict of 1980s–90s, 63–64, 66; report, stage built for announcement of, 84–85; report by, 203n29; on responsibility for deaths, 46; on social hierarchy in conflict, 5

tuberculosis: drug-resistant, in Peru, 195nn1–2; in Lomas de Carabayllo, 23, 24, 55, 56

Túpac Amaru Revolutionary Movement. *See* MRTA

Uccello, Francesca Labarthe, 60, 64, 202n21, 203n27, 204n35

Ulfe, Maria Engenia, 84–85

United Nations. *See* Convention on the Rights of the Child (CRC)

United States: Black feminist love-politics in, 210n9; Black girlhood

studies in, 192n21, 207n17; and child labor laws in Peru, 141, 159; indigenous land dispossession in, 206n7; neoliberalism in, 214n24; and reproductive justice activism, 190–91n15

Velasco, Juan, 82–83

violence: definition of, 14; intersectional, obscuring of, by logic of colonial thought, 11; legacies of, influence despite recent laws, 16; legacies of, shaping Lomas de Carabayllo, 43–50, 150, 200n56; legacy of colonial dispossession as, 14–15, 25, 40–41; multiple forms employed by Peruvian state, 4, 5, 11, 190n15; Peruvian children's understanding of, multimethod approach needed to reveal, 207n10; state's obligation to provide life free from, 5–6; against women, high levels in Peru, 16. *See also* political violence; structural violence

visual images, and subconscious participation of reader, 206n8

visual political propaganda in Peru: capitalist goals underlying, 83; children as vessels for nationalism in, 84–85; family planning campaign, racialized messages of, 84; history of, 82–85; state's instrumental use of women in, 84; targeting of children in, 83–84

visual practices in social sciences, 198n28

wage labor, as form of violence and technique of governance, 31

Walker, Tamara, 43, 94, 196n6, 207n10

water contamination, children's expression of concern about, 35

water, 35, 36, 39, 45, 54, 79, 82, 87, 101, 177, 186–87

Webster, Crystal Lynn, 6, 84, 192n21

Weeks, Kathi, 197n18,

White, Sarah, 212n33

248   Index

women: denial of genuine citizenship to, 214n25; forced sterilization under Fujimori, 165; state's instrumental use in visual propaganda, 84; violence toward, 16, 67–68, 101, 204n42, 208n31

Women's Ministry (PROMUDEH): creation of, 174–75; focus on women's traditional roles, 175; move of SNAINA to, as means of reducing its power, 174–76; move of SNAINA to, as subordination of children's issues within family issues, 174, 175. *See also* Ministerio de la Mujer y Poblaciones Vulnerables (MIMPV), Ministry of Women and Social Development (MIMDES)

women's reproductive rights: conflict with children's rights beginning at conception, 190n15; and reproductive justice, 190n15

Workers' Union of Lima, International Workers' Day march in Lima (2014), 107–8, *108*